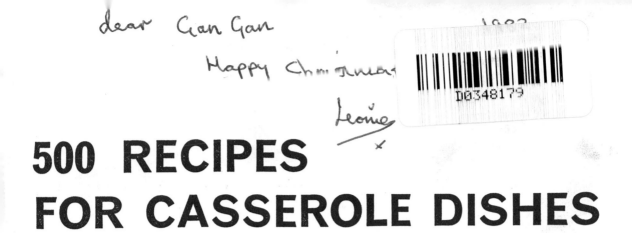

dear Gan Gan
Happy Christmas
Leonie
x

500 RECIPES
FOR CASSEROLE DISHES

by Catherine Kirkpatrick

Page 36
Page 10
Page 21

HAMLYN

LONDON · NEW YORK · SYDNEY · TORONTO

Contents

Introduction   2

Basic Method of Making Casseroles   2

Some Useful Facts and Figures   4

Beef Casseroles   6

Veal Casseroles   21

Lamb Casseroles   26

Pork and Bacon Casseroles   36

Offal Casseroles   44

Chicken Casseroles   50

Game Casseroles   60

Fish Casseroles   65

Vegetable, Egg and Cheese Casseroles   75

Recipes for Reference   84

Desserts   87

Index   91

Cover photograph by Paul Williams

Published by The Hamlyn Publishing Group Limited
London · New York · Sydney · Toronto
Astronaut House, Feltham, Middlesex, England

© Copyright The Hamlyn Publishing Group
Limited 1965

First published 1965
Revised edition 1971
Eleventh impression 1982

ISBN 0 600 31706 4

Printed and bound in Great Britain by
R. J. Acford

Introduction

It is not until someone asks what a casserole is that one realizes how we have come to accept this word as part of our everyday cookery language. The *Oxford Dictionary* defines a casserole as an 'ovenware dish in which meat and other ingredients are cooked'. I feel that this is an injustice. To me a casserole is many things: this word conjures up a picture of an attractive oval or round dish – the warm comforting brown of the casserole dish loved by the French, the brilliant blue and orange of the Scandinavian dishes and the essentially practical clear glass of the British variety. No matter what type you choose, all these casserole dishes are so good looking that you will be proud to use them in the oven and to serve straight from them at the table. If you are going to buy a casserole dish – and you will certainly need one if you are going to try out the dishes in this book – do make sure that it has a well fitting lid.

Casserole also means a one dish meal, the standby of all busy housewives. A dish that has so many advantages. It can be prepared in advance, put straight in the oven from the refrigerator, doesn't spoil if it is kept waiting and requires little or no attention once it is in the oven. In fact for this kind of cooking, it is really the oven that does all the work once the ingredients are prepared.

Yet another meaning for this versatile word: 'to casserole'. In this way it is used to describe the long slow method of cooking usually applied to meat, which is used to render the cheaper cuts more tender. All thrifty housewives will know that cheaper meat cooked in this way is nutritious and tasty.

Basic Method of Making Casseroles

There is a basic method of cooking a casserole and once you get the rules in your mind, this method of cooking leaves plenty of scope for the ingenious cook. Meat or fish vegetables and stock are required, with added flavouring of herbs and seasoning to your own taste. It is usually necessary to thicken the stock before the dish is served and this can be done quite easily with cornflour.

The preparation of stock for a casserole is no problem with beef and chicken stock cubes. Simply add boiling water to a cube and you have a well flavoured stock containing a balanced amount of seasoning.

If you are the kind of clever cook who makes the best use of short cuts to good cooking, you will find that packet soups make an excellent addition to casserole dishes. Packet soups containing dehydrated ingredients not only provide a well flavoured and seasoned stock but the vegetables, once the moisture has been replaced, are just as good as fresh. As they are already chopped, this is an easy way of adding flavour, food value and colour to a casserole dish. To most people a casserole is just a meat stew, although if they stop to think about it, they would quickly realize that fish and vegetables also make excellent casserole additions.

To the inexperienced cook, a casserole might seem to be a meat and vegetable mixture cooked in the oven, with perhaps less liquid than one would use with a stew. Asked what a stew is, the answer would be much the same mixture cooked in a saucepan on top of the stove but with more liquid.

Now that so many casserole dishes can be used on direct heat one could say that the terms 'stew' and 'casserole' are interchangeable. From a practical point of view it is important to remember that when the mixture is cooked on direct heat, no matter what sort of pan or dish is used, more liquid is required than when it is cooked in the oven.

Meat Casseroles

Any cut of beef, lamb, mutton or veal sold for stewing can be used to make a casserole. Pork is not much used because of the amount of fat.

For a general recipe for making a casserole, simply cut the meat into cubes; brown in oil or dripping and remove from the pan. Add the prepared vegetables chosen to give flavour – for example, onion, carrots or celery – and brown quickly. Put browned meat in the dish with the vegetables. Pour in enough stock to give about ¾-inch depth of liquid. Cover and cook on a low shelf in a cool oven at about 300°F. until the meat and vegetables are tender. The time taken will depend on the quality of the meat and the size of the pieces.

A large almost full casserole dish can be left in a very slow oven on the lowest shelf for about 8 hours without coming to any harm. In this case, the meat and vegetables should be cut into fairly large pieces and a little more liquid should be used. To ensure that there is no chance of the liquid evaporating, cover the top of the casserole with aluminium foil before putting on the lid.

Before this dish is served, the stock should be thickened, using ½ oz. cornflour to 1 pint liquid. Alternatively, the meat may be tossed in seasoned cornflour before browning and should not then require any further thickening. If you are making a casserole with 'white' meat (veal, chicken or turkey) do not brown the meat and do not add vegetables other than onions. When the meat is cooked, strain the juices from the dish and use these to make a sauce which can be poured back into the casserole before serving.

Fish Casseroles

There is not a tremendous advantage or time-saving here, since fish cooks so much more quickly than meat; this is, however, such a convenient method to use that many people will not cook fish in any other way. There is far less likelihood of a fishy smell throughout the house. All the nutritive values of the fish are conserved and there is far less washing up!

Mock Casseroles

Many dishes are cooked in casseroles simply as a convenience – although there is not the necessity for long slow cooking – as this is such an easy way of heating through to finish off a dish. Canned sweet corn and canned prawns, for example, stirred into cheese sauce, may be poured into a casserole and heated through in a moderate oven for about 20 minutes. Served with boiled rice, this dish can be proudly served as a **Prawn Casserole** and no one but you need know how it was done.

Accompaniments

Although in most cases the casserole is a 'meal in a dish', you may want to serve extra vegetables, but do remember for economy to choose vegetables that can be cooked in the oven at the same time as the main dish.

Baked potatoes, braised celery, onions, conservatively cooked carrots or turnips – all of these may be cooked slowly in the oven.

Rice is an excellent accompaniment to a casserole and it is important to cook it properly.
For 2 servings: allow 4 oz. Patna rice, ½ pint water and 1 teaspoon salt. Bring the water to the boil with the salt added. Add rice, cover and cook gently for 10–15 minutes until all the water is absorbed and each grain is separated. Remove the lid and allow the rice to dry off: stir lightly with a fork to ensure the grains remain separated.

Lemon rice – add rice to a large pan full of briskly boiling salted water, add also ½ a small lemon. Cook, stirring occasionally for 15–17 minutes. Test the rice for 'tenderness' after 12 minutes. When ready, drain well removing lemon and dot with butter. Toss lightly. Cover with a clean cloth and allow to stand in a warm oven for 10–15 minutes. Add freshly chopped parsley and serve.

Fried rice – boil and dry rice by usual method. When required, melt butter (½ oz.–4 oz. rice). Fry 1 small onion, finely chopped, and half a clove of garlic. Fry for 5 minutes without allowing the onion to brown. Add the rice and continue to fry gently, until the rice becomes golden, about 10 minutes. Stir in 1 dessertspoon finely chopped fresh herbs.

Risotto–chop 1 small onion finely and fry gently in 1½ oz. of butter for 5 minutes. Add rice and allow to cook for 2 minutes. Stir in ⅛ pint dry white wine and ¼ pint stock. Cover with buttered paper and well fitting lid, and cook for 16 minutes at 375°F. Gas Mark 5. Fork extra butter through the rice before serving, if liked.

Risotto with Parmesan–prepare as above, omitting wine, and stir in 1 tablespoon concentrated tomato purée with the stock. When the rice is cooked, sprinkle with 1½ oz. finely grated Parmesan cheese.

If you are fighting the eternal battle to keep weight down, meat or fish and vegetables cooked in an unthickened stock is a satisfying way of getting protein without surplus calories. If, however, you have to satisfy the hearty appetites of a growing family, small savoury dumplings could be made (see page 86), or forcemeat or stuffing balls made according to the recipe on page 86. Place these in foil, dot with butter and cook in the bottom of the oven for about 1½ hours.

Puddings

When choosing a casserole from the varied selection in this book, prepare a pudding that can be cooked in the oven at the same time.
Stewed fruit, baked custard, rice pudding, caramel custard, fruit crumble, baked stuffed apples, compote of dried fruit, are among the familiar puddings that can always be given a new look or a new taste.

Pineapple rice (see cover picture) is plain boiled rice transformed by canned pineapple rings, the centre of each filled with jam.

Fine shred marmalade stirred into hot rice–grated plain chocolate or coconut mixed with grated orange peel sprinkled on to baked custard or cornflour pudding–apples stuffed with mincemeat or chunky marmalade mixed with breadcrumbs–all add new flavours.
There is a section on Desserts at the end of the book.

Cooking by remote control

If you possess a cooker with an auto-timer, leave the dish in the oven, setting the dial switch on and off at the appropriate times. The meal will be ready with only a last-minute gravy or sauce making to be done when you come home.

To make the best use of your auto-timer

See that the cooker is switched on, and arrange oven shelves to suit the dish to be cooked.
If necessary set the clock to the correct time.
Set timer to hour the meal is required.
Regulate the auto-timer to give the necessary cooking time.
Set the dial switch for automatic cooking.
Turn thermostat to the temperature required.
When preparing a casserole, the preliminary frying of the meat and vegetables should be done the evening before.
Fry the meat so it is cooked through, then allow it to become cold. If possible, leave it in the refrigerator until it is put in the oven.
Most of your favourite recipes can be adapted for cooking automatically. When cooking from cold, allow extra 10 minutes on cooking time.
The auto-timer is so valuable to the busy housewife that it is worth while using it whenever you are using the oven so that you will feel completely confident about it when you are away from the house.
Do read the manufacturers' instructions and make sure you are quite familiar with the placing of the shelves and zones of heat before starting to use the oven.

Some Useful Facts and Figures

Comparison of Weights and Measures

English weights and measures have been used throughout the book. 3 teaspoonfuls equal 1 tablespoon. The average English teacup is ¼ pint. The average English breakfast cup is ½ pint. When cups are mentioned in recipes they refer to a B.S.I. measuring cup which holds ½ pint or 10 fluid ounces. In case it is wished to translate quantities into American or metric counterparts the following give a comparison.

Liquid measure

The American pint is 16 fluid ounces, as opposed to the British Imperial pint and Canadian pint which are 20 fluid ounces. The American ½-pint measuring cup is therefore equivalent to ⅖ British pint. In Australia the British Imperial pint, 20 fluid ounces, is used.

Solid measure

British	American
1 lb. butter or other fat	2 cups
1 lb. flour	4 cups
1 lb. granulated or castor sugar	2 cups
1 lb. icing or confectioners' sugar	3½ cups
1 lb. brown (moist) sugar (firmly packed)	2 cups
12 oz. golden syrup or treacle	1 cup
14 oz. rice	2 cups
1 lb. dried fruit	3 cups
1 lb. chopped or minced meat (firmly packed)	2 cups
1 lb. lentils or split peas	2 cups
2 oz. soft breadcrumbs	1 cup
½ oz. flour	2 tablespoons
1 oz. flour	¼ cup
1 oz. sugar	2 tablespoons
½ oz. butter	1 tablespoon
1 oz. golden syrup or treacle	1 tablespoon
1 oz. jam or jelly	1 tablespoon

All U.S. standard measuring cups and tablespoons

To help you understand metrication

You will see from the chart that 1 oz. is approximately 28 grammes but can be rounded off to the more convenient measuring unit of 25. Also the figures in the right hand column are not always increased by 25. This is to reduce the difference between the convenient number and the nearest equivalent. If in a recipe the ingredients to be converted are 1 oz. of margarine and 6 oz. of flour, these are the conversions: 25 grammes margarine and 175 grammes flour.

The conversion chart

Ounces	Approx. g and ml to nearest whole number	Approx. to nearest unit of 25
1	28	25
2	57	50
3	85	75
4	113	125
5	142	150
6	170	175
7	198	200
8	226	225
12	340	350
16	456	450

Note: When converting quantities over 16 oz. first add the appropriate figures in the centre column, not those given in the right hand column, THEN adjust to the nearest unit of 25 grammes. For example, to convert 1¾ lb. add 456 grammes to 340 grammes which equals 796 grammes. When rounded off to the convenient figure it becomes 800 grammes.

Approximate liquid conversions

¼ pint – 150 ml   1,000 millilitres – 1 litre
½ pint – 275 ml   1 litre – 1¾ pints
¾ pint – 425 ml   ½ litre – ¾ pint plus 4 tablespoons
1 pint – 575 ml   1 dl (decilitre) – 6 tablespoons

Note: If solid ingredients give scant weight using the 25 unit conversion, the amount of liquid allowed must also be scant. For example, although 575 ml is nearer to 1 pint (20 fluid oz.) when making a white pouring sauce use 550 ml of milk to 25 grammes each of butter and flour for a better consistency.

Oven Temperatures

The following chart gives conversions from degrees Fahrenheit to degrees Celsius (formerly known as Centigrade). This chart is accurate to within 3° Celsius, and can therefore be used for recipes which give oven temperatures in metric.

Description	Electric Setting	Gas Mark
Very Cool	225°F–110°C	¼
	250°F–130°C	½
Cool	275°F–140°C	1
	300°F–150°C	2
Moderate	325°F–170°C	3
	350°F–180°C	4
Moderately Hot	375°F–190°C	5
	400°F–200°C	6
Hot	425°F–220°C	7
	450°F–230°C	8
Very Hot	475°F–240°C	9

Note: This table is an approximate guide only. Different makes of cooker vary and if you are in any doubt about the setting it is as well to refer to the manufacturer's temperature chart.

Beef Casseroles

Angelino's beef casserole

you will need for 4 servings:

1 tablespoon oil
1 tablespoon lard
8 oz. fat salt pork, diced
1 medium-sized onion, peeled and sliced
1 clove garlic, chopped
2 lb. lean stewing beef
salt, freshly ground pepper
pinch marjoram
pinch rosemary
¼ pint red wine
4 tablespoons tomato purée (see page 85)
½ pint water

1 Heat oil and lard together, add pork, onion and garlic and sauté all together until onion is lightly browned.
2 Cut meat into small pieces and sprinkle with salt, pepper, marjoram and rosemary.
3 Put into pan and cook till well browned.
4 Transfer to a casserole.
5 Put wine into pan in which meat was browned and boil until reduced by half.
6 Add the tomato purée and water. Bring to boiling point, and pour over contents of casserole.
7 Add a little extra water if required. The meat should be just covered.
8 Cover and cook in a slow oven (350°F.–Gas Mark 3) about 2 hours.

Beef à la grecque

you will need for 4 servings:

1½ lb. stewing steak
3 tablespoons oil
1 lb. small white onions
1 medium-sized onion, peeled and stuck with 4 cloves
1 2-inch stick of cinnamon
1 can tomato purée
3 tablespoons cider vinegar
1 pint water
salt, freshly ground black pepper

1 Trim meat, cut into pieces and brown all over in hot oil.
2 Put into a casserole with onions and cinnamon.
3 Mix tomato purée, vinegar and water together and bring to boiling point. Add salt and pepper and pour over contents of casserole.
4 Cover and cook in a slow oven (350°F.–Gas Mark 3) for about 2½ hours.

Beef and onion casserole

you will need for 4 servings:

1 oz. dripping
1½ lb. minced steak
2 onions, chopped
1 10½-oz. can condensed cream of tomato soup
12 oz. potatoes, peeled and sliced
½ oz. butter

1 Melt dripping and brown steak, stirring all the time.
2 Add onion and cook for about 5 minutes.
3 Dilute soup as directed on the can, add to meat mixture, stirring well.

4 Arrange half the sliced potatoes in the bottom of a casserole.
5 Cover with meat mixture and arrange remaining potatoes on top. Dot with butter.
6 Cook in a moderate oven (375°F.–Gas Mark 4) for 40 minutes.

Variation

Onion ring casserole–use only 6 oz. potatoes raw, cook remaining 6 oz. and mash. After 30 minutes' cooking, remove casserole, pipe creamed potato round edge of dish, brush lightly with beaten egg and decorate with lightly fried onion rings. Return to oven for 7–10 minutes.

Beef and orange casserole No. 1

you will need for 4 servings:

1½ lb. stewing steak
1½ oz. cornflour
salt, pepper
2 onions
1 clove garlic
2 tablespoons corn oil
2 carrots
2 oranges
½ pint cider
water
2 beef stock cubes
blanched green pepper, sliced

1 Trim meat and cut into cubes.
2 Coat well with seasoned cornflour.
3 Sauté meat in oil with sliced onions and finely chopped garlic. Remove to a casserole. Add carrots, sliced.
4 Thinly peel oranges, remove white membrane, blanch peel for a few minutes, cut in thin strips.
5 Add half peel to meat and vegetables and reserve remainder for garnish.
6 Squeeze out juice from oranges and add to cider. Add stock cubes and enough boiling water to make quantity to 1½ pints. Stir well.
7 Pour over meat and vegetables, cover and cook for 1–1½ hours in a moderate oven (375°F.–Gas Mark 4).
8 Serve garnished with remaining orange rind and green pepper.

Beef and sausage casserole

you will need for 4 servings:

1 lb. stewing beef
8 oz. pork sausages
1 tablespoon flour
salt, pepper
1 lb. potatoes, peeled and sliced
8 oz. tomatoes, peeled and sliced
1 apple, peeled, cored and chopped
1 large onion, peeled and chopped
stock (see page 84) or water

1 Cut meat and sausages into pieces and coat with seasoned flour.
2 Arrange all ingredients in layers in a deep casserole, starting and finishing with vegetables.

3 Add salt and pepper and enough stock or water to come about $\frac{2}{3}$ up the casserole.

4 Cover closely and cook in a very slow oven (325°F.– Gas Mark 2) about $2\frac{1}{2}$ hours.

Beef au gratin

you will need for 4 servings:

12 oz. potatoes, peeled and thickly sliced	$\frac{1}{2}$ oz. flour
1 lb. chuck steak	1 beef stock cube
8 oz. onions, sliced thinly	$\frac{2}{3}$ pint water
1 small green pepper, seeded and chopped finely	3 tablespoons red cooking wine
2 oz. butter	3 tomatoes, peeled and sliced
	breadcrumbs
	extra butter

1 Put potatoes into a greased casserole.

2 Put meat on top.

3 Brown onion and pepper in butter and put with meat.

4 Add flour and crumbled stock cube to remaining fat and mix well. Add water and stir till boiling. Add wine. Pour this over meat and cover with tomatoes.

5 Sprinkle fairly thickly with breadcrumbs and dot with butter.

6 Cover and cook in a slow oven (350°F.– Gas Mark 3) for about 2 hours.

7 Remove lid, increase heat a little, and cook until breadcrumbs are nicely browned.

Beef cobbler

you will need for 4 servings:

2 lb. stewing beef	1 teaspoon salt
1 oz. well-seasoned flour	$\frac{1}{4}$ pint water
1 oz. cooking fat	**cobbler topping:**
2 medium-sized onions, peeled and thinly sliced	8 oz. self-raising flour
	1 teaspoon salt
2 medium-sized tomatoes, skinned and chopped (optional)	2 oz. margarine and cooking fat mixed
	1 teaspoon parsley, finely chopped
	6–8 tablespoons milk

1 Cube meat and toss in seasoned flour.

2 Melt fat, add vegetables and fry until golden.

3 Add meat and fry for 5 minutes.

4 Turn into 2–3 pint casserole, add tomatoes, salt and water.

5 Cover and cook in the centre of a cool oven (325°F.– Gas Mark 2) for 2–2$\frac{1}{2}$ hours.

To make topping

1 Sift flour and salt, rub in fat and add parsley.

2 Mix to a soft dough with milk and turn on to a floured surface.

3 Knead lightly and roll out to $\frac{1}{2}$-inch thickness.

4 Cut into 10 rounds with a biscuit cutter and cut out centre of each round with a smaller cutter.

5 Take casserole from oven. Arrange scone rounds on top of meat.

6 Brush scones with milk and return to top of a moderately hot oven (400°F.– Gas Mark 5) for 20–25 minutes until scones are well risen and brown.

Beef and orange casserole No. 2

you will need for 4 servings:

1$\frac{1}{2}$ lb. stewing steak	1 oz. flour
1 oz. fat	1 beef stock cube
8 oz. onions, peeled and chopped	1 pint water
	$\frac{1}{4}$ pint cider
2 carrots, peeled and chopped	2 oranges
	seasoning
small clove garlic, chopped	

1 Trim and cut up meat and brown on all sides in hot fat. Put into a casserole.

2 Add vegetables and garlic to remaining fat and sauté for a few minutes, then put with meat.

3 Put flour and crushed stock cube into pan in which meat was browned and mix well. Add water, stir till boiling.

4 Add cider and orange juice and pour over contents of the casserole.

5 Blanch rind of 1 orange, remove all white pith and shred thinly. Put half into the casserole and keep the rest for garnish.

6 Cover and cook in a very slow oven (325°F.– Gas Mark 2) for about 2 hours.

7 Before serving, correct seasoning and sprinkle with remaining orange peel.

Beef and mushroom casserole

you will need for 4 servings:

1$\frac{1}{2}$ lb. lean stewing steak	8 oz. carrots, peeled and cut into slices lengthways
1 tablespoon flour	
salt, pepper	1 small red or green pepper, seeded and thinly sliced
1$\frac{1}{2}$ oz. dripping	
2 medium-sized onions, peeled and sliced thinly	$\frac{1}{2}$ pint stock (see page 84) or water
4 oz. mushrooms	

1 Cut meat into pieces and coat with seasoned flour.

2 Heat dripping, add onions and fry till golden brown. Put into a casserole with all other vegetables.

3 Fry meat in remaining fat and when brown remove to the casserole.

4 Add stock to any remaining fat and sediment in the pan. Stir till boiling then pour over contents of casserole.

5 Cover and cook in a slow oven (350°F.– Gas Mark 3) for 2–2$\frac{1}{2}$ hours.

6 Correct seasoning before serving.

Beef and tomato casserole

you will need for 6 servings:

2 oz. dripping	1 beef stock cube
2–3 lb. topside beef	$\frac{1}{2}$ pint water
8 oz. onions, peeled and sliced	salt, pepper
	8 oz. spaghetti
12 oz. carrots, peeled and sliced	$\frac{1}{2}$ oz. butter
	1 tablespoon grated cheese
1 lb. tomatoes, peeled and thickly sliced	

1 Heat dripping in a heavy saucepan. Put in meat and brown well on all sides. [*continued*

2 Put into a casserole and surround with vegetables and tomatoes.
3 Drain off any surplus fat from pan, leaving any sediment from the meat. Add stock cube and water and stir till boiling.
4 Pour over contents of casserole. Add a little seasoning, cover and cook in a slow oven (325°F.—Gas Mark 2) for about 3 hours.
5 About 20 minutes before the end of the cooking, put spaghetti into boiling salted water and cook till tender. Drain, then add butter and sprinkle with cheese.
To serve, put the meat on to a large dish and arrange spaghetti and vegetables round.

Beef and potato hot pot

you will need for 4 servings:

1½ lb. stewing steak	4 tomatoes, peeled and
1 oz. flour	sliced
salt, pepper	3 carrots, peeled and
2 oz. fat	sliced
1 large onion, peeled	2–3 sticks celery,
and sliced	chopped
1 beef stock cube	¼ teaspoon basil
¾ pint water	¼ teaspoon marjoram
	8 oz. potatoes

1 Trim meat and cut into pieces.
2 Coat with seasoned flour.
3 Heat fat, put in meat and brown well. Remove to a casserole.
4 Brown onion and put with meat.
5 Add stock cube and remaining flour to remaining fat in the pan, mix well, add water, tomatoes, carrots, celery and herbs and stir till boiling. Pour over contents of casserole.
6 Slice potatoes and put on top, sprinkle with salt and pepper.
7 Cover and cook about 2 hours in a very slow oven (325°F.—Gas Mark 2).
8 Remove lid for the last 30 minutes.

Beef olives

you will need for 4 servings:

stuffing:	1–1½ lb. stewing steak
2 oz. fresh breadcrumbs	2 tablespoons oil
½ small onion, peeled	1 onion, peeled and
and chopped	sliced
1 teaspoon mixed herbs	1 carrot, peeled and
1 teaspoon chopped	sliced
parsley	1 beef stock cube
salt, pepper	¾ pint water
1 oz. butter	3 tablespoons red wine
1 egg	1 bay leaf
	1 tablespoon cornflour

1 Mix all ingredients for stuffing together and bind with beaten egg.
2 Cut meat into thin slices, put a little stuffing on each and roll up. Tie with thin string.

3 Heat oil and fry the meat till brown, then remove to casserole.
4 Sauté onion and carrot in remaining oil and put with meat.
5 Crumble stock cube into pan, add water and wine and stir till boiling. Pour over contents of casserole.
6 Add bay leaf, cover and cook in a slow oven (325°F.—Gas Mark 2) for 1–1½ hours.
7 When cooked, add cornflour mixed smoothly with a little cold water and cook a further 5 minutes.
8 Remove string and correct seasoning before serving.

Beef Neapolitan

you will need for 4 servings:

1½ lb. lean stewing beef	1 carrot, sliced thinly
salt, pepper	½ small clove garlic,
1 tablespoon oil	crushed
1 6-oz. can tomato	8 oz. small macaroni or
purée	spaghetti
½ pint water	2 oz. grated cheese
1 tablespoon lemon	1 oz. butter
juice	1 tablespoon chopped
pinch sugar	parsley
pinch marjoram or	
oregano	

1 Cut meat into small pieces, sprinkle with salt and pepper and brown in hot oil. Transfer to a casserole.
2 Mix tomato purée, water and lemon juice together, add sugar and pour over meat.
3 Add marjoram, carrot and garlic.
4 Cover and cook for 2 hours in a slow oven (350°F.—Gas Mark 3). Add a little extra stock or water during the cooking if the sauce becomes too thick.
5 About 15 minutes before the end of the cooking, cook the macaroni in boiling salted water. Drain well, add cheese, butter and parsley.
6 Put meat and sauce into a serving dish and arrange the macaroni round.

Beef provençale No. 1

you will need for 4 servings:

1½ lb. stewing steak	pinch sugar
1 oz. flour	¼ pint red wine
salt, pepper	¼ pint stock (see
2 tablespoons oil	page 84) or water
2 rashers streaky bacon	*bouquet garni* (see
12 small white onions	page 85)
2 oz. mushrooms	little chopped parsley

1 Trim and cut up meat and coat well with seasoned flour.
2 Heat oil and brown meat well on all sides. Transfer to a casserole.
3 Add chopped bacon, onions and sliced mushrooms to remaining oil. Add sugar and cook all together for a few minutes, then put into casserole.
4 Add wine and stock to any remaining fat and sediment in the pan and stir till boiling.
5 Pour over contents of casserole. Add *bouquet garni*.

6 Cover and cook in a slow oven (350°F. – Gas Mark 3) about 2 hours.

7 Before serving, remove *bouquet garni*, check seasoning and sprinkle with parsley.

Beef suprême

you will need for 4 servings:

1 lb. stewing steak	4 oz. runner beans, sliced
1 oz. flour	2 sticks celery, chopped
salt, pepper	1 beef stock cube
2 tablespoons oil	½ pint water
1 large onion, peeled and sliced	1 tablespoon soy sauce
1 green pepper, seeded and sliced	4 oz. mushrooms, sliced
1 tablespoon pimento, chopped	

1 Cut meat into pieces, coat with seasoned flour.

2 Heat oil, add meat and cook till brown. Remove to a casserole.

3 Add onion, pepper, pimento, beans and celery to remaining oil and cook all together for about 5 minutes. Put into casserole with the meat.

4 Put stock cube and any remaining flour into pan. Add water and soy sauce and stir till boiling.

5 Pour over contents of casserole, add mushrooms, cover and cook in a slow oven (325°F. – Gas Mark 2) for 1½–2 hours.

Braised beef bourguignon No. 1

you will need for 4 servings:

1½ lb. topside beef	4 tablespoons oil
salt, freshly ground black pepper	2 oz. streaky bacon
3–4 onions, peeled and sliced	1 tablespoon flour
1 bay leaf	1 beef stock cube
1 sprig thyme	½ pint water
strip of lemon peel	1 clove garlic
¼ pint red wine	*bouquet garni* (see page 85)
	1 lemon

1 Trim meat and cut into fairly large pieces.

2 Put into a dish and sprinkle with salt and pepper. Add a little of the onion, bay leaf, thyme and lemon peel. Pour over wine and 2 tablespoons oil. Leave to marinate for about 3 hours.

3 Heat remaining oil, add bacon, cut into pieces and remaining onion and cook till onion is slightly coloured, then move to a casserole.

4 Remove meat from marinade, drain, coat with flour and brown in the remaining oil, then put into casserole.

5 Strain marinade and pour into pan in which meat was browned, add stock cube, water, garlic and *bouquet garni*. Bring all to boiling point, then pour over contents of casserole.

6 Cover and cook in a slow oven (325°F. – Gas Mark 2) about 2½ hours. Before serving, remove garlic and *bouquet garni* and correct seasoning. Garnish with wedges of lemon.

Beef bourguignon No. 2

(for special occasions)

you will need for 4 servings:

2–2½ lb. buttock steak	1 tablespoon tomato purée (see page 85)
1 tablespoon flour	¾ pint red wine
salt, pepper	4 oz. button mushrooms
3–4 tablespoons oil	½ oz. butter
4 tablespoons brandy	½ oz. flour
4 oz. streaky bacon	½ oz. brown sugar
4 oz. button onions	parsley
1 clove garlic	

1 Trim and cut meat into pieces, coat with seasoned flour and fry in hot oil till well browned.

2 Add brandy and ignite. When flames die down, transfer meat to a casserole.

3 Cut up bacon and fry in remaining oil with peeled onions and crushed garlic, then put with the meat.

4 Add tomato purée, wine, mushrooms and enough water to just cover the meat.

5 Cook in a slow oven (325°F. – Gas Mark 2) about 2½ hours.

6 Mix butter with flour and stir into casserole. Correct seasoning and add sugar.

7 Continue cooking for 30 minutes and sprinkle with parsley before serving.

Braised beef casserole

you will need for 4–6 servings:

2½–3 lb. braising steak	2 onions, peeled and grated
1 oz. dripping or bacon fat	1 stick celery, chopped
2 carrots, peeled and grated	1 leek, chopped
2 turnips, peeled and grated	1 bay leaf
1 parsnip, peeled and grated	salt, pepper
	1 tablespoon water

1 Grease bottom and sides of a large casserole.

2 Brown meat on all sides in hot dripping.

3 Mix all vegetables and bay leaf together and put half into casserole; sprinkle with a little salt and pepper. Put meat on top and cover with remaining vegetables.

4 Add water and cover securely with foil, then put on the lid. (It is important that no moisture is lost.)

5 Cook in a very moderate oven (350°F. – Gas Mark 3) for 4–4½ hours.

Braised silverside of beef

you will need for 6 servings:

about 3 lb. silverside	3–4 sticks of celery, chopped
2 oz. dripping	*bouquet garni* (see page 85)
8 oz. onions, peeled and sliced	½ pint stock (see page 84) or water
8 oz. carrots, peeled and sliced	salt, pepper
1 turnip, peeled and chopped	1 tablespoon chopped parsley

1 Wipe meat, and leave in one piece.

2 Heat dripping in a large pan, put in meat and brown on all sides.

3 Put all vegetables into a deep casserole, place meat on top. Add *bouquet garni*, and stock and season well.

4 Cover closely and cook in a slow oven (325°F. – Gas Mark 2) until the meat is tender, about 2–2½ hours.

5 To serve, put meat on to a dish and arrange vegetables round. Sprinkle with parsley.

Swedish casserole

you will need for 4 servings:

1 lb. minced beef	4 oz. streaky bacon,
1 oz. fresh breadcrumbs	chopped
pinch mixed herbs	1 carrot, chopped
1 tablespoon chopped	1 packet tomato soup
onion	1 pint water
1 level teaspoon salt	1 12-oz. can butter
1 egg, beaten	beans
1 oz. cornflour	
2 tablespoons corn oil	

1 Mix together the beef, breadcrumbs, herbs, onion and salt. Bind together with the egg.

2 Shape into 12 balls and coat with the cornflour. Heat the corn oil and brown the meat balls. Remove to a casserole.

3 Sauté the bacon and carrot in the remaining corn oil and add the contents of the packet of tomato soup.

4 Stir in the water and bring to the boil stirring all the time. Drain the butter beans and add to the sauce.

5 Pour the sauce over the meat balls in the casserole. Cover and bake in a moderately hot oven (375°F. – Gas Mark 4) for 45 minutes.

Canadian steak

you will need for 4 servings:

1½ lb. stewing steak	¾–¾ pint water
1 oz. cornflour	8 oz. carrots, peeled
salt, pepper	and diced
2 oz. fat	1 small can mushroom
1 medium-sized onion,	soup
peeled and chopped	

1 Trim meat, cut into pieces and coat with seasoned cornflour.

2 Melt fat, add onion and fry till brown, then put into a casserole.

3 Add meat to remaining fat and brown on all sides. Put with onion.

4 Add water, carrots and mushroom soup. Cover and cook in a slow oven (325°F. – Gas Mark 2) for about 2 hours.

5 Correct seasoning before serving.

Burgundian meat balls

you will need for 4 servings:

for the meat balls:	for the sauce:
1 lb. raw minced beef	3 tablespoons oil
2 oz. white	½ oz. flour
breadcrumbs	1 beef stock cube
salt, pepper	¾ pint water
1 teaspoon dried basil	¼ pint red wine
½ teaspoon grated	4 oz. mushrooms,
lemon rind	sliced
1 small onion, peeled	
and finely chopped	

1 Mix all ingredients for meat balls together and shape into 8–9 balls with floured hands.

2 Heat oil, brown meat balls and put into a casserole.

3 Mix flour with remaining oil and cook for 2–3 minutes. Add stock cube, water and wine and stir till boiling.

4 Pour over contents of casserole, add mushrooms.

5 Cover and cook about 1 hour in a slow oven (325°F. – Gas Mark 2).

Californian beef casserole

you will need for 4 servings:

1½ lb. lean stewing beef	6 olives
1 oz. flour	1 beef stock cube
salt, pepper	8 oz. potatoes, peeled
1 large onion, peeled	and sliced
and sliced	½ oz. butter
2 oz. prunes, soaked	
overnight	

1 Trim meat and cut into pieces.

2 Coat with seasoned flour and put into a casserole.

3 Cover with onion, and add prunes, stoned and stuffed with olives.

4 Use water in which prunes were soaked, and make quantity up to ¾ pint with boiling water.

5 Dissolve beef cube in this and pour over ingredients in casserole.

6 Cover with potatoes, sprinkle with salt and pepper and dot with butter.

7 Cover and cook in a slow oven (325°F. – Gas Mark 2) for about 2 hours. Remove lid for the last 20–30 minutes to allow potatoes to brown.

Cantonese beef with ginger rice

you will need for 4 servings:

	for ginger rice:
1½ lb. stewing beef	6 oz. Patna rice
1 tablespoon soy sauce	1 small onion, peeled
3 tablespoons sherry	and chopped
2 teaspoons sugar	1 tablespoon oil
pinch cinnamon	1 tablespoon preserved
1 beef stock cube	ginger
¾ pint boiling water	
½ oz. cornflour	
bean shoots for garnish,	
optional	

1 Trim meat and cut into cubes.

2 Mix soy sauce, sherry, sugar and cinnamon, pour over meat and leave for about 1 hour, stirring frequently.

3 Put meat and marinade into a casserole.

4 Dissolve stock cube in water and pour over meat.

5 Cover and cook in a slow oven (325°F. – Gas Mark 2) for about 1¾–2 hours.

6 Mix cornflour smoothly with a little cold water and stir into casserole – cook a further few minutes.

7 Before serving, correct seasoning and garnish with bean shoots.

To make ginger rice

1 Cook rice for 12 minutes in boiling salted water, drain, rinse and keep hot.
2 Fry onion in oil till soft, then mix with rice.
3 Add preserved ginger, chopped into small pieces, and toss all together.

Casseroled beef with peppers

you will need for 4 servings:

1½ lb. stewing beef	1 beef stock cube
1 oz. flour	1 pint water
salt, freshly ground black pepper	¼ pint red wine
2 tablespoons oil	1 red pepper, seeded and diced
2 onions, peeled and sliced	1 green pepper, seeded and diced
1 clove garlic, crushed	2 oz. mushrooms
2 carrots, peeled and chopped	black olives for garnish, optional

1 Trim meat and cut into cubes; coat with seasoned flour.
2 Heat oil and sauté meat, onions and garlic, then remove to a casserole and add carrots.
3 Put remaining flour and crumbled stock cube into pan, mix well, then add water and wine. Stir till boiling and pour over contents of casserole.
4 Cover and cook in a slow oven (350°F. – Gas Mark 3) for 1½ hours.
5 Add peppers and mushrooms and continue cooking for 45 minutes.
6 Before serving, correct seasoning and add black olives.

Casseroled beef Palermo

you will need for 4 servings:

1 lb. stewing steak	1 small clove garlic, chopped
1 tablespoon flour	½ pint stock or water
salt, pepper	1 small can peeled tomatoes
2 tablespoons oil	
8 oz. onions, peeled and sliced	pinch sugar
2 carrots, peeled and sliced	little vinegar
	few black olives

1 Cut meat into pieces and coat with seasoned flour.
2 Heat oil, and fry meat till browned. Remove to a casserole.
3 Fry onion, carrots and garlic in remaining oil and put with meat.
4 Add any remaining flour to pan, add water and tomatoes and stir till boiling.
5 Correct seasoning; add sugar and vinegar to improve the flavour.
6 Pour over meat and vegetables in casserole, cover tightly and cook in a very slow oven (325°F. – Gas Mark 2) for about 2 hours.
7 Just before serving, add olives.

Stuffed steak

you will need for 6 servings:

1½ lb. stewing steak	little chopped parsley
1 packet leek soup	little chopped green pepper
1 pint water	salt and pepper
	1 egg
for the stuffing:	
2 oz. breadcrumbs	pepper rings and tomato for garnish
pinch of basil	
pinch of sage	

1 Cut the meat into 2 flat pieces.
2 Make the stuffing by mixing all the dry ingredients together, bind with the egg.
3 Spread this on to one piece of the steak, place the other on top and place in a casserole.
4 Empty the contents of the packet of soup into a saucepan, stir in the pint of water and bring to the boil. Pour over the meat in the casserole, cover and cook in a moderately hot oven (375°F. – Gas Mark 4) for 1½–2 hours, until meat is tender.
5 Garnish with pepper rings and tomato slices.

Crusty beef stew

you will need for 4 servings:

1½ lb. stewing steak	½ pint stock (see page 84) or water
1 oz. flour	
salt, pepper	**for the crusty top:**
1 oz. fat	8 oz. self-raising flour
2 medium-sized onions, peeled and sliced	1 teaspoon salt
	1 oz. margarine
1 large carrot, peeled and sliced	1 oz. lard
2 tomatoes, peeled and chopped	milk

1 Trim and cut meat into pieces, coat with seasoned flour.
2 Melt fat and fry meat till brown, then put into a casserole.
3 Add all vegetables to remaining fat and sauté for 5 minutes, then put with meat in casserole.
4 Add a little seasoning and water or stock.
5 Cover and cook in a very slow oven (325°F. – Gas Mark 2) for about 2½ hours.

For crusty top

1 Sift flour and salt into a bowl, rub in fats. Mix to a soft dough with a little milk and knead lightly. Roll out to about ¼ inch thick and cut into rounds with a small plain cutter.
2 Remove casserole from oven, and arrange scones round the edge, just overlapping each other. Brush with milk and return to oven.
3 Increase heat to 400°F. – Gas Mark 5 for 20–25 minutes until scones are risen and browned.

Dolmas

you will need for 4 servings:

2 lb. raw minced beef
1 small onion, peeled
   and chopped finely
salt, freshly ground
   pepper
2 tablespoons cooked
   rice

1 cabbage
flour
stock (see page 84)
1 bay leaf
1 small can tomato
   purée
chopped parsley

1 Mix meat, onion, seasoning and rice very thoroughly and moisten with a little water.
2 Remove coarse outside leaves from cabbage and discard them.
3 Remove more tender leaves carefully, wash, then put into a pan of cold water, bring to the boil and boil for 3 minutes.
4 Drain and dab leaves dry with a cloth, then remove any hard stalk.
5 Put spoonful meat mixture on each leaf and roll up to form a sausage.
6 Roll lightly in flour and arrange in layers in a casserole. Barely cover with stock, add bay leaf and a little salt and pepper.
7 Cover and cook in a moderate oven (375°F.–Gas Mark 4) about 1¼ hours.
8 Carefully drain off some stock and use it to dilute the tomato purée, then pour back into the casserole and continue cooking for 15–20 minutes. Sprinkle with parsley before serving.

Exeter stew

you will need for 4 servings:

1 lb. stewing beef
1 oz. fat
1 onion
2–3 carrots
1 beef stock cube
¾ pint water
bouquet garni (see
   page 85)

for the dumplings:
4 oz. flour
1½ oz. finely chopped
   suet
1 teaspoon chopped
   parsley
¼ small onion, peeled
   and finely chopped
¼ teaspoon baking
   powder
salt, pepper

1 Trim meat, remove excess fat and cut into pieces.
2 Heat fat, add onion and fry till brown.
3 Add meat and brown on all sides.
4 Put meat into a casserole with onion and carrots.
5 Add flour and crumbled stock cube to remaining fat and mix well.
6 Add water and stir till boiling.
7 Pour over contents of casserole and add *bouquet garni*. Cover and cook in a slow oven (325°F.–Gas Mark 2) for about 1½ hours.
8 Make dumplings by mixing all ingredients together. Add enough cold water to form a soft dough. Shape into about 12 small balls. Put into casserole and continue cooking for 1 hour.

Chilli con carne

you will need for 4 servings:

1 lb. lean stewing
   beef
8 oz. pork
1¼ oz. fat, preferably
   bacon fat
1 medium-sized
   onion, peeled and
   chopped
1 clove garlic,
   crushed

½ pint stock (see
   page 84)
1 tablespoon flour
2 tablespoons chilli
   powder
½ teaspoon oregano
1 bay leaf
salt, freshly ground
   black pepper

1 Cut meat into small pieces and brown in hot fat. Remove to a casserole.
2 Brown onion and garlic in remaining fat and put with meat.
3 Barely cover with stock, cover and cook in a very slow oven (325°F.–Gas Mark 2) about 1 hour.
4 Mix flour and chilli powder smoothly with a little stock or water and stir into casserole.
5 Add oregano, bay leaf and seasoning and continue cooking a further 30 minutes–1 hour.
Before serving, correct seasoning and serve with red kidney beans and boiled rice.

Farmhouse pot roast

you will need for 4 servings:

4 oz. streaky bacon
1 tablespoon dripping
2 lb. beef brisket,
   chuck or skirt
2 onions, peeled and
   chopped
12 oz. carrots, peeled
   and sliced

¼ head of celery,
   chopped
½ oz. flour
1 beef stock cube
¾ pint water
sprig parsley
1 bay leaf
1 small clove garlic

1 Dice bacon, put into a pan and fry until fat runs out. Remove bacon to a casserole.
2 Heat dripping with bacon fat, tie meat into a good shape, then brown on all sides in hot fat. Put into casserole.
3 Add onions, carrots and celery to remaining fat and cook for about 5 minutes, then remove to casserole.
4 Put flour and crumbled stock cube into pan with any remaining fat and meat sediment, mix well, then add water and stir till boiling.
5 Pour over contents of casserole and add parsley, bay leaf and garlic.
6 Cover tightly with foil or greaseproof paper and then with the casserole lid.
7 Cook in a slow oven (350°F.–Gas Mark 3) for 2½–3 hours.

Flemish hot pot

you will need for 4 servings:

2 oz. dripping or 2 tablespoons oil
1½ lb. stewing steak
2 medium-sized onions, peeled and sliced
2 carrots, peeled and sliced

1 bay leaf
pinch mixed herbs
salt, pepper
1–1½ pints water or stock (see page 84)
1 slice bread, cut thickly
little made mustard

1 Heat fat, cut up the meat and brown well. Remove to a casserole.
2 Add onions and carrots to remaining fat and sauté for a few minutes. Put into casserole with meat.
3 Add bay leaf, herbs, seasoning and water.
4 Cover and cook in a slow oven (350°F. – Gas Mark 3) for about 2 hours.
5 Remove crust from bread, spread on both sides with mustard and place on top of stew.
6 Return to oven for 10 minutes, then stir bread into stew.
7 Correct seasoning before serving.

Goulash

you will need for 4 servings:

1½ lb. stewing steak
1 oz. fat
2 onions, peeled and chopped
2 carrots, peeled and chopped
1 oz. flour

1 beef stock cube
3 tablespoons tomato purée (see page 85)
2 teaspoons paprika
1 pint water
3 tablespoons yoghurt

1 Trim and cut up meat and brown in hot fat. Remove to a casserole.
2 Put onions and carrots into pan and sauté until lightly browned, then put with meat.
3 Put flour, crumbled stock cube and tomato purée into pan, adding a little more fat if necessary.
4 Cook for a few minutes, then add paprika and water and stir till boiling.
5 Pour into casserole, cover closely and cook in a very slow oven (325°F. – Gas Mark 2) for about 2 hours.
6 Just before serving, correct seasoning and stir in yoghurt.

Note: Sauerkraut or buttered noodles (page 87) are excellent with goulash.

Haricot beef

you will need for 4 servings:

8 oz. butter or haricot beans (soaked overnight)
1½ lb. stewing steak
½ oz. flour
salt, pepper
1 oz. dripping
2 onions, peeled and chopped

2 carrots, peeled and chopped
2–3 potatoes, peeled and sliced
8 oz. tomatoes, peeled and sliced
1 bay leaf
2 beef stock cubes
1½ pints boiling water

1 Cook beans until almost tender, then drain.
2 Cut meat into pieces and coat with seasoned flour.
3 Heat dripping and fry meat till well browned, then remove to a deep casserole.
4 Brown onions and carrots in remaining fat and put with meat.
5 Put potatoes, tomatoes, beans and bay leaf into casserole.
6 Dissolve stock cubes in boiling water and pour into casserole.
7 Cover and cook in a slow oven (350°F. – Gas Mark 3) for 2½–3 hours.

Huntsman's steak

you will need for 4 servings:

1 lb. stewing steak
salt, pepper
4 oz. mushrooms, sliced
1 onion, peeled and chopped
1 carrot, peeled and chopped
2 rashers streaky bacon

1 small can baked beans
1 tablespoon tomato purée (see page 85)
about ⅓ pint stock (see page 84) or water
8 oz. tomatoes, peeled and sliced

1 Cut meat into small pieces, put into a casserole and add a little seasoning.
2 Add vegetables and bacon, cut into strips.
3 Add beans and tomato purée and enough stock to barely cover.
4 Arrange tomato slices on top.
5 Cover and cook in a slow oven (325°F. – Gas Mark 2) about 1½ hours. Correct seasoning.

Italian beef stew

you will need for 4 servings:

2 tablespoons oil
4 oz. salt pork
1 small onion, peeled and sliced
1 clove garlic, crushed
1 lb. stewing beef

salt, pepper
pinch marjoram
⅛ pint red wine
2 tablespoons tomato purée (see page 85)
½ pint water

1 Heat oil, add pork cut into pieces, onion and garlic and sauté for a few minutes. Put into a casserole.
2 Trim and cut up beef, sprinkle with salt, pepper and marjoram and fry till brown in remaining oil, then put with pork.
3 Put wine into pan and reduce a little, then add tomato purée and water. Stir till boiling, then pour over ingredients in casserole. The liquid should barely cover meat.
4 Cover and cook in a slow oven (325°F. – Gas Mark 2) about 2 hours.

Hungarian herb stew

you will need for 4 servings:

1½ lb. stewing beef	2 tablespoons red
1 oz. flour	wine
salt, pepper	1 bay leaf
1½ oz. fat, preferably	1 tablespoon chopped
bacon fat	parsley
2 medium-sized	pinch caraway seeds
onions, peeled and	1 tablespoon paprika
chopped	¼ teaspoon marjoram
¾ pint stock	

1 Trim meat and cut into pieces. Coat with seasoned flour.
2 Heat fat, and brown meat on all sides. Remove to a casserole.
3 Add onions to remaining fat and brown well, then put with meat.
4 Add stock and wine.
5 Add bay leaf, cover and cook in a slow oven (325°F. – Gas Mark 2) for about 1½ hours.
6 Add all herbs and continue the cooking for 1 hour.
7 Correct seasoning and consistency before serving.

Hungarian beef

you will need for 4 servings:

1½ oz. fat	2 tablespoons tomato
2 medium-sized	purée (see page 85)
onions, peeled and	½ pint stock (see page
chopped	84) or water
1 tablespoon paprika	1 lb. potatoes
1½ lb. stewing steak	salt
1 teaspoon caraway	½ green pepper, thinly
seeds	sliced
¼ raw potato, grated	

1 Melt fat and fry onions till brown, stir in paprika.
2 Cut meat into small pieces, put with onions and add caraway seeds and potato.
3 Cook for a few minutes, stirring occasionally.
4 Add tomato purée and stock and transfer all into a casserole.
5 Cover and cook in a slow oven (350°F. – Gas Mark 3) for about 1½ hours.
6 Add the potatoes, peeled and cut into small cubes, add a little salt, and continue cooking for 30 minutes.
7 Before serving, correct seasoning and garnish with green pepper.

Jugged beef

you will need for 4 servings:

2 lb. leg or shin of	4 oz. streaky bacon
beef	1 carrot, peeled and
	chopped
for the marinade:	2 strips orange peel
3 tablespoons oil	1 apple, peeled and
salt	chopped
freshly ground black	½ pint stock (see page
pepper	84)
1 slice onion	1 oz. butter
1 bay leaf	¾ oz. cornflour
1 clove garlic	1 tablespoon
3 tablespoons red	redcurrant jelly
wine or vinegar	

1 Cut meat into small pieces.

2 Mix together all ingredients for marinade. Pour over meat and leave overnight.
3 Next day, fry bacon to extract fat, remove meat from marinade, and brown in bacon fat. Remove to a casserole.
4 Add carrot, orange peel, apple, marinade and stock. Cover and cook in a slow oven (325°F. – Gas Mark 2) for about 2½ hours.
5 Heat butter in pan in which meat was browned, add cornflour and mix well. Gradually add strained liquor from casserole, stir till boiling and boil for 1 minute.
6 Add redcurrant jelly, correct seasoning and pour back into casserole.
7 Return to oven and continue cooking for 1 hour or until meat is tender.

Meat balls with noodles

you will need for 4 servings:

2 oz. stale bread	3 tablespoons oil
1 lb. lean beef	tomato sauce (see
¼ onion or small piece	page 85) or
garlic	condensed
1 teaspoon salt	tomato soup
¼ teaspoon pepper	8–12 oz. noodles
2 eggs	

1 Soak bread in cold water for 5 minutes. Squeeze dry and mash well.
2 Mince beef finely with onion or garlic (if garlic is used, chop very finely).
3 Thoroughly mix bread, meat mixture, seasoning and eggs.
4 With wet hands, shape mixture into about 16 small balls.
5 Make tomato sauce.
6 Heat oil and brown meat balls, frequently shaking pan.
7 Drain off excess oil and transfer meat balls to casserole.
8 Pour in tomato sauce or soup (add only ½ can water if soup is used).
9 Cook, covered, in a slow oven (325°F. – Gas Mark 2) for 45 minutes.
10 Cook noodles in boiling salted water until tender and serve separately.

Mexican minced beef

you will need for 4 servings:

1 tablespoon oil	1 small can baked
1 clove garlic,	beans
crushed	¾ oz. flour
2 medium-sized	1 beef stock cube
onions, peeled and	½ pint water
chopped	2 teaspoons
1 lb. stewing beef,	Worcestershire
minced	sauce
8 oz. tomatoes,	
peeled and sliced	
thickly	

1 Heat oil, add garlic and onions and fry till lightly browned.
2 Add meat and brown lightly.

14

3 Transfer meat and onions to a casserole. Add tomatoes and baked beans.

4 Put flour and crumbled stock cube into pan in which meat was browned, mix well, then add water and stir till boiling. Add Worcestershire sauce and pour over contents of casserole.

5 Cover and cook in a slow oven (350°F. – Gas Mark 3) for about 1¼ hours. Correct seasoning.

Minced beef Marguerite

you will need for 4 servings:

1 tablespoon oil	2 oz. seedless raisins
1 large onion, peeled and chopped	1 beef stock cube
1½ lb. minced beef	⅜ pint boiling water
salt, pepper	½ oz. cornflour
¼ teaspoon grated nutmeg	2 hard-boiled eggs, fried croûtons for garnish
1 bay leaf	

1 Heat oil, add onion and meat and sauté for 5 minutes.

2 Put into a casserole with salt, pepper, nutmeg, bay leaf and raisins.

3 Dissolve stock cube in boiling water and pour into casserole.

4 Cover and cook in a slow oven (350°F. – Gas Mark 3) for about 45 minutes.

5 Mix cornflour smoothly with a little cold water and stir into casserole. Continue cooking for 15 minutes.

6 Serve garnished with croûtons of toast, or fried bread and quartered eggs.

Provençal stew

you will need for 4 servings:

1 lb. stewing steak	2 carrots, sliced
1 oz. cornflour	1 pint beef stock
salt and pepper	¼ pint red wine (optional)
2 tablespoons corn oil	1 small red pepper, diced
2 onions, sliced	1 small green pepper, diced
clove of garlic, finely chopped	

1 Trim the meat and cut into cubes, coat well with cornflour, seasoned with salt and pepper.

2 Heat the corn oil and lightly sauté the meat, onions, garlic and carrots.

3 Add the beef stock, wine and peppers, cover and simmer gently for 1–1¼ hours or until the meat is tender.

Mock duck

you will need for 4 servings:

1½ lb. stewing beef, in one piece	small piece green pepper
stuffing:	salt, pepper
2 oz. white breadcrumbs	1 tablespoon oil
pinch basil and sage	
1 teaspoon chopped parsley	1 can condensed mushroom soup

1 Cut meat into two flat pieces.

2 Mix all ingredients for stuffing together, with enough oil to bind.

3 Spread stuffing on half the meat, place the other piece on top and put into a casserole.

4 Pour mushroom soup over.

5 Cover and cook in a slow oven (350°F. – Gas Mark 3) about 1½ hours.

Prune hot pot

you will need for 4 servings:

1 lb. stewing steak	8 oz. onions, peeled and sliced
1 oz. flour	4 oz. cooked stoned prunes
salt, pepper	1 beef stock cube
1 lb. potatoes, peeled and sliced	⅜ pint boiling water

1 Trim meat and cut into pieces.

2 Coat with seasoned flour.

3 Arrange meat, vegetables and prunes in layers in a casserole, leaving enough potatoes for the top layer.

4 Dissolve stock cube in water and pour over contents of casserole.

5 Top with potato slices.

6 Cover closely and cook in a slow oven (350°F. – Gas Mark 3) for about 2 hours.

Moussaka

you will need for 4 servings:

3 tablespoons oil	8 oz. tomatoes, peeled and sliced
1 oz. butter	chopped parsley
8 oz. onions, peeled and sliced	
2 aubergines, sliced	**sauce:**
1 lb. potatoes, peeled and sliced	1 oz. butter
1 lb. minced beef	1 oz. flour
salt, pepper	½ pint milk and water
	1 egg
	2 oz. grated cheese

1 Heat oil and butter, add onions and cook until beginning to look transparent.

2 Add aubergines and potatoes and cook for a few minutes.

3 In another pan, melt butter for sauce.

4 Add flour and mix well. Remove from heat and add milk.

5 Return to heat, stir till boiling and boil for 1 minute.

6 Season, and leave to cool a little, then stir in beaten egg and cheese.

7 Put a layer of onion, potato and aubergine into a deep casserole. Add meat, cover with tomato and some sauce.

8 Cover with remaining onion mixture and add remaining sauce.

9 Cover and cook in a slow oven (325°F. – Gas Mark 2) for about 2 hours.

10 Sprinkle with parsley before serving.

Old English beef hot pot

you will need for 4 servings:

1 pint ale, beer or
  or cider
¼ pint beef stock (see
  page 84) or 1 beef
  stock cube
  dissolved in ½ pint
  water
8 oz. onions, peeled
  and sliced
2 lb. leg or shin of
  beef
2 medium-sized
  carrots, peeled and
  chopped
2 oz. mushrooms,
  sliced
1 stick celery, chopped
1 leek, chopped
small piece of turnip,
  peeled and
  chopped
salt, pepper
pinch nutmeg
1 strip lemon peel
1 bay leaf
1 tablespoon chopped
  parsley

1 Boil ale until reduced by half, add stock and boil a further 5 minutes.
2 Put a layer of onions in a large casserole, then fill about three-quarters full with layers of meat, cut into small pieces, and vegetables.
3 Sprinkle each layer with a little seasoning and add nutmeg, lemon peel and bay leaf.
4 Add hot reduced liquid.
5 Cover tightly with foil and then put lid on.
6 Cook in a slow oven (350°F. – Gas Mark 3) for 4–4½ hours.
7 Before serving, sprinkle with parsley and remove bay leaf and lemon peel.

Ragoût of beef No. 1
(for special occasions)

you will need for 4 servings:

1½ lb. stewing beef
2 tablespoons oil
12 small button
  onions, peeled
1 dessertspoon flour
4 tablespoons red
  wine
1–1½ pints stock (see
  page 84)
salt, pepper
bouquet garni (see
  page 85)
1 small clove garlic,
  crushed
1 oz. walnuts
1 head celery,
  chopped
½ oz. butter
1 tablespoon orange
  peel, blanched and
  shredded

1 Cut meat into pieces and brown in hot oil. Transfer to a casserole.
2 Brown onions and put with meat.
3 Add flour to remaining fat and cook for a few minutes. Remove from heat, add wine and 1 pint stock. Return to heat and stir till boiling. Add salt and pepper and pour over meat.
4 Add *bouquet garni*, garlic and, if necessary, a little more stock so meat is just covered.
5 Cover tightly and cook in a slow oven (325°F. – Gas Mark 2) about 1 hour.
6 Toss walnuts and best part of the celery in butter for a few minutes. Add to casserole and continue cooking for 1 hour.
7 Before serving, correct seasoning and sprinkle with orange peel.

Ragoût of beef No. 2

you will need for 4 servings:

1½ lb. stewing steak
2 tablespoons oil
2 onions, peeled and
  finely chopped
2 carrots, peeled and
  chopped
½ oz. cornflour
2 beef stock cubes
1½ pints water
bouquet garni (see
  page 85)
1 small head celery
2 tablespoons sherry
2 oz. browned
  almonds, shredded

1 Trim and cut up meat, brown on all sides in hot oil, then put into a casserole.
2 Brown onions and carrots and put with meat.
3 Add cornflour and crumbled stock cubes to remaining fat, mix well and cook for a few minutes.
4 Add water and stir till boiling, then pour over contents of casserole.
5 Add *bouquet garni*, cover and cook in a slow oven (325°F. – Gas Mark 2) for about 1 hour.
6 Add chopped celery and continue cooking for 1 hour or until meat is tender.
7 Before serving, correct seasoning, add sherry and sprinkle with almonds.

Russian beef casserole

you will need for 4 servings:

1½ lb. lean stewing
  beef
½ oz. flour
salt, pepper
¼ teaspoon curry
  powder
1½ oz. butter
2–3 onions, peeled
  and sliced thinly
1 beef stock cube
1 pint water
2 tablespoons tomato
  purée (see page 85)
2 tablespoons sour
  cream

1 Cut meat into small pieces.
2 Mix flour, salt, pepper and curry powder and toss meat in it.
3 Heat butter, add meat and fry till golden brown. Transfer to a casserole.
4 Put onions into remaining fat, brown well, then put into casserole with meat.
5 Put any remaining flour into pan, add crumbled stock cube and mix well.
6 Add water and tomato purée, stir till boiling.
7 Cool a little, stir in sour cream and pour over contents of casserole.
8 Cover and cook for 2–2½ hours in a slow oven (325°F. – Gas Mark 2).

Steak and kidney casserole

you will need for 4 servings:

1 lb. stewing steak
2 lamb's kidneys
½ oz. flour
salt, pepper
2 tablespoons oil
1 lb. potatoes
1 onion, peeled and
  sliced
1 carrot, peeled and
  sliced
4 oz. mushrooms,
  peeled and sliced
½ oz. cornflour
1 beef stock cube
¾ pint water

1 Remove any excess fat from steak and cut into pieces.

2 Skin kidneys, cut in half and remove cores.

3 Coat with seasoned flour.

4 Heat oil and brown steak and kidney.

5 Peel and slice potatoes, reserve enough for top of the casserole and put the rest in the bottom with onion, carrot and mushrooms.

6 Arrange meat and kidney on top, add seasoning.

7 Mix cornflour and stock cube in pan in which meat was fried. Add water and stir till boiling.

8 Pour over contents of casserole.

9 Arrange remaining potato slices neatly on top.

10 Cover closely and cook in a slow oven (325°F. – Gas Mark 2) for about 2 hours. For a golden brown top, the lid can be removed about 30 minutes before the end of cooking.

Beef paprika

you will need for 4 servings:

1 lb. stewing steak	2 level tablespoons
1 oz. cornflour	sultanas
salt and pepper	1 2¼-oz. can tomato
2 level teaspoons	purée
paprika pepper	1 beef stock cube
2 tablespoons corn	¼ pint water
oil	4 oz. mushrooms,
2 onions, chopped	sliced
2 carrots, sliced	
½ small green pepper, sliced	

1 Trim the steak and cut into 1 inch cubes.

2 Coat in the cornflour to which salt, pepper and paprika pepper have been added.

3 Heat the corn oil and sauté the meat and onions until lightly browned. Remove to a casserole.

4 Add the carrots, green pepper and sultanas to the meat.

5 Reheat the remaining corn oil and add remaining cornflour.

6 Add the tomato purée and beef stock cube, mix well. Gradually stir in the water and bring to the boil, stirring well. Pour over the ingredients in the casserole.

7 Cover and cook in a moderate oven (375°F. – Gas Mark 4) for 2 hours.

8 Fifteen minutes before the end of cooking time, add the mushrooms.

Beef in red wine

you will need for 4 servings:

2 lb. topside beef	*bouquet garni* (see
4 rashers bacon	page 85)
1 tablespoon chopped	salt, pepper
parsley	½ pint red wine
1 clove garlic, minced	2 teaspoons tomato
1 tablespoon oil	purée (see page 85)
4 oz. onions, peeled	2 teaspoons cornflour
and sliced	
8 oz. carrots, peeled and sliced	

1 Wipe meat and cut into 2-inch squares.

2 Remove rind from bacon and cut into 2-inch strips.

3 Mix parsley and garlic and roll bacon strips in it.

4 Using a sharp pointed knife, insert a strip of bacon into each piece of beef.

5 Heat oil, and sauté onion and carrot until onion is well browned.

6 Add meat, *bouquet garni*, seasoning and wine and bring to boiling point.

7 Cover very tightly and cook in a slow oven (325°F. – Gas Mark 2) about 3½ hours.

8 When meat is tender, put on to a serving dish with vegetables.

9 Strain off liquor into a small pan, add tomato purée and cornflour mixed, stir till boiling and boil for 3 minutes. Correct seasoning and serve in a sauce boat.

Beef bourgeoise

you will need for 4 servings:

1½ lb. stewing steak	12 onions
1 oz. flour	1 tablespoon tomato
salt, pepper	purée (see page 85)
1 oz. dripping	1 pint stock (see page
8 oz. French beans,	84)
cut in diamonds	*bouquet garni* (see
3–4 carrots, peeled	page 85)
and sliced	
1 turnip, peeled and chopped	

1 Cut meat into pieces, coat with seasoned flour.

2 Heat dripping and brown meat on all sides, then remove to a casserole.

3 Add all vegetables to meat.

4 Add remaining flour to fat left in pan and mix well. Add tomato purée and stock and stir till boiling. Pour over contents of casserole.

5 Add *bouquet garni*, cover and cook in a slow oven (350°F. – Gas Mark 3) about 2 hours. Remove *bouquet garni* and correct seasoning before serving.

Spiced beef casserole

you will need for 4 servings:

4 oz. ox kidney	1 teaspoon mixed
1 lb. stewing beef	spice
2 tablespoons oil	2 onions, peeled and
3 tablespoons red	sliced
wine	2 carrots, peeled and
1 clove garlic,	sliced
crushed	1 can tomato Juice
1 bay leaf	salt, pepper
pinch nutmeg	

1 Cut kidney into pieces, cover with cold salted water and leave for 5 minutes, then drain and dry.

2 Trim and cut beef into pieces.

3 Mix oil, wine and spices and herbs together, pour over meat and kidney. Leave overnight in a cool place.

4 Next day, put meat and kidney into a casserole with onions and carrots, add strained marinade and tomato juice. Season lightly with salt and pepper.

5 Cover and cook in a slow oven (325°F. – Gas Mark 2) for about 3 hours. Correct seasoning before serving.

Steak and bacon casserole

you will need for 4 servings:

1½ lb. lean stewing steak	½ pint beer
8 oz. lean bacon	¼ pint stock (see page 84) or water
2 oz. dripping	
8 oz. onions, peeled and sliced	1 teaspoon made mustard
1 oz. flour	2 teaspoons sugar
salt, pepper	*bouquet garni* (see page 85)

1 Cut meat and bacon into thin strips.
2 Heat dripping and fry onions until golden brown. Put into a casserole.
3 Coat meat with seasoned flour and fry in remaining fat till well browned. Add to casserole.
4 Put any remaining flour into pan and mix with sediment from meat.
5 Add beer and stock and stir till boiling.
6 Add mustard, sugar and seasoning as required and pour over meat.
7 Add *bouquet garni*.
8 Cover and cook in a slow oven (350°F. – Gas Mark 3) about 2 hours.

Beef and spaghetti casserole

you will need for 4 servings:

3 tablespoons oil	salt, pepper
8 oz. beef sausages	8 oz. stewing beef, minced
1 onion, peeled and chopped	2 lb. tomatoes, peeled and chopped
1 green pepper, seeded and chopped	8 oz. spaghetti
1 clove garlic, crushed	3 oz. Parmesan cheese, grated

1 Heat oil, slice sausages and brown lightly then remove to a plate.
2 Add onion, green pepper and garlic and sauté until onion is transparent.
3 Add meat and cook, stirring frequently until meat is brown. Season carefully.
4 Add sausages and tomatoes, bring all to boiling point, then transfer to a casserole. Cover and cook in a slow oven (325°F. – Gas Mark 2) about 35 minutes.
5 Cook spaghetti in boiling salted water, drain well and chop.
6 Stir into casserole with half the cheese and continue cooking for 1 hour.
7 Uncover for the last 10–15 minutes and sprinkle with remaining cheese before serving.

Beef stew

you will need for 4 servings:

2 lb. lean stewing steak	1 pint beef stock (see page 84)
3 oz. bacon fat or lard	¼ pint shelled broad beans or 1 packet frozen broad beans
1½ lb. onions, peeled and sliced	
3 tablespoons paprika	¼ pint sour cream
garlic salt, pepper	1 oz. flour
1 14- oz. can tomatoes	

1 Wipe and trim meat and cut into small cubes.
2 Heat bacon fat, add meat and cook till well browned, then remove to a casserole.
3 Add onions to remaining fat and fry till lightly browned, then put with meat.
4 Stir paprika, garlic salt and pepper into remaining fat in pan and mix well. Add tomatoes and a little of the stock and cook for a few minutes, then pour over contents of casserole.
5 Add enough stock to just cover the meat. Cover casserole and cook in a very slow oven (325°F. – Gas Mark 2) about 2 hours.
6 Add broad beans and cook a further 20 minutes.
7 Mix sour cream and flour smoothly with a little liquor from the casserole.
8 Stir into casserole and cook a further 5 minutes, but do not allow to boil. Serve with mashed potatoes or noodles.

Casserole of beef, bacon and mushrooms

you will need for 4 servings:

1½ lb. stewing steak	2 rounded teaspoons concentrated tomato purée
1 onion	
4 oz. streaky bacon	
4 oz. mushrooms	½ pint water
1–1½ oz. butter	salt and pepper
1½ oz. flour	

1 Trim meat and cut into 1-inch cubes.
2 Peel and slice onion.
3 Remove rind from bacon, cut into pieces 1 inch in length.
4 Peel mushrooms if necessary.
5 Fry onion, bacon and mushrooms in butter for 3 minutes. Remove from pan, and fry steak until browned. Remove steak.
6 Place steak with onion, bacon and mushroom in casserole.
7 Stir flour into pan, adding more butter if necessary to make a roux. Allow to cook for 3 minutes.
8 Add tomato purée, and gradually stir in water. Bring to boil. Allow to boil for 3 minutes. Pour into casserole.
9 Cover and cook for 1½ hours (350°F. – Gas Mark 3). Season to taste with salt and pepper and serve.

Brown stew

you will need for 4 servings:

2 lb. chuck steak	1 pint cider
1 oz. flour	1 tablespoon tomato purée (see page 85)
salt, pepper	
1½ oz. dripping	½ pint stock (see page 84)
2 large onions, peeled and sliced	
1 lb. carrots, peeled and sliced	1 small packet frozen peas
1 small can mushrooms or 2 oz. fresh mushrooms	1 small packet frozen beans
	1 small packet frozen broad beans

1 Cut meat into cubes, coat with seasoned flour and brown in heated dripping.

2 Transfer meat to a large casserole and brown onions in remaining dripping, then put with meat.

3 Add carrots, mushrooms and cider.

4 Mix tomato purée with stock and add to other ingredients.

5 Cover and cook in a slow oven (325°F.–Gas Mark 2) for 2 hours.

6 Add remaining vegetables and continue cooking for 30 minutes.

Correct seasoning and consistency before serving.

Carbonnade of beef

you will need for 4 servings:

1½ lb. topside beef	½ pint beer
1 oz. flour	½ pint beef stock (see
salt, pepper	page 84)
1 oz. butter	chopped parsley
8 oz. onions, peeled and chopped	

1 Wipe meat and cut into good size pieces.

2 Toss in seasoned flour and brown on all sides in heated butter. Transfer meat to a casserole.

3 Add onions to remaining fat, and sauté until transparent, then put with meat in casserole.

4 Add beer and stock.

5 Cover and cook in a slow oven (325°F.–Gas Mark 2) about 2½ hours.

Correct seasoning and sprinkle with parsley before serving.

Casseroled roast of beef

you will need for 6 servings:

3 lb. fresh brisket	salt, pepper
1 tablespoon dry mustard	4 tablespoons water
2 tablespoons oil	1 large onion, peeled and sliced
1½ oz. dripping	½ oz. flour

1 Wipe meat.

2 Mix mustard smoothly with oil and rub well into meat.

3 Heat dripping and brown meat on all sides.

4 Put meat and any remaining fat and sediment into a casserole, sprinkle with salt and pepper, add onion and water.

5 Cover with foil or greaseproof paper and put lid tightly on casserole.

6 Cook for 2½–3 hours in a slow oven (350°F.–Gas Mark 3).

7 When meat is cooked, remove to a serving dish.

8 Pour off any excess fat from liquor left in casserole, add flour mixed smoothly with a little water and stir till boiling. Add a little extra stock or water if sauce is too thick.

Chuck wagon casserole

you will need for 4 servings:

2 lb. chuck steak	1 tablespoon lemon juice
2 oz. cooking fat	2–3 sticks celery, chopped
1 medium-sized onion, peeled and chopped	8 oz. carrots, peeled and quartered
1 clove garlic, crushed	8 oz. button onions, peeled
salt, pepper	3 potatoes, peeled and sliced
1½ pints water or stock (see page 84)	1 8-oz. can tomatoes
1 teaspoon sugar	2 oz. flour
1 teaspoon Worcestershire sauce	

1 Trim meat and cut into small pieces.

2 Heat fat, add meat and brown on all sides.

3 Add onion and garlic and sauté for a few minutes.

4 Add water or stock, seasoning, sugar, Worcestershire sauce and lemon juice. Bring to boiling point, then transfer to a casserole.

5 Cover and cook in a slow oven (325°F.–Gas Mark 2) about 2 hours.

6 Add celery, carrots, onions and potatoes and cook for 30 minutes.

7 Mix flour smoothly with contents of the can of tomatoes, stir into stew and continue cooking for 30 minutes. Correct seasoning before serving.

Daube of beef

you will need for 4 servings:

1½ lb. topside of beef	2 onions, peeled and chopped
1 tablespoon chopped parsley	1 sprig thyme
1 clove garlic, crushed	1 bay leaf
6 tablespoons white wine	3–4 tomatoes, peeled and chopped
3 tablespoons oil	*bouquet garni* (see page 85)
8 oz. belly of pork	
2 carrots, peeled and chopped	

1 Wipe meat and cut into pieces, sprinkle with parsley and garlic.

2 Blend wine and oil, pour over meat and leave for at least 1 hour.

3 Cut pork into pieces and arrange alternating layers of beef, pork and vegetables in a casserole. Add herbs, tomatoes and *bouquet garni*.

4 Pour over the wine and oil.

5 Cover top of casserole with foil, then put on the lid.

6 Cook in a slow oven (325°F.–Gas Mark 2) about 2½ hours. Correct seasoning before serving.

Priest's goulash

This is an old recipe, so called because the parish priest was able to go on his rounds and leave his lunch cooking unattended.

you will need for 4 servings:

1½–2 lb. chuck steak	2 pints stock (see
1 tablespoon flour	page 84) or water
salt, pepper	2 onions, peeled and
2 teaspoons paprika	chopped
2 oz. cooking fat	3 carrots, peeled and
1 clove garlic,	chopped
chopped	4 tomatoes, peeled
1 bay leaf	and chopped
6 coriander seeds,	½ teaspoon caraway
crushed	seeds

1 Wipe meat and cut into pieces.
2 Mix flour, salt, pepper and paprika together and toss meat in it.
3 Heat fat, add meat and garlic and fry till well browned.
4 Add bay leaf, coriander seeds and stock and stir till boiling, then transfer all to a casserole.
5 Cover and cook in a slow oven (325°F.–Gas Mark 2) for 1½ hours.
6 Add vegetables, tomatoes and caraway seeds and continue the cooking for 1½–2 hours. Correct seasoning before serving.

Casserole Napoli

you will need for 4 servings:

1 lb. stewing steak	¾ pint water
2 tablespoons corn	4 oz. mushrooms
oil	8 oz. cooked peas
2 level tablespoons	4 oz. shell noodles,
cornflour	cooked and drained
½ level teaspoon salt	¼ pint single cream,
1 packet tomato soup	optional
½ pint milk	

1 Trim the meat and cut into thin strips 1–1½ inches long. Heat the corn oil and sauté the meat strips for 5 minutes.
2 Add the cornflour, salt and the contents of the packet of tomato soup.
3 Stir in the milk and water. Bring to the boil, stirring all the time. Cover and cook in a moderate oven (375°F.–Gas Mark 4) for 1 hour.
4 Add the mushrooms, peas and the noodles and cook for a further 10 minutes.
5 Stir in the cream and serve.

Sweet-sour meat balls

you will need for 4 servings:

1 lb. stewing beef,	1 egg
minced	2 oz. sultanas
1 small onion, peeled	1½ oz. sugar
and minced	1 lemon, peeled and
salt, pepper	thinly sliced
pinch oregano	¾ pint stock (see
2 tablespoons grated	page 84)
cheese	½ oz. flour
1 tablespoon	
breadcrumbs	

1 Mix meat, onion, seasoning, cheese and breadcrumbs together and bind with beaten egg. Shape into small balls.
2 Put sultanas, sugar and lemon into a casserole. Arrange meat balls on top and pour hot stock over.
3 Cover and cook in a slow oven (325°F.–Gas Mark 2) about 40 minutes.
4 Mix flour smoothly with a little of the liquid, pour into casserole and cook for 5–10 minutes. Correct seasoning before serving.

Stewed steak and onions

you will need for 4 servings:

1½ lb. stewing steak	8 oz. onions, peeled
1 oz. flour	and sliced
salt, pepper	½ pint water or stock
2 oz. fat	(see page 84)

1 Trim meat and cut into fairly large pieces.
2 Coat well with seasoned flour.
3 Heat fat, brown meat on all sides, then put into a casserole.
4 Add onions to remaining fat and cook till well browned. Put with meat.
5 Add remaining flour to sediment in pan. Add water and stir till boiling.
6 Pour over ingredients in casserole, cover and cook in a slow oven (325°F.–Gas Mark 2) for about 2 hours. Correct seasoning before serving.

Simple stroganoff

you will need for 4–6 servings:

1½ lb. grilling steak	1 clove garlic,
pinch of salt and	chopped
pepper	2 oz. mushrooms
2 level tablespoons	1 beef stock cube
flour	½ pint water
2 oz. butter	5 fluid oz. soured
1 small onion, sliced	cream

1 Cut meat into strips, toss in seasoned flour.
2 Heat the butter in a flame-proof casserole, brown the meat. Add the onion, garlic and mushrooms, and fry gently for 5 minutes.
3 Add the stock cube made up with ½ pint boiling water. Cover and cook in a moderate oven until meat is tender, approximately 30 minutes.
4 Stir in sour cream and cook for a further 10 minutes. Serve with boiled rice.

Tyrolean beef casserole

you will need for 4 servings:

1 lb. braising beef
2 oz. dripping
2 large onions, peeled and sliced
½ oz. flour
salt, pepper
¼ teaspoon brown sugar
1 teaspoon vinegar
pinch nutmeg
small clove garlic, crushed
½ pint beer
stock (see page 84) or water
4 slices of bread
little French or German mustard

1 Trim meat and cut into pieces.
2 Heat dripping, put in meat and brown on all sides. Transfer to a casserole.
3 Fry onions till well browned in remaining fat and put with meat.
4 Put flour, seasonings and spices into pan and mix. Add beer and about ¼ pint stock, and stir till boiling. Pour over meat and add a little extra stock if meat is not quite covered.
5 Cover casserole and cook in a slow oven (325°F.– Gas Mark 2) for about 2 hours.
6 Skim off any fat and pour it over bread. Spread with mustard and arrange on top of meat.
7 Return to oven uncovered, until bread is crisp.

Beef provençale No. 2

you will need for 4 servings:

1 lb. stewing beef
1 oz. cornflour
salt and pepper
2 tablespoons corn oil
1 onion, sliced
3 carrots, sliced
1 clove garlic, chopped
1 beef stock cube
¾ pint boiling water
2 tablespoons red wine
8 oz. tomatoes, peeled and cut in quarters
a few black olives

1 Cut the meat into cubes. Coat with the cornflour, to which salt and pepper have been added. Heat the corn oil and brown the meat.
2 Remove to a casserole. Sauté the onion, carrots and garlic in the remaining corn oil, and place with the meat in the casserole.
3 Dissolve the stock cube in the water and bring to the boil with the wine.
4 Pour over the ingredients in the casserole, cover and cook in a slow oven (325°F.– Gas Mark 2) for 2–2½ hours.
5 Add the tomatoes and olives 10 minutes before the end of the cooking time.

Veal Casseroles

Haricot veal

you will need for 4–6 servings:

2 lb. best end neck veal
2 medium onions, peeled and sliced
2 oz. butter
1 oz. flour
1 chicken stock cube
1 pint water
1 small cauliflower
1 teaspoon lemon juice

forcemeat balls:
4 oz. breadcrumbs
2 oz. suet, chopped finely
1 tablespoon chopped parsley
1 teaspoon mixed herbs
little grated lemon rind
salt, pepper
egg or milk to bind

1 Trim meat and divide into cutlets.
2 Fry onions in hot fat till lightly browned, then put into a casserole.
3 Brown meat in remaining fat and put with onions.
4 Add flour and stock cube to pan in which meat was browned and mix well.
5 Add water and stir till boiling.
6 Pour over ingredients in the casserole.
7 Cover and cook in a slow oven (350°F.– Gas Mark 3) 1¼ hours.
8 Divide cauliflower into small flowerets, add to casserole and continue the cooking for 45 minutes.
9 While meat is cooking, make the forcemeat balls. Mix all ingredients and bind with egg or milk. Shape into small balls, roll in flour and fry in hot fat.

10 To serve, put meat and vegetables on to a hot dish. Add lemon juice to sauce, correct seasoning and strain over meat. Garnish with forcemeat balls.

Braised veal

you will need for 3 servings:

1 lb. fillet of veal
2 oz. butter
1 medium-sized onion, peeled and chopped
2 small turnips, peeled and chopped
2 carrots, peeled and chopped
1 blade mace
1 bay leaf
salt, pepper
2 oz. macaroni
½ oz. cornflour
½ pint stock (see page 84)

1 Trim meat, heat butter and brown meat on both sides. Remove to a casserole.
2 Fry vegetables in remaining fat and put with meat.
3 Add mace, bay leaf, seasonings and macaroni broken into small pieces.
4 Mix cornflour with sediment and any remaining fat in the pan in which the meat and vegetables were browned. Add stock and stir till boiling.
5 Pour over ingredients in the casserole.
6 Cover and cook in a slow oven (350°F.– Gas Mark 3) about 1½–2 hours until the veal is tender.
7 Remove mace and bay leaf and correct seasoning before serving.

Casseroled breast of veal

you will need for 4–6 servings:

2½–3 lb. breast of veal
½ teaspoon mixed
  herbs
2 teaspoons chopped
  parsley
2 tablespoons
  breadcrumbs

salt, pepper
8 oz. streaky bacon
4 oz. onions, peeled
  and chopped
1 dessertspoon flour
½ pint stock (see
  page 84)

1 Bone veal (the butcher will do this for you). Put bones into a pan, just cover with water, and simmer to make stock.
2 Flatten meat, remove any skin or gristle and sprinkle with herbs, parsley and breadcrumbs.
3 Season with salt and pepper, arrange bacon on top and roll up. Tie securely with string.
4 Heat a little bacon fat and brown meat lightly on all sides, then remove to a casserole.
5 Brown onions lightly and put with meat.
6 Mix flour with remaining fat and meat sediment in the pan, cook for a few minutes, then add veal stock. Stir till boiling and pour over contents of casserole.
7 Cover tightly and cook in a slow oven (325°F. – Gas Mark 2) about 3 hours.

Casserole of veal

you will need for 4–6 servings:

2 lb. stewing veal
1 oz. butter
2 large carrots, peeled
  and chopped
1 onion, peeled and
  chopped
¾ oz. cornflour

1 chicken stock cube
¾ pint water
salt, pepper
strip lemon peel
1 tablespoon chopped
  parsley

1 Trim and cut meat into pieces and put into a casserole.
2 Heat butter and fry carrot and onion until well browned. Put with meat.
3 Add cornflour and stock cube to remaining fat and mix well. Add water and stir till boiling. Pour over ingredients in casserole.
4 Add a little extra seasoning if required and lemon peel.
5 Cover, and cook in a slow oven (350°F. – Gas Mark 3) about 2 hours.
6 Sprinkle with parsley before serving.

Fricassée of veal

you will need for 3 servings:

1 lb. fillet of veal
1 small onion, peeled
  and chopped
bouquet garni
  (see page 85)
¼ pint white stock
  (see page 84) or
  water

salt, pepper
strip lemon peel
¼ pint milk
¼ oz. cornflour
lemon juice
bacon rolls, grilled
lemon wedges

1 Trim meat, cut into small pieces and put into a casserole.

2 Add onion, *bouquet garni*, stock, seasoning and lemon peel
3 Cover and cook in a slow oven (350°F. – Gas Mark 3) about 1¼ hours.
4 Remove *bouquet garni* and lemon peel and strain off liquor.
5 Put ¼ pint in a pan with milk.
6 Add cornflour, mixed smoothly with a little milk, and stir till boiling. Correct seasoning, add lemon juice to taste.
7 Pour over meat and continue cooking for 15 minutes.
8 Garnish with bacon rolls and lemon wedges.

Neck of veal with forcemeat balls

you will need for 4–5 servings:

2 lb. neck of veal
2 onions
1 carrot
1 oz. fat or oil
1 oz. flour
1 pint stock (see
  page 84)

½ teaspoon salt
½ teaspoon pepper
veal forcemeat (see
  page 86)

1 Cut veal into joints.
2 Peel and slice onions and carrot.
3 Heat fat or oil in a casserole and brown the meat.
4 Remove veal and sauté vegetables.
5 Sprinkle in flour, mix and cook for 1–2 minutes.
6 Stir in stock, bring to the boil and add seasoning and veal.
7 Cover and cook in a slow oven (325°F. – Gas Mark 2) for 1 hour.
8 Make forcemeat and divide into small balls. Remove lid, add to casserole and cook for 30 minutes.

Ossobuco

you will need for 4 servings:

1½–2 lb. stewing veal
1 oz. flour
salt, pepper
1 tablespoon oil
1 oz. butter
8 oz. onions, peeled
  and sliced
8 oz. carrots, peeled
  and chopped
1 stick celery,
  chopped

3 tomatoes, peeled
  and chopped
bouquet garni (see
  page 85)
grated rind and juice
  1 lemon
1 tablespoon tomato
  purée (see page 85)
¼ pint dry white wine
¼ pint water
chopped parsley

1 Cut meat into fairly large pieces, coat with seasoned flour.
2 Heat oil and butter together, add meat, cook for a few minutes, then remove to a casserole.
3 Add onions to remaining fat, fry till golden brown, then put with the meat.
4 Put carrots, celery, tomatoes and *bouquet garni* in the pan. Toss for a minute or two and then add lemon rind and juice, tomato purée, wine and water. Stir till boiling and pour into the casserole.
5 Cover and cook in a slow oven (350°F. – Gas Mark 3) for about 2½ hours.

6 To serve, put meat on to a dish. Rub sauce through a sieve. Reheat, correct seasoning and pour over meat. Sprinkle with chopped parsley.

Spanish veal casserole

you will need for 4 servings:

3 tablespoons oil	1 chicken stock cube
1½ lb. stewing veal	½ pint water
2 cloves garlic, crushed	½ teaspoon mixed herbs
1 onion, peeled and sliced	1 teaspoon chopped parsley
8 oz. carrots, peeled and sliced	6 stuffed olives
½ oz. flour	3 tablespoons sherry

1 Heat oil, add meat, cut into pieces, and fry lightly for a few minutes. Transfer to a casserole.

2 Fry garlic, onion and carrot till brown in remaining fat, then put with meat.

3 Put flour and stock cube into pan. Mix together and add water. Stir till boiling.

4 Add herbs and parsley and pour over contents of casserole.

5 Cover and cook in a slow oven (350°F. – Gas Mark 3) about 1¾ hours.

6 Remove meat to a serving dish, strain sauce into a clean pan and reheat.

7 Add sliced olives and sherry and pour over meat.

Veal and bacon casserole

you will need for 3 servings:

1 lb. loin of veal	3 sticks celery, chopped
6 oz. bacon	bouquet garni (see page 85)
1 carrot, peeled and diced	salt, pepper
1 onion, peeled and chopped	small piece mace
1 turnip, peeled and diced	½ pint stock (see page 84) or water
	squeeze lemon juice

1 Trim meat, remove any fat or gristle and cut into pieces. Chop bacon.

2 Put meat and vegetables into a casserole and add bouquet garni, seasoning and mace.

3 Add stock and lemon juice.

4 Cover and cook in a slow oven (350°F. – Gas Mark 3) for about 1¼–1½ hours.

5 Before serving, remove bouquet garni and mace and correct seasoning.

Veal chops lyonnaise

you will need for 4 servings:

4 veal chops	8 oz. potatoes, peeled and sliced
½ oz. flour	1 chicken stock cube
salt, pepper	¾ pint water
½ teaspoon grated lemon rind	1 teaspoon sugar
2 oz. butter	1 tablespoon chopped parsley
8 oz. onions, peeled and sliced	

1 Trim chops, mix flour with a little pepper and salt and lemon rind, and coat chops well.

2 Heat butter and fry chops on both sides till lightly browned. Remove to a casserole.

3 Add onions and potatoes, sauté for about 5 minutes, then put with chops.

4 Crumble chicken stock cube into pan, add water and stir till boiling.

5 Add sugar and pour over contents of casserole.

6 Cover and cook in a slow oven (350°F. – Gas Mark 3) about 1 hour.

7 Sprinkle with parsley before serving.

Veal rolls

you will need for 4 servings:

	for the sauce:
4 thin fillets of veal	1 oz. butter
1 oz. butter, melted	1 small onion, grated or very finely chopped
salt, pepper	
2 teaspoons finely chopped onion	½ small apple, peeled and grated
2 teaspoons finely chopped parsley	2 teaspoons cornflour
1 teaspoon grated lemon rind	1 small can tomato purée
	1 chicken stock cube
	¾ pint water

1 Brush fillets with a little butter, sprinkle each with salt and pepper, onion, parsley and lemon rind and roll up tightly. Secure with a small skewer or thin string. Put into a casserole.

2 *To make the sauce:* heat butter, add onion and apple and sauté for a few minutes without browning.

3 Stir in cornflour, tomato purée and crumbled chicken stock cube and mix well together.

4 Add water and stir till boiling. Boil for 2 minutes, then pour over veal rolls.

5 Cover and cook in a slow oven (325°F. – Gas Mark 2) for about 2 hours.

Veal Marengo

you will need for 4 servings:

1½ lb. neck of veal	½ pint water or stock (see page 84)
½ oz. cornflour	
salt, pepper	8 oz. tomatoes, peeled and chopped
1 teaspoon grated lemon rind	2 oz. mushrooms, sliced
3 tablespoons oil	croûtons of fried bread, or toast for garnish
2 shallots, peeled and chopped finely	

1 Trim meat and cut into pieces.

2 Mix cornflour, salt, pepper and lemon rind and coat the meat well.

3 Heat oil, add meat and fry till golden brown, then put into a casserole.

4 Add shallots to remaining oil and cook till soft and lightly browned.

5 Add stock, tomatoes and mushrooms, bring to boiling point, then pour all into casserole. *[continued*

6 Cover and cook in a slow oven (350°F. – Gas Mark 3) for about 1¼–1½ hours.

7 Check seasoning and serve with croûtons or toast.

Veal and orange casserole

you will need for 4 servings:

1½ lb. stewing veal	2 small onions,
1½ oz. cornflour	peeled and sliced
salt, pepper	1 clove garlic, finely
2 tablespoons oil	chopped
2 medium-sized	2 oranges
carrots, peeled and	1½ pints chicken stock
sliced	(see page 85)

1 Trim veal and cut into cubes.

2 Coat with seasoned cornflour.

3 Heat oil, add meat, vegetables and garlic and sauté for a few minutes, then remove to a casserole.

4 Add remaining cornflour to oil left in the pan and mix well. Add orange juice and stock, stir till boiling and pour over contents of the casserole.

5 Remove pith from orange peel and blanch for a few minutes, then drain, and cut into thin strips.

6 Add half to meat.

7 Cover the casserole and cook in a slow oven (325°F. – Gas Mark 2) about 1–1¼ hours.

8 Garnish with remaining orange strips.

Veal paprika

you will need for 4 servings:

1½ lb. stewing veal	½ oz. flour
1 oz. butter	½ pint stock (see
8 oz. onions, peeled	page 84) or water
and sliced	3 tablespoons tomato
1 clove garlic,	purée (see page 85)
crushed	¼ pint yoghurt
1 tablespoon paprika	

1 Cut meat into pieces and brown in hot butter. Remove to a casserole.

2 Add onion and garlic and fry for a few minutes.

3 Add paprika and flour and cook for a few minutes, stirring, over low heat.

4 Add stock and tomato purée and stir till boiling.

5 Pour over meat in casserole, cover and cook for 2 hours in a slow oven (350°F. – Gas Mark 3).

6 Add yoghurt and correct seasoning. Serve with buttered noodles (see page 87).

Veal goulash

you will need for 4 servings:

1 oz. butter	salt, pepper, pinch
8 oz. onions, peeled	paprika
and sliced	2 teaspoons tomato
1½ lb. stewing veal	purée (see page 85)
¾ pint white stock	1 teaspoon flour
(see page 84)	¼ pint sour cream

1 Heat butter, add onions and cook till soft but not brown. Remove to a casserole.

2 Cut meat into pieces and sauté for a few minutes in remaining fat, then put into casserole with onions.

3 Add stock, salt, pepper and paprika.

4 Cover and cook in a slow oven (350°F. – Gas Mark 3) for 1–1¼ hours.

5 Mix the tomato purée, flour and sour cream and stir into casserole. Cook a further few minutes. Serve with buttered noodles (see page 87).

Italian veal casserole

you will need for 4 servings:

1½–2 lb. leg of veal	¼ pint tomato purée
2 tablespoons oil	(see page 85)
salt, pepper	6 tablespoons white
2 cloves garlic,	wine
chopped	2 sprigs rosemary

1 Cut meat into 2-inch pieces.

2 Heat oil, sprinkle meat with salt and pepper and brown in oil, then transfer to a casserole.

3 Brown garlic in remaining oil and put with meat.

4 Put tomato purée, wine and rosemary in pan, bring to boiling point, then pour over contents of casserole.

5 Cook about 1½ hours in a slow oven (350°F. – Gas Mark 3).

6 Before serving, correct consistency and seasoning.

Veal chops with mushrooms

you will need for 4 servings:

4 veal chops	1 small onion, peeled
salt, pepper	and sliced
2 tablespoons oil	4 tablespoons white
4 medium-sized	wine
carrots, peeled and	2 tomatoes, peeled
sliced	and sliced
4 oz. mushrooms,	
sliced	

1 Trim chops and sprinkle with salt and pepper.

2 Heat oil, brown chops on both sides, then transfer to a casserole.

3 Add all other ingredients, cover and cook in a slow oven (350°F. – Gas Mark 3) about 1 hour.

4 Correct seasoning before serving.

Veal chops with wine

you will need for 4 servings:

4 veal chops	1 onion, peeled and
(preferably with	chopped
kidney)	4 oz. mushrooms,
1½ oz. flour	sliced
salt, pepper	¼ pint white wine
2 tablespoons oil	

1 Trim chops and coat with seasoned flour.

2 Heat oil, brown chops on both sides, then transfer to a casserole.

3 Add onion to remaining oil and cook till lightly brown. Add remaining flour and mix well. Add mushrooms and wine and bring to boiling point, stirring all the time.

4 Pour sauce over chops in the casserole. Cover, and cook about 1 hour in a slow oven (350°F.–Gas Mark 3).

Veal and tomato casserole

you will need for 4 servings:

1 oz. butter	1 can whole carrots
1 onion, peeled and sliced	salt, pepper
	pinch rosemary
1 lb. stewing veal	cooked or frozen peas
1 oz. flour	
1 14-oz. can tomatoes	

1 Heat butter, and sauté onion until golden.
2 Trim and cube veal, fry till well browned.
3 Add flour, mix well, then add tomatoes, carrots and liquid from both cans.
4 Stir till boiling. Add seasoning.
5 Transfer all to a casserole, sprinkle with rosemary, cover, and cook in a slow oven (325°F.–Gas Mark 2) about 2¼ hours.
6 Just before serving, correct seasoning and add peas to give colour.

Veal Romano

you will need for 4 servings:

4 veal chops	2 tablespoons parsley, chopped
2 tablespoons oil	1 oz. grated Parmesan cheese
3 oz. breadcrumbs	
salt, pepper	1 can peeled tomatoes
1–2 stick celery, chopped	

1 Trim chops, brush with oil and coat with seasoned breadcrumbs.
2 Put remaining oil in a casserole, add chops and sprinkle with celery, parsley, cheese and remaining breadcrumbs.
3 Add tomatoes, cover and cook in a slow oven (350°F.–Gas Mark 3) about 1 hour.

Veal Portugaise

you will need for 4 servings:

8 oz. onions, chopped	1 large green pepper
1 clove garlic, chopped	8 oz. tomatoes
	1 teaspoon sugar
2 oz. bacon, chopped	1 level teaspoon salt
3 oz. butter	5 fluid oz. yoghurt
1½ lb. boned breast of veal	

1 Gently fry onion, garlic and bacon in butter for 5 minutes.
2 Cut veal into 2-inch cubes, add to pan, and fry briskly for a further 5 minutes, stirring all the time.
3 Remove seeds and cut pepper into strips. Skin

tomatoes and chop roughly. Add with sugar and salt to veal.
4 Cover and cook in a moderate oven (375°F.–Gas Mark 4) for 1–1¼ hours until veal is tender.
5 Remove from oven, stir in yoghurt and serve immediately.

Veal sauté

you will need for 4 servings:

1½ lb. shoulder or breast of veal	3 tomatoes, peeled and chopped
½ oz. flour	½ pint chicken stock (see page 85)
salt, pepper	
2 tablespoons oil	¼ pint dry white wine
8 oz. mushrooms, sliced	lemon juice
	1 tablespoon chopped parsley
2 small onions, peeled and chopped	

1 Trim meat and cut into small pieces.
2 Coat with seasoned flour and sauté for a few minutes in hot oil. Remove to a casserole.
3 Add mushrooms, onions and tomatoes to remaining oil and cook for a few minutes.
4 Add stock and wine and stir till boiling.
5 Pour all over the meat in casserole.
6 Cover and cook in a slow oven (350°F.–Gas Mark 3) about 1½ hours.
7 Before serving, correct seasoning, add lemon juice and parsley.

Casseroled knuckle of veal

you will need for 4–6 servings:

2½–3 lb. knuckle of veal	¼ pint white wine
	white stock (see page 84) or water
2 tablespoons oil	
3–4 carrots, peeled and chopped	1 sprig thyme
	1 bay leaf
1–2 sticks celery	2 strips lemon peel
1 oz. flour	salt, pepper
¼ pint tomato pulp	parsley

1 Ask your butcher to saw the bones into 2-inch lengths (if they are chopped the marrow is inclined to fall out).
2 Heat oil in a large pan, put in pieces of knuckle and brown well, then transfer to a casserole.
3 Add carrots, celery and flour to remaining oil and sauté for about 5 minutes.
4 Add tomato pulp and wine, stir till boiling, then pour into casserole.
5 Add enough stock just to cover.
6 Add thyme, bay leaf, lemon peel and seasoning.
7 Cover and cook in a slow oven (325°F.–Gas Mark 2) about 2 hours.
8 Remove thyme, bay leaf and lemon peel, add parsley and correct seasoning before serving.

Veal Mozzarella

you will need for 4 servings:

4 escalopes veal
¼ oz. flour
salt, pepper
1 egg
breadcrumbs
2 tablespoons oil
1 small onion, peeled
and chopped
1 clove garlic,
crushed
2 rashers streaky
bacon
8 oz. tomatoes,
peeled and sliced
8 oz. Mozzarella
cheese
1 oz. grated
Parmesan cheese

1 Cut each escalope into 4, coat with seasoned flour, then with egg and breadcrumbs.
2 Heat oil, brown escalopes on both sides, then remove from pan.
3 Add onion, garlic, chopped bacon and tomatoes to remaining oil and sauté for 5 minutes. Add any remaining flour and mix well.
4 Put half the veal into a casserole, cover with half the tomato mixture and then the Mozzarella cheese, sliced.
5 Add another layer of veal and remaining tomato mixture.
6 Sprinkle with Parmesan cheese, cover and cook about 40 minutes in a slow oven (350°F.–Gas Mark 3).

Sherry veal with cream

you will need for 4 servings:

1½ lb. boned breast
of veal
2 oz. butter
1 medium onion,
chopped
2 stalks celery,
chopped
4 oz. mushrooms,
sliced
½ teaspoon mixed
herbs
4 tablespoons dry
sherry
salt and pepper
¼ pint double cream

1 Cut veal in 1-inch cubes. Fry gently in butter, until lightly browned on all sides.
2 Add onion, celery, mushrooms and herbs. Fry gently for 5 minutes.
3 Stir in sherry and season to taste with salt and pepper.
4 Cover and cook in a moderate oven (375°F.–Gas Mark 4) for 1–1¼ hours until veal is tender.
5 Remove from oven, stir in cream and serve at once.

Variation

Veal paprika with lemon–omit sherry, add 1 level teaspoon paprika and 2 tablespoons lemon juice with the mixed herbs.

Lamb Casseroles

American casserole

you will need for 4 servings:

4 chump chops
¼ oz. flour
salt, pepper
2 oz. butter
8 oz. onions, peeled
and sliced thinly
1 small clove garlic,
crushed
4 tomatoes, peeled
and sliced
1 lb. potatoes, peeled
and sliced
3–4 tablespoons
stock (see page 84)
or water

1 Coat chops with flour to which a little salt and pepper has been added and brown both sides in 1 oz. butter. Remove from pan.
2 Put onions and garlic into the same pan and fry for a few minutes.
3 Arrange meat in a casserole with layers of onion, tomatoes and potatoes, finishing with potatoes.
4 Add seasoning and stock and dot with the remaining butter.
5 Cover and cook for about 2 hours in a slow oven (325°F.–Gas Mark 2).
6 About 15 minutes before the end of the cooking, remove lid to allow potatoes to brown.

Barley lamb casserole

you will need for 4–6 servings:

2 lb. scrag end of lamb
2 large carrots
2 medium-sized
onions
seasoned flour
1 oz. dripping
salt, pepper
1 tablespoon pearl
barley
½ pint stock (see page
84) or water
2 large potatoes
chopped parsley
freshly ground pepper

1 Trim meat, remove excess fat.
2 Chop into 8 pieces.
3 Finely slice carrots and onions.
4 Dip meat in seasoned flour.
5 Melt fat and brown the meat. Remove meat and brown carrots and onions lightly. Season.
6 Place in a casserole. Arrange meat on top and sprinkle with pearl barley. Pour over stock or water.
7 Cover with layer of thinly sliced potatoes. Cover with tightly fitting lid and cook in a very cool oven (200°F.–Gas Mark ¼) for 2 hours.
8 Remove lid and raise heat to 425°F.–Gas Mark 7 to allow potatoes to brown.
9 Serve dusted with pepper and parsley.

Braised lamb and green peas

you will need for 4 servings:

1 onion	1 lump sugar
4 lamb cutlets	little water
2–3 diced young	8 oz. green peas
turnips	chopped parsley
seasoning	

1 Slice onion thinly and put into a casserole.
2 Wipe and trim cutlets and lay them on top.
3 Add turnips, seasoning and sugar.
4 Add enough water almost to cover.
5 Cover casserole and cook in a moderate oven (375°F. – Gas Mark 4) for 30 minutes.
6 Add peas and cook for 30 minutes.
7 Serve very hot, sprinkled with parsley.

Bitter sweet lamb casserole

you will need for 4–6 servings:

2 lb. middle neck of lamb	$\frac{1}{8}$ teaspoon freshly ground black pepper
2 tablespoons oil	pinch dry mustard
$\frac{1}{2}$ pint water	pinch paprika
3 tablespoons vinegar	$\frac{1}{2}$ teaspoon each, celery seed, basil, oregano
1 8-oz. can orange juice	3–4 cloves
1 dessertspoon Worcestershire sauce	2 teaspoons sugar
$\frac{1}{2}$ teaspoon salt	boiled rice

1 Trim and cut meat into pieces, and brown in hot oil.
2 Put into a casserole with water and vinegar. Cover and cook about 1 hour in a slow oven (350°F. – Gas Mark 3).
3 Put orange juice, sauce, flavourings, seasonings and sugar into a small pan and simmer, uncovered, for 10 minutes.
4 When meat has cooked for 1 hour, stir in orange juice mixture and continue cooking for 1 hour. Serve with boiled rice.

Braised mutton ménagère

you will need for 6–8 servings:

2$\frac{1}{2}$–3 lb. loin of mutton	1 tablespoon chopped parsley
$\frac{1}{2}$ oz. fat	seasoning
2 large onions, peeled and chopped	12 small white onions
12 oz. sausage meat	3–4 carrots
$\frac{1}{2}$ teaspoon each chopped fresh thyme, marjoram and savory, or pinch of mixed dried herbs	1 pint stock (see page 84) or water
	1 clove garlic
	1 lb. potatoes

1 Bone meat, remove any surplus fat.
2 Heat fat, add onions and sauté until beginning to soften, then mix with sausage meat, herbs and seasonings.
3 Spread this mixture on the meat, roll up and tie with string.
4 Add a little extra fat if necessary to the pan in which the onion was browned. Put in the meat and brown on all sides, then remove to a casserole.
5 Add small onions and carrots, peeled and sliced.
6 Add stock and garlic. Cover and cook in a slow oven (350°F. – Gas Mark 3) for 1$\frac{1}{2}$ hours.
7 Meanwhile, peel and quarter potatoes, brown in remaining fat, add to casserole.
8 Continue cooking for 30 minutes.
9 To serve, remove meat and vegetables. Reduce liquor, correct seasoning and serve separately.

Casseroled breast of lamb

you will need for 4 servings:

8 oz. bacon rashers	$\frac{1}{4}$ teaspoon chopped thyme, or pinch dried thyme
2 onions, peeled and cut into quarters	1 teaspoon chopped parsley
8 oz. carrots, peeled and sliced	1 pint stock (see page 84)
1$\frac{1}{2}$ lb. breast of lamb, boned	
salt, pepper	

1 Put 4 oz. bacon into a casserole with half the onions and carrots.
2 Tie meat into a neat shape and put on top. Add remaining vegetables.
3 Sprinkle with pepper and salt, add the thyme and parsley.
4 Cover with remaining bacon.
5 Add stock, cover and cook in a slow oven (350°F. – Gas Mark 3) about 2 hours.

Casserole of lamb with rice

you will need for 4 servings:

2 oz. butter	12 oz. cooked sliced lamb
1 large onion, peeled and chopped finely	pinch nutmeg
4 oz. rice	8 oz. tomatoes, peeled and sliced
2 chicken stock cubes	
1$\frac{1}{2}$ pints water	

1 Heat butter, add onion and cook till soft, but not brown.
2 Add rice and cook for a few minutes.
3 Add crumbled stock cubes and water and stir till boiling. Cook for about 10 minutes or until rice has absorbed most of the liquid.
4 Add lamb and nutmeg, then transfer all to a casserole.
5 Top with tomato, cover and cook in a slow oven (350°F. – Gas Mark 3) for about 40 minutes.

Canterbury casserole

you will need for 4–6 servings:

½ leg lamb, fillet end
8 oz. onions, peeled and sliced
4 oz. mushrooms, sliced
8 oz. carrots, peeled and, if large, sliced
2 tablespoons chopped parsley
salt, pepper
½ pint hot stock from lamb
2 tablespoons red wine or vinegar
little chopped mint

1 Remove bone from meat, put it into a pan with ½ pint water and boil to make stock.
2 Cut meat into 4–5 thick slices and put into a casserole with onions, mushrooms, carrots and parsley, sprinkling each layer with a little salt and pepper.
3 Add hot stock and wine. Cover and cook in a slow oven (350°F. – Gas Mark 3) for 2 hours.
4 Sprinkle with mint before serving.

Casserole of shoulder of mutton

you will need for 6–8 servings:

6 small onions
1 sprig thyme
1 bay leaf
2 sprigs parsley
½ oz. butter
½ oz. lard
3–4 lb. shoulder of mutton
½ pint stock (see page 84) or water
½ teaspoon salt
¼ teaspoon pepper

1 Peel onions, tie herbs together with fine thread.
2 Heat fats in a casserole.
3 Brown meat, add stock, onions, herbs and seasoning.
4 Cover and cook in a very slow oven (300°F. – Gas Mark 1) for 2 hours.
5 During cooking, baste the joint 3 or 4 times with the liquid.
6 Remove meat and place on a hot plate. Skim fat from gravy and pour over meat after carving.

Country casserole

you will need for 4 servings:

for the stuffing:
1 oz. breadcrumbs
1 small apple, chopped
½ oz. onion, chopped
pinch sage
seasoning
1 beaten egg
1 oz. butter
8 oz. onions, sliced
4 oz. carrots, sliced
½ pint stock (see page 84)
salt, pepper
parsley
1 bay leaf

1½ lb. middle neck of lamb, boned

1 Mix stuffing ingredients and bind with egg.
2 Spread over half the meat, fold over the other half and tie in place.
3 Melt butter, brown onions, carrots and meat.
4 Add stock, seasoning and herbs.
5 Cover and cook in a very slow oven (300°F. – Gas Mark 1) for 1½–2 hours. Remove lid 20 minutes before the end of cooking time.
6 Remove meat to a hot plate, then reduce the liquid by boiling until it is thick.

7 Coat meat with thickened gravy, or meat glaze, and serve sliced.

Creamy lamb casserole

you will need for 4 servings:

2 lb. middle neck lamb
2 onions, peeled and chopped
2 cloves
1 lemon
salt, pepper
1 bay leaf
2 oz. butter
2 oz. flour
1 pint milk
2–3 tablespoons thin cream

1 Trim meat and cut into pieces, removing excess fat.
2 Put into a pan, cover with cold water, bring to boiling point, then skim carefully. Transfer to a casserole.
3 Add onions, cloves, thinly pared lemon rind, seasoning and bay leaf. Cover and cook in a slow oven (350°F. – Gas Mark 3) about 1¼ hours.
4 Melt butter, add flour and cook for a few minutes. Remove from heat and add 1¼ pints stock from casserole.
5 Stir till boiling and boil for 3 minutes.
6 Add meat, onions and milk and bring to boiling point again. Correct seasoning and stir cream in.

Hungarian mutton

you will need for 4 servings:

1½ lb. stewing mutton
2 tablespoons oil
1 large onion, peeled and sliced
1 sweet red pepper, seeded and sliced
1 oz. flour
2 teaspoons paprika
1 chicken stock cube
1 pint water
4 oz. haricot beans, soaked overnight
3–4 potatoes, peeled and sliced

1 Trim meat and cut into small pieces.
2 Heat oil, add meat, onion and pepper and sauté for a few minutes. Transfer to a casserole.
3 Add flour, paprika and crumbled stock cube to remaining oil in pan and mix well. Add water and stir till boiling. Add haricot beans and cook for 5 minutes.
4 Pour all over contents of the casserole.
5 Cover and cook for 2 hours in a slow oven (350°F. – Gas Mark 3).
6 Arrange potatoes on top of casserole and cook for 25–30 minutes or until potatoes are tender.

Curried mutton

you will need for 4 servings:

2 lb. best end or middle neck of mutton
1 oz. coconut
1½ oz. fat
1 onion, peeled and chopped
1 apple, peeled, cored and chopped
2 tablespoons curry powder
2 oz. flour
¾ pint stock (see page 84) or water
1 teaspoon sugar
salt
lemon juice
2 oz. sultanas
1 tomato, peeled and quartered
rice

1 Trim and bone meat, cut into pieces.
2 Cover coconut with boiling water.
3 Heat fat, brown meat, then remove to a casserole.
4 Add onion, apple, curry powder and flour to remaining fat and cook, stirring, for about 5 minutes.
5 Add stock and water from coconut and stir till boiling, then pour over meat.
6 Add sugar, salt and lemon juice to taste.
7 Cover and cook in a slow oven (325°F. – Gas Mark 2) about 2 hours. Add sultanas and tomato.
Serve with plainly boiled rice.

Devonshire casserole

you will need for 4 servings:

2 oz. butter	½ pint stock (see
4 loin chops	page 84) or water
1 lb. potatoes, peeled	salt, pepper
and sliced	¼ pint cider
8 oz. onions, peeled	1 lb. apples
and sliced	2 tablespoons grated
½ oz. flour	cheese

1 Heat butter and brown chops on both sides.
2 Remove meat and sauté vegetables for a few minutes.
3 Put half the vegetables into a casserole, put meat on top, then cover with remaining vegetables.
4 Put flour into pan with remaining fat and stir till lightly browned.
5 Add stock and stir till boiling.
6 Add seasoning and cider and pour into casserole.
7 Cover with apples, peeled, cored and sliced, sprinkle with cheese.
8 Cover and cook for about 1½ hours in a moderate oven (375°F. – Gas Mark 4).

Holiday stew

you will need for 4 servings:

2 lb. boned shoulder	1 12-oz. can whole
of lamb	kernel corn
salt	2 tomatoes, peeled
freshly ground black	and sliced
pepper	1 tablespoon
6 rashers streaky	Worcestershire
bacon	sauce
2 medium-sized	2 oz. melted butter
onions, peeled and	1 tablespoon chopped
sliced	parsley
3 medium-sized	¼ pint dry white wine
potatoes, peeled	
and sliced	

1 Wipe meat, cut into small cubes and sprinkle with salt and pepper.
2 Put half the bacon into a deep casserole, add half the meat and half the onions.
3 Add remaining bacon and cover with potato.
4 Add rest of meat, onion, sweet corn and tomatoes.
5 Mix sauce, butter, parsley and wine, season with salt and pepper and pour over contents of casserole.
6 Cover tightly and cook in a very slow oven (300°F. – Gas Mark 1) about 3½–4 hours.

Imperial lamb cutlets

you will need for 4 servings:

8 lamb cutlets	2 sticks celery,
2 tablespoons vinegar	chopped
¼ pint water	½ pint stock (see page
2 small onions,	84)
peeled and sliced	8 oz. cooked rice
1 teaspoon chopped	2–3 oz. seedless
mint	raisins
salt, pepper	1–2 oranges
1 oz. flour	mint jelly (see page
2 oz. cooking fat	85)
2 carrots, peeled and	
diced	

1 Trim the chops.
2 Put vinegar, water, onions, mint, salt and pepper into a casserole, add cutlets and leave for 1 hour.
3 Remove cutlets, drain and dab dry.
4 Coat with flour to which a little salt and pepper has been added and fry in the heated fat till brown on both sides, then return to casserole.
5 Add carrots and celery, cover, and cook about 1 hour in a slow oven (350°F. – Gas Mark 3).
6 Remove cutlets.
7 Mix remaining flour smoothly with stock, add to liquor left in the casserole, bring to boiling point and boil for 3 minutes.
8 Mix raisins with hot rice and pile on to a serving dish. Arrange cutlets on top and coat with some sauce.
9 Garnish with slices of orange brushed with mint jelly and serve remaining sauce separately.

Irish stew

you will need for 4 servings:

2 lb. neck or scrag of	8 oz. onions, peeled
mutton	and sliced
3 lb. potatoes, peeled	salt, pepper
and roughly	water
chopped	

1 Divide meat into neat pieces and put into a casserole in alternate layers with potatoes and onions. Sprinkle salt and pepper between layers.
2 Barely cover with water, then cover tightly and cook in a slow oven (325°F. – Gas Mark 2) for about 3 hours.

Jugged lamb cutlets

you will need for 4 servings:

1 lb. lamb cutlets	salt, pepper, celery
1 oz. butter	salt
1 onion, peeled and	juice of 1 lemon
quartered	1 teaspoon redcurrant
2 tomatoes, peeled	jelly
¼ oz. flour	½ glass port wine
¼ pint stock (see	parsley
page 84)	

1 Trim cutlets and remove excess fat.
2 Heat butter and brown cutlets on both sides, then put into a casserole.
3 Brown onion and put with meat, add tomatoes.

[continued

4 Put flour into remaining fat and stir over low heat until it begins to colour.

5 Add stock and stir till boiling.

6 Add salt, pepper, celery salt and lemon juice and pour over contents of the casserole.

7 Cover tightly and cook in a slow oven (325°F. – Gas Mark 2) for 2 hours.

8 About 10 minutes before the end of the cooking, add redcurrant jelly and port wine. Sprinkle with parsley before serving.

Lamb cutlets soubise

you will need for 4 servings:

1½–2 lb. best end neck or loin of lamb	salt, pepper
1 oz. butter	1 bay leaf
2 medium-sized onions, peeled and chopped	⅛ pint white wine or stock (see page 84)
	½ pint white sauce (see page 85)

1 Divide meat into cutlets, trim and remove any surplus fat.

2 Heat butter and fry cutlets very gently for about 5 minutes. Do not allow to brown. Remove to a casserole.

3 Put onions into pan and sauté till they begin to soften but not colour, then put with cutlets.

4 Add seasoning, bay leaf and wine. Cover and cook in a moderate oven (375°F. – Gas Mark 4) for 30–45 minutes.

5 Remove cutlets to a serving dish and keep warm.

6 Pass onion and liquor left in the casserole through a fine sieve and add to sauce. Reheat and pour over cutlets.

Lamb chop casserole

you will need for 4 servings:

4 lamb chops	2 oz. mushrooms, sliced
1 oz. dripping or cooking fat	salt, pepper
2 large onions, peeled and sliced	¼ oz. flour
8 oz. carrots, peeled and sliced	1 beef stock cube
2–3 sticks celery	¼ pint water
8 oz. tomatoes, peeled and quartered	8 oz. garden peas or 1 small packet frozen peas

1 Trim chops and fry in the hot dripping till lightly browned on both sides. Transfer to a casserole.

2 Fry onions and carrots and put with chops.

3 Add celery, cut into 2-inch lengths, tomatoes and mushrooms. Season with salt and pepper.

4 Put flour and crumbled stock cube into pan in which meat and onions were fried. Cook for a few minutes, add water and stir till boiling.

5 Pour over contents of casserole, cover and cook in a slow oven (350°F. – Gas Mark 3) about 2 hours.

6 Add peas, continue cooking for 30 minutes.

Lamb casserole with peas

you will need for 4 servings:

2 lb. best end neck of lamb	3 oz. butter
1 pint shelled green peas	stock (see page 84)
	seasoning
2 large lettuce, washed, and shredded	1 oz. flour
	chopped mint

1 Trim meat and cut into small squares.

2 Put into a casserole with peas, lettuce, 2 oz. butter and a little stock.

3 Season lightly, cover and cook in a slow oven (350°F. – Gas Mark 3) about 2 hours.

4 15 minutes before serving, add remaining butter mixed with flour.

5 Correct seasoning and sprinkle with mint.

Lamb hot pot

you will need for 4 servings:

1 lb. neck of lamb	salt, pepper
8 oz. onions	pinch mixed herbs
1 large carrot	½ pint stock (see page 84) or water
2 lb. potatoes	
1–2 sticks celery	

1 Cut meat into pieces.

2 Peel and slice onion and carrot thinly.

3 Peel and cut potatoes into fairly thick slices, chop celery.

4 Put alternate layers of vegetables, meat and seasoning into a casserole, finishing with vegetables and arranging the top layer of potatoes in neat circles.

5 Add stock, cover and cook for 1½–2 hours in a slow oven (325°F. – Gas Mark 2).

6 Remove lid for the last 30 minutes to allow potatoes to brown.

Lamb chops créole

you will need for 4 servings:

1 oz. butter	1 can condensed tomato soup
4 oz. onions, peeled and chopped	½ teaspoon dried marjoram or rosemary
4 loin chops	
salt, pepper	8 oz. plain boiled rice
¼ oz. flour	

1 Melt butter and fry onions till lightly browned. Put into a casserole.

2 Trim excess fat from chops, coat with seasoned flour and brown on both sides in remaining fat.

3 Put into casserole with onions and pour the soup round. Sprinkle with herbs.

4 Cover and cook in a slow oven (350°F. – Gas Mark 3) about 1¼ hours. Serve with rice.

Lamb curry

you will need for 4 servings:

1½ lb. lean lamb	1 pint beef stock (see
½ oz. curry powder	page 84)
¾ oz. flour	*bouquet garni* (see
salt, pepper	page 85)
1 oz. lard	1 oz. sultanas
1 onion, peeled and	1 tart apple, peeled
chopped	and chopped

1 Trim meat, remove excess fat and cut into cubes.
2 Mix curry powder, flour, salt and pepper, coat meat well and brown in heated lard with onion.
3 Add stock and *bouquet garni*, bring to boiling point and skim.
4 Pour all into a casserole, add sultanas and apple.
5 Cook in a slow oven (350°F. – Gas Mark 3) about 1½ hours.
6 Remove any excess fat, correct seasoning and consistency and serve with plain boiled rice.

Lamb curry with yoghurt

you will need for 4 servings:

1½ lb. lean lamb	2½ fl. oz. yoghurt
2 oz. butter	¼-inch cinnamon
1 large onion, peeled	stick
and chopped	2 cloves
¼ clove garlic	3–4 cardamom seeds,
1 oz. curry powder	if available
salt	1 bay leaf
cayenne pepper	stock (see page 84)
1 tablespoon tomato	
purée (see page 85)	

1 Trim meat, remove excess fat and cut into small pieces.
2 Heat butter, brown meat on all sides, then remove to a casserole.
3 Brown onion and garlic in remaining butter. Add curry powder, salt and cayenne and cook for 3 minutes.
4 Add tomato purée and yoghurt and pour all over the meat.
5 Tie cinnamon, cloves, cardamom seeds and bay leaf loosely in a piece of muslin and put into casserole.
6 Barely cover with stock.
7 Cover tightly and cook in a slow oven (350°F. – Gas Mark 3) about 1½ hours.
   Serve with plain boiled rice.

Lamb and kidney casserole

you will need for 4–6 servings:

2 lb. best end neck	2 oz. mushrooms,
lamb	sliced
4 lamb's kidneys	4 tomatoes, peeled
2 onions, peeled and	and sliced
chopped	½ oz. flour
2 oz. dripping or oil	1 pint stock (see
1 green pepper,	page 84) or water
seeded and	salt, pepper
chopped	

1 Trim meat and cut into pieces, skin and core kidneys and cut into quarters.
2 Heat fat, fry the meat and kidneys till brown, then transfer to a casserole.
3 Brown onions in remaining fat, then put with meat.
4 Add green pepper, mushrooms and tomatoes and cook for a few minutes, add flour and mix well.
5 Add stock or water and stir till boiling.
6 Add seasoning and pour over contents of casserole.
7 Cover and cook for 2½–3 hours in a slow oven (325°F. – Gas Mark 2).

Lamb and macaroni casserole

you will need for 6–8 servings:

1 lb. macaroni	1 tablespoon curry
1 lb. stewing lamb	powder
2 tablespoons oil	1 teaspoon capers
1 oz. flour	1 pint milk
	salt, pepper

1 Cook macaroni in boiling salted water till tender, then drain.
2 Wipe and cut up meat, brown lightly in hot oil, then remove to a plate.
3 Add flour, curry powder and capers to remaining oil and cook for a few minutes. Add milk, stir till boiling and boil for 3 minutes. Add seasonings.
4 Put half macaroni into a casserole. Arrange remaining meat on top, pour over sauce and cover with remaining macaroni.
5 Cover tightly and cook in a moderate oven (375°F. – Gas Mark 4) about 1½ hours.

Lamb and potato casserole

you will need for 4 servings:

1½ lb. neck of lamb	3 carrots, peeled and
1 oz. flour	sliced
salt, pepper	1½ lb. potatoes,
½ level teaspoon	peeled and sliced
ground ginger	juice of ½ lemon
1 tablespoon oil	¼ pint stock (see page
3 medium-sized	84) or water
onions, peeled and	
sliced	

1 Trim meat, removing excess fat, and cut into cubes.
2 Mix flour, salt, pepper and ginger and roll meat in it.
3 Heat oil, fry the meat till brown on all sides.
4 Put alternate layers of meat, vegetables and seasoning in a casserole, finishing with potatoes.
5 Add lemon juice and stock.
6 Cover, and cook in a slow oven (350°F. – Gas Mark 3) about 2 hours.
   Remove the lid for the last 40–45 minutes to brown the potatoes.

Spicy lamb noisettes

you will need for 4–6 servings:

1½ lb. best end neck
    of lamb, boned and
    rolled
1 dessertspoon corn
    oil
2 onions, chopped
1–2 sticks celery,
    chopped
3 tomatoes, peeled
    and sliced

½ small green pepper,
    sliced thinly
¼ level teaspoon
    paprika pepper
salt and pepper
1 chicken stock cube
½ pint boiling water
2 oz. rice

1 Slice the meat into 4–6 noisettes and secure each
   noisette with a cocktail stick.
2 Heat the corn oil and lightly brown the meat.
3 Remove the meat to a casserole, sauté the onions in
   the remaining corn oil and add to the meat with the
   celery, tomatoes and pepper.
4 Season with paprika pepper, salt and pepper.
5 Dissolve the chicken stock cube in the water, stir in
   the rice and pour over the ingredients in the casserole.
   Cover and cook in a moderate oven (375°F. – Gas
   Mark 4) for 2–2½ hours.

Navarin of lamb

you will need for 4 servings:

4 loin chops
2 oz. butter
8 small button onions,
    peeled
1 carrot, peeled and
    diced
2 medium-sized
    potatoes, peeled
    and diced

¼ pint shelled peas
½ small turnip, peeled
    and diced
1 small can tomato
    purée
½ pint thin brown
    stock (see page 84)
    or gravy
salt, pepper

1 Trim chops and remove excess fat.
2 Heat butter, brown chops on both sides, then remove
   to a plate.
3 Brown onions in remaining butter.
4 Arrange meat and vegetables in alternate layers in a
   casserole.
5 Mix tomato purée with stock and pour on top.
6 Add seasoning, cover and cook about 1 hour in a
   slow oven (325°F. – Gas Mark 2).

Marinated lamb casserole

you will need for 4–6 servings:

2 lb. shoulder of
    lamb
2 onions, peeled and
    sliced
2 cloves garlic
½ pint white wine
½ oz. flour
salt, pepper
2 tablespoons oil
1 pint stock (see
    page 84)

2–3 carrots, peeled
    and diced
2 small potatoes,
    peeled and diced
1–2 sticks celery,
    chopped
1–2 tablespoons
    green peas

1 Trim meat and cut into 2-inch cubes.
2 Add onions, garlic and wine and leave to marinate
   about 3 hours.

3 Discard garlic, remove meat and coat well with
   seasoned flour.
4 Heat oil and brown meat, then put into a casserole.
5 Add stock and onions and wine used for marinating.
   Cover and cook in a slow oven (350°F. – Gas Mark 3)
   about 1½ hours.
6 Add vegetables and continue cooking for 30 minutes
   or until vegetables are tender. Correct the seasoning
   before serving.

Lamb stew

you will need for 4 servings:

1 large or 2 small
    breasts of lamb
1 oz. fat
8 oz. onions, peeled
    and sliced
8 oz. carrots, peeled
    and chopped

1 chicken stock cube
1 pint water
4 oz. rice
1 small carton frozen
    peas
4 oz. mushrooms
½ pint red wine

1 Have meat boned, then cut into pieces.
2 Heat fat, brown the meat on all sides. Put into a
   casserole.
3 Add onions to remaining fat and brown.
4 Add carrots, crumbled stock cube and water, stir till
   boiling.
5 Pour all over meat in casserole and add washed rice.
6 Cover and cook in a slow oven (350°F. – Gas Mark 3)
   for about 1½ hours, stirring occasionally.
7 Add peas, mushrooms and wine and continue cooking for a further 30 minutes or until meat and rice are
   tender. Correct seasoning.

Paprika lamb

you will need for 4 servings:

1½ lb. middle or best
    end neck of lamb
1½ oz. butter
6 oz. onion, minced
1 lb. tomatoes,
    skinned and sliced

1 tablespoon parsley,
    chopped
2 teaspoons paprika
salt, pepper
¼ pint sour cream or
    yoghurt

1 Score and trim meat free of excess fat, cut into chops.
2 Heat butter in a casserole and brown chops on both
   sides.
3 Remove chops and sauté onion until beginning to
   brown.
4 Add tomatoes, parsley, paprika and seasoning. Replace chops.
5 Cover and cook in a slow oven (350°F. – Gas Mark 3)
   for about 2 hours.
6 Remove lid, stir in sour cream or yoghurt, adjust
   seasoning and bring to simmering point.

Quick haricot cutlets

you will need for 4 servings:

8 lamb cutlets
2 oz. butter
8 small button onions
8 rashers streaky
    bacon

4 oz. cooked haricot
    beans
salt, pepper
¾ pint brown stock
    (see page 84)

1 Trim cutlets and remove excess fat.
2 Heat butter, brown cutlets on both sides and remove to a casserole.
3 Brown onions in remaining butter, then put into the casserole with bacon rolls, haricot beans and seasoning.
4 Add stock, cover and cook in a very slow oven (325°F.–Gas Mark 2) about 45 minutes.

Lamb with noodles

you will need for 4 servings:

1½ lb. breast or shoulder of lamb
1 tablespoon oil
8 oz. leeks, chopped
3 onions, peeled and chopped
1 lb. tomatoes, peeled and sliced or 1 large can
¾ pint stock (see page 84) or water
salt, pepper
pinch rosemary or pinch mixed herbs
6–8 oz. ribbon noodles
1–2 oz. butter

1 Have meat boned, cut into small cubes.
2 Heat oil, add leeks and onions and fry till lightly browned.
3 Add meat and brown, and then transfer all to a casserole.
4 Add tomatoes, stock, seasoning and herbs.
5 Cover and cook in a slow oven (350°F.–Gas Mark 3) about 1½ hours.
6 About 30 minutes before the end of the cooking, put noodles into boiling salted water and cook for 15–20 minutes. Drain, then rinse in hot water. Drain thoroughly and mix with butter.

Variation
With **cheese** – a little grated cheese may be sprinkled over the noodles before serving.

Lamb with sweet red pepper

you will need for 4 servings:

1 tablespoon oil
1 onion, peeled and chopped
1 sweet red pepper, seeded and chopped
1½ lb. stewing mutton, cut into pieces
4 oz. haricot beans, soaked overnight in cold water
1 oz. flour
1 pint stock (see page 84) or water and 1 chicken stock cube
salt, pepper
3–4 potatoes, peeled and sliced

1 Heat oil, add onion, red pepper and meat and cook for a few minutes, then transfer to a casserole and add drained haricot beans.
2 Add flour to remaining fat in pan, and mix well. Add stock or stock cube and water, stir till boiling and boil for 1 minute. Season.

3 Pour into casserole. Cover and cook in a slow oven (350°F.–Gas Mark 3) about 2 hours.
4 Remove lid and arrange potatoes on top. Continue cooking a further 30 minutes or until potatoes are tender. Correct seasoning.

Lancashire hot pot

you will need for 4 servings:

2 lb. potatoes, peeled and sliced thickly
1½–2 lb. middle neck or scrag end mutton
2 sheep's kidneys
1 large onion, peeled and sliced
salt, pepper
½ pint water
1 oz. fat

1 Grease a casserole and put in a layer of potatoes.
2 Trim and cut meat into pieces and put on top.
3 Remove core from kidneys, slice, and put with meat.
4 Add onion, seasoning and water.
5 Arrange remaining potatoes on top, completely covering the meat, dot with fat.
6 Cover and cook in a slow oven (325°F.–Gas Mark 2) about 2½ hours.
7 Remove lid for the last 20–30 minutes to brown the top.

Note: It is traditional to serve a dish of pickled red cabbage with Lancashire hot pot.

Shank of mutton casserole

you will need:

veal forcemeat (see page 86)
piece boned shank of mutton
1 onion
1 carrot
1 turnip
2 oz. fat or oil
bouquet garni (see page 85)
1 teaspoon salt
1–2 peppercorns
½ pint water or stock (see page 84)
1 dessertspoon cornflour

1 Make forecemeat and stuff the meat.
2 Tie securely with coarse white cotton or string.
3 Peel onion, carrot and turnip and slice coarsely.
4 Heat fat or oil in casserole large enough to take the meat.
5 Fry meat in it until brown all over; remove and pour off fat.
6 Put in vegetables, *bouquet garni* and seasonings and meat.
7 Add water or stock, cover and cook in a slow oven (350°F.–Gas Mark 3) according to weight of meat (45 minutes per lb.).
8 10 minutes before end of cooking time, stir in cornflour which has been blended smoothly with ¼ pint cold water.

Note: Add more water or stock if meat seems to become dry during cooking.

Lamb and tomato casserole

you will need for 4 servings:

1½ lb. middle or best end neck of lamb
1½ oz. butter
2 medium-sized onions, peeled and chopped
1 lb. tomatoes, peeled and sliced
2 teaspoons paprika
salt, sugar
¼ pint yoghurt or sour cream
1 tablespoon chopped parsley

1 Trim excess fat from meat and cut into chops.
2 Heat butter, brown chops on both sides, then put into a casserole.
3 Add onion to remaining fat, cook till lightly browned.
4 Add tomatoes and paprika, season carefully with a little salt and a pinch of sugar.
5 Pour over chops, cover, and cook in a slow oven (325°F. – Gas Mark 2) about 1¼ hours.
6 Stir in yoghurt, correct seasoning and sprinkle with parsley before serving.

Raisin-stuffed shoulder of lamb

you will need:

3 oz. Patna rice
1 beef stock cube dissolved in ½ pint water
1 tablespoon onion, finely chopped
1 tablespoon raisins
1 dessertspoon parsley, chopped
1 teaspoon grated lemon rind
salt, pepper
1 shoulder of lamb, boned
½ oz. flour
1 oz. dripping

1 Parboil the rice in stock. After 10 minutes, add onion, raisins, parsley, lemon rind, salt and pepper.
2 Mix well and use to stuff the shoulder. Tie securely with string.
3 Sprinkle the joint with flour, put into a casserole, dot with dripping and cover.
4 Cook in a slow oven (350°F. – Gas Mark 3) and calculate time according to weight of meat (30 minutes per lb.).

Spring casserole

you will need for 4 servings:

1½ lb. middle neck of lamb
1 onion
1½ lb. potatoes
8 oz. new carrots
1 small cauliflower
3–4 leeks
seasoning
water

1 Prepare meat, remove excess fat. Cut into chops.
2 Prepare and slice onion, potatoes and carrots. Break cauliflower into sprigs. Cut leek into 1½-inch lengths.
3 Place alternating layers of potatoes, onion and meat in a casserole, finishing with potatoes. Season layers with salt and pepper and add enough water to half cover.
4 Cover casserole and cook in a moderate oven (375°F. – Gas Mark 4) for 1 hour.

5 Remove lid and add cauliflower, carrots and leeks. Cover again and cook for 1–1½ hours.

Scotch hot pot

you will need for 4 servings:

1½–2 lb. neck of lamb
stock (see page 84) or water
2 medium-sized onions
salt, pepper
8 oz. shelled peas
8 oz. shelled broad beans
4 small carrots, peeled and chopped
4 small turnips, peeled and chopped
1 small cauliflower
2 tablespoons chopped parsley

1 Trim meat, cut into fairly large pieces.
2 Put into a pan, just cover with stock or water, add salt and pepper and onions peeled and coarsely chopped.
3 Bring slowly to boiling point, skim carefully and transfer all to a casserole.
4 Add half the peas, beans, turnips and carrots, cover and cook in a slow oven (325°F. – Gas Mark 2) about 2 hours.
5 Add remaining peas and cauliflower divided into small flowerets and continue cooking for 1 hour. Correct seasoning and add parsley before serving.

Spanish lamb casserole

you will need for 4–6 servings:

2½ lb. fillet end leg of lamb
3 tablespoons oil
salt, pepper
1 bay leaf
¼ pint white wine
2 oz. butter
1 red pepper, seeded and chopped finely
1 clove garlic, minced or chopped finely
1 dessertspoon chopped parsley

1 Wipe meat, brush with oil and put into a deep casserole with remaining oil. Sprinkle with salt and pepper and add bay leaf.
2 Cover, and put into a hot oven (450°F. – Gas Mark 8) for 10 minutes until meat begins to brown.
3 Pour wine over meat, cover, reduce heat to 350°F. – Gas Mark 3 and cook, basting occasionally, for 1½–2 hours until meat is tender.
4 About 15 minutes before serving, heat butter, add the red pepper and garlic and cook for a few minutes. Add parsley and liquor from casserole. Mix all well and bring to boiling point. Cook for a few minutes, then pour back over meat.
5 Leave in oven for 10 minutes before serving.

Thursday lamb

you will need for 4 servings:

1½ lb. middle neck of lamb
1 large carrot
1 medium-sized parsnip
1 leek
1 oz. flour
¼ oz. dripping
2 rounded teaspoons concentrated tomato purée
1 chicken stock cube
¾ pint water
8 oz. can butter beans
salt and pepper

1 Trim meat and cut into serving portions.
2 Peel carrot and parsnip. Slice carrot into rings, cut parsnip into large cubes. Wash and slice leek.
3 Toss meat in flour, fry in dripping until browned. Remove from pan.
4 Add remaining flour to pan, stir into dripping to form a roux.
5 Add tomato purée and stock cube, blend all together. Stir in water, adding also liquid from butter beans. Bring to the boil and allow to boil for 3 minutes.
6 Replace meat, add vegetables.
7 Cover and cook in a moderate oven (375°F. – Gas Mark 4) for 1 hour.
8 Add butter beans and cook for further 15 minutes. Season to taste with salt and pepper and serve.

Stuffed breast of lamb en casserole

you will need for 4 servings:

for the stuffing:	2 lb. boned breast of
½ oz. butter	lamb
1 small apple, peeled	salt, pepper
and chopped	8 oz. carrots, peeled
8 oz. sausage meat	and sliced
2 oz. cooked rice	8 oz. onions, peeled
1 teaspoon chopped	and sliced
parsley	1 small turnip, peeled
1 teaspoon chopped	and sliced
fresh mint or ½	1–2 sticks celery,
teaspoon mixed	chopped
herbs	water
salt, pepper	

1 Heat butter, add apple and sausage meat and cook for a few minutes. Add all other ingredients and mix well.
2 Sprinkle meat with a little salt and pepper, spread with the stuffing and roll up.
3 Secure with a piece of string.
4 Put vegetables into a fairly deep casserole, add salt and pepper, then put meat on top.
5 Add a small quantity of water, cover and cook for about 2 hours in a slow oven (325°F. – Gas Mark 2).
To serve: put meat on to a dish, remove string and arrange the vegetables round. Thicken gravy left in the casserole and serve separately.

Summer casserole

you will need for 4–6 servings:

2–2½ lb. neck of	1 small turnip, peeled
lamb	and chopped
1 oz. dripping or	1 pint stock (see
butter	page 84) or water
1 medium-sized	salt, pepper
onion, peeled and	1 sprig mint
chopped finely	1 sprig thyme
8 oz. carrots, peeled	4 oz. cooked green
and sliced	peas

1 Trim meat and cut into pieces.

2 Heat dripping and brown meat, then put into a casserole.
3 Fry onion till lightly browned and put with meat.
4 Put vegetables into casserole, add stock and season carefully. Add mint and thyme.
5 Cover and cook in a slow oven (350°F. – Gas Mark 3) for about 1½ hours.
6 About 15 minutes before serving, add peas.
7 When ready to serve, remove mint and thyme and correct seasoning.

Braised lamb with vegetables

you will need for 6 servings:

salt and pepper	1 oz. butter
flour	½ pint water
half leg of lamb,	8 oz. tomatoes
about 2 lb.	2 rounded teaspoons
12 oz. carrots	cornflour
12 oz. leeks	

1 Add a good pinch of salt and pepper to flour and rub flour into surface of lamb.
2 Peel and quarter carrots, wash leeks and cut into short lengths. Fry carrots and leeks in butter for 2–3 minutes. Place into large casserole.
3 Brown lamb in butter, and place on top of vegetables. Add water, cover and cook in a moderate oven (350°F. – Gas Mark 3) for 1½ hours until lamb is tender.
4 Skin tomatoes and cut into quarters.
5 Remove lamb, carrots and onions to a warm serving dish.
6 Blend cornflour with a little water, stir into casserole. Add tomatoes.
7 Bring to boil, allow to boil for 1 minute, until cornflour thickens liquid. Add salt and pepper if necessary.
8 Pour into warmed sauceboat and serve with lamb.

Spicy lamb hot pot

you will need for 4 servings:

1½–2 lb. best end	½ green pepper,
neck lamb	chopped
1 oz. fat	¼ teaspoon paprika
2 medium-sized	¼ teaspoon mixed
onions, peeled and	spice
chopped	2 oz. rice
¼ clove garlic,	stock (see page 84)
crushed	or water
1–2 sticks celery,	salt, pepper
chopped	1 tablespoon chopped
3 tomatoes, peeled	parsley
and chopped	

1 Trim meat, remove excess fat and cut into pieces.
2 Heat fat and brown meat, then put into a casserole.

[continued

3 Add onion and garlic to remaining fat and fry till lightly browned. Put with meat.

4 Add remaining vegetables and spices.

5 Wash rice and mix with other ingredients.

6 Add stock or water to barely cover.

7 Cover and cook in a slow oven (350°F. – Gas Mark 3) for about 2 hours.

8 Correct seasoning before serving and sprinkle with chopped parsley.

Welsh cowl

you will need for 4 servings:

1½ lb. best end neck of mutton
2 pints water
salt, peppercorns
2 oz. pearl barley

2 carrots, peeled and chopped
1 lb. small potatoes, peeled
3 leeks, chopped
parsley, chopped

1 Trim and cut meat into joints.

2 Put into a pan with water, salt, few peppercorns, blanched barley and carrots.

3 Bring to boiling point and skim.

4 Transfer all to a casserole, cover tightly and cook in a slow oven (350°F. – Gas Mark 3) about 1½ hours.

5 Add potatoes whole and leeks and continue cooking for 1 hour.

6 Before serving, sprinkle with parsley.

✗ Lazy lamb

you will need:

4 lamb chops
1 lb. small potatoes
8 oz. small onions
1 dessertspoon instant stock powder

2 oz. butter
1 heaped tablespoon chopped parsley
¼ pint water

1 Trim excess fat off chops and peel potatoes and onions.

2 Cut four 18-inch squares of kitchen foil.

3 Place 1 lamb chop on each piece of foil, sprinkle with stock powder.

4 Divide the potatoes and onions between the four pieces of foil, also the butter and parsley.

5 Bring up the edges of each piece of foil, to make a parcel, adding 2 tablespoons water to each.

6 Seal edges, and place parcels on a baking tray.

7 Bake above the centre of a moderately hot oven (375°F. – Gas Mark 4) for about 45 minutes, until lamb and vegetables are tender.

To serve: open parcels carefully, tip contents on to warmed dinner plates.

Variations

With tomatoes – prepare as above, using 1 lb. skinned tomatoes instead of potatoes. Reduce water to 1 tablespoon and add a good pinch of sugar to each parcel.

With garlic – prepare either recipe, adding a good puff of powdered garlic to each parcel before sealing.

Pork and Bacon Casseroles

Pork and beans

you will need for 4 servings:

1½ lb. belly of pork
1 oz. bacon fat or butter
2 medium-sized onions, peeled and sliced
1 oz. flour
1 can beans in tomato sauce

1 teaspoon mustard
pinch of curry powder
1 tablespoon Worcestershire sauce
½ pint water
salt, pepper

1 Cut meat into small pieces.

2 Heat fat, add meat and fry for a few minutes, then remove to a casserole.

3 Put onions into pan with remaining fat and cook until beginning to look transparent, then put with meat.

4 Put flour into pan, mix with any remaining fat and sediment from meat and cook for a few minutes. Add contents of can of beans, and all other ingredients. Bring to boiling point, stirring all the time.

5 Pour into casserole. Cover and cook in a slow oven (350°F. – Gas Mark 3) for about 2 hours.

Devonshire pork chops

you will need for 4 servings:

4 pork chops
1 oz. soft brown sugar
1 teaspoon dry mustard
1½ oz. butter
¾ oz. cornflour
1 orange

cider
salt, pepper
1 clove garlic, crushed and chopped
4 olives, sliced
4 cloves

1 Trim chops, remove any excess fat.

2 Mix sugar and mustard together and coat both sides of chops.

3 Heat butter and brown chops on both sides. Remove to a casserole.

4 Add cornflour to remaining fat, mix well and cook for 1 minute.

5 Squeeze juice from orange and add enough cider to make the quantity up to ¾ pint. Add to cornflour, stir till boiling and boil 1 minute.

6 Add seasoning, garlic, olives and cloves and pour over chops.

7 Cover and cook in a slow oven (350°F. – Gas Mark 3) about 30 minutes or until chops are tender.

Casseroled pork chops

you will need for 4 servings:

4 spare-rib pork chops	4 oz. mushrooms, sliced
1 tablespoon oil	2 tablespoons tomato purée (see page 85)
2 medium-sized onions, peeled and chopped	juice ½ lemon
1 small can pimentos, chopped	¼ pint stock (see page 84) or water
	salt, pepper
	1 teaspoon dried basil

1 Trim chops and brown on both sides in hot oil. Transfer to a casserole.

2 Put onions, pimento and mushrooms into pan in which chops were browned and sauté for a few minutes.

3 Add tomato purée, lemon juice, stock and seasoning and bring to boiling point.

4 Pour over meat and sprinkle basil on top.

5 Cover and cook in a slow oven (350°F. – Gas Mark 3) about 1 hour.

Casserole of pork

you will need for 4 servings:

4 lean pork chops	8 prunes
salt, pepper	good pinch rosemary or sage
1 oz. dripping	¼ pint cider
2 medium-sized cooking apples	¼ pint water
8 oz. onions	

1 Trim chops, removing excess fat, season, and brown on both sides in hot dripping.

2 Peel and slice apples and onions and put half into a casserole. Place meat on top.

3 Cover prunes with hot water and leave for a few minutes, then remove stones and put into casserole.

4 Add rosemary and a little seasoning, then cover with remaining apple and onion.

5 Mix cider and water together and pour into casserole.

6 Cover with a piece of buttered paper and then with a tight fitting lid.

7 Cook in a slow oven (325°F. – Gas Mark 2) about 2 hours.

Pork and prune casserole

you will need for 4–6 servings:

2½–3 lb. loin of pork, boned	1 apple, peeled and chopped
salt, pepper	2 oz. butter
8 oz. prunes, soaked overnight	1 pint chicken or veal stock (see page 85)
pinch ground ginger	

1 Flatten meat on a board and sprinkle lightly with seasoning.

2 Stone prunes and mix with apple and ginger. Spread over meat, roll up and tie securely.

3 Heat butter and brown meat on all sides, then transfer to a casserole.

4 Pour hot stock over, cover and cook in a very slow oven (325°F. – Gas Mark 2) about 2 hours or until the meat is tender.
Serve with apple sauce.

Pork and macaroni casserole

you will need for 4 servings:

4 oz. macaroni	2 sticks celery, chopped finely
3 oz. butter	6 oz. grated cheese
4 pork chops	salt, pepper
½ oz. flour	4 oz. mushrooms, sliced
½ pint milk	
1 small onion, peeled and chopped	

1 Cook macaroni in boiling salted water.

2 Heat 1½ oz. butter and fry chops until brown on both sides.

3 Make a sauce with remaining butter, flour and milk.

4 Add onion, celery, cheese and seasoning and cook till cheese has melted. Add macaroni and mushrooms.

5 Pour sauce into a casserole and arrange chops on top. Cover and cook in a slow oven (350°F. – Gas Mark 3) about 1 hour. Add a little extra milk or stock if necessary during the cooking.

Savoury pork chops

you will need for 4 servings:

2 tablespoons corn oil	8 oz. cooking apples, peeled and sliced
4 pork chops	1 packet onion sauce
4 tomatoes, skinned and sliced	salt and pepper
	¼ pint milk

1 Heat the corn oil and brown the chops.

2 Place the tomatoes and apples in the bottom of a fireproof dish. Place the chops on top. Season.

3 Make up the onion sauce as directed on the packet using ½ pint milk and pour over the chops. Cover and cook in a moderate oven (350°F. – Gas Mark 3) for 1½ hours, until chops are tender.

Pork with peppers

you will need for 4 servings:

1 lb. spare rib of pork	1 green pepper, seeded and chopped
2 oz. butter	1 red pepper, seeded and chopped
2 medium-sized onions, peeled and chopped	4 tomatoes, peeled and chopped
1 oz. brown sugar	1 clove garlic, crushed
½ oz. cornflour	pinch basil
1 chicken stock cube	
1 pint water	
1 tablespoon soy sauce	

1 Trim and cube pork.

2 Heat butter, sauté pork for a few minutes, then remove to a casserole.

3 Add onions to remaining fat and cook till golden brown. Put into casserole with meat. [continued

4 Put sugar, cornflour and chicken stock cube into the pan in which the meat was sautéed. Add water and soy sauce and stir till boiling.
5 Pour over meat and onions.
6 Add peppers, tomatoes, garlic and basil.
7 Cover and cook in a slow oven (350°F. – Gas Mark 3) about 1½ hours. Correct seasoning.

Belly of pork casserole

you will need for 4 servings:

1 large onion, peeled and sliced	1 chicken stock cube
1 large cooking apple, peeled and sliced	¾ pint boiling water
1½ lb. belly of pork	pinch freshly ground pepper
2 tablespoons tomato purée	pinch sage

1 Put onion and apple into a casserole and put meat on top.
2 Mix tomato purée and stock cube together, add boiling water and stir till stock cube has dissolved.
3 Pour over meat in casserole, add pepper and sage.
4 Cover and bake in a slow oven (325°F. – Gas Mark 2) about 2 hours.

Pork chops Milanese

you will need for 4 servings:

4 pork chops	½ small onion, peeled and minced
salt, pepper	½ clove garlic, minced
3 tablespoons oil	1 can peeled tomatoes
1½ oz. breadcrumbs	
2 oz. grated cheese	

1 Trim chops, season and brush both sides with oil.
2 Mix breadcrumbs and cheese together and coat chops with mixture.
3 Heat oil, add onion and garlic and brown lightly.
4 Add chops and brown on both sides then transfer all to a casserole.
5 Add tomatoes, cover and cook about 1¼ hours in a slow oven (350°F. – Gas Mark 3). Correct seasoning before serving.

Pork chops Italienne

you will need for 4 servings:

4 pork chops	4 oz. breadcrumbs
2 tablespoons oil	1 small onion, peeled and chopped
1 small green pepper, seeded and chopped	1 egg
1 can creamed corn	salt, pepper

1 Trim chops and brown on both sides in hot oil, then transfer to a casserole.
2 Mix all other ingredients together, adding a little milk or stock if mixture is too thick.
3 Spread over chops, cover and cook about 1¼–1½ hours in a slow oven (350°F. – Gas Mark 3).

Oriental pork chops

you will need for 4 servings:

4 pork chops	¾ pint water
2 tablespoons oil	pinch mixed herbs
1 small onion, peeled and chopped	2 oz. prunes, soaked overnight
½ green pepper, seeded and sliced	1 small can mandarin oranges, drained
8 oz. Patna rice	salt, pepper
1 chicken stock cube	

1 Trim chops, removing excess fat.
2 Heat oil, and brown chops on both sides, remove to a casserole.
3 Add onion, pepper and rice to remaining oil and cook for a few minutes.
4 Add stock cube, water and herbs and stir till boiling. Pour over chops.
5 Add prunes, stoned and halved.
6 Cover and cook in a slow oven (350°F. – Gas Mark 3) about 1 hour.
7 30 minutes before serving, add mandarin oranges and correct seasoning.

Piquant pork chops

you will need for 4 servings:

4 pork chops	1 dessertspoon tomato purée (see page 85)
1 tablespoon oil	1 beef stock cube
1 small onion, peeled and chopped	½ pint water
1 tablespoon brown sugar	1 tablespoon Worcestershire sauce
1 tablespoon dry mustard	2 tablespoons lemon juice

1 Put chops in a baking tin or a wide shallow casserole and bake uncovered in a moderate oven (375°F. – Gas Mark 4) for about 20 minutes.
2 Meanwhile, heat oil, add onion and fry till browned.
3 Add sugar, mustard, tomato purée and crumbled beef stock cube, mix well, then add water and stir till boiling. Add Worcestershire sauce and lemon juice and check seasoning.
4 Pour off any excess fat from chops, and pour sauce over them.
5 Cover and continue cooking in a slow oven (350°F. – Gas Mark 3) for about 40–45 minutes.

Pork hot pot

you will need for 4 servings:

1½ lb. boneless lean pork	1 cooking apple, peeled and sliced
1 lb. potatoes, peeled and sliced	1 teaspoon sage
8 oz. onions, peeled and sliced	salt, pepper
4 oz. prunes, soaked overnight, and stoned	about ½ pint stock (see page 84)

1 Cut meat into small pieces and arrange in a casserole in layers with vegetables, prunes and apple.

2 Sprinkle salt and pepper and sage between layers.

3 Add stock to come about ⅔ up the casserole.

4 Cover and cook in a slow oven (350°F. – Gas Mark 3) for about 2 hours.

5 Correct seasoning before serving.

Ragoût of pork

you will need:

1 oz. bacon fat or butter	1 small can tomato purée
8 oz. onions, peeled and chopped	1 beef stock cube
4 pork chops	½ pint water
¾ oz. flour	1 bay leaf

1 Heat fat and fry onion until lightly browned, remove to a casserole.

2 Brown chops on both sides and put into casserole with onions.

3 Add flour to remaining fat and mix well. Add tomato purée, beef stock cube and water and stir till boiling.

4 Pour over chops, add bay leaf.

5 Cover and cook in a moderate oven (375°F. – Gas Mark 4) about 1 hour.

Pork and quince casserole

(An old Greek recipe)

you will need for 4 servings:

1½ lb. boneless lean pork	salt, pepper
½ oz. bacon fat or butter	pinch cinnamon
8 oz. tomatoes, peeled and sliced	stock (see page 84) or water
	2 lb. quinces
	3 oz. sugar

1 Trim and cut meat into pieces.

2 Heat fat and brown meat on all sides.

3 Put meat into a casserole with tomatoes, seasoning and cinnamon. Barely cover with stock or water. Cover and cook for about 1 hour in a slow oven (350°F. – Gas Mark 3).

3 Meanwhile, peel and slice quinces, sprinkle with sugar and leave for at least 30 minutes.

5 When meat has cooked for 1 hour, remove from oven, arrange slices of quince on top and add liquid drawn from them.

6 Cover, return to oven and continue cooking for 1 hour.

Quick pork goulash

you will need for 4 servings:

2 tablespoons oil or pork fat	1 small can tomato purée (see page 85)
1 lb. cooked lean pork, cut into cubes	1 sprig thyme or pinch dried thyme
2 onions, peeled and sliced	¼ teaspoon ground ginger
1 clove garlic, crushed	3 tablespoons sour cream
¼ pint stock (see page 84) or water	buttered noodles (see page 87)

1 Heat oil, brown meat lightly, then transfer to a casserole.

2 Cook onion and garlic till just beginning to look transparent, then put with meat.

3 Mix stock and tomato purée and pour over meat.

4 Add thyme and ginger and stir in cream.

5 Cover and cook in a moderate oven (375°F. – Gas Mark 4) about 30 minutes.

6 Correct seasoning and serve with buttered noodles.

Sausage and bean casserole

you will need for 4 servings:

1 lb. pork sausages	½ teaspoon oregano
4 oz. cooked ham	pinch marjoram
2 tablespoons oil	1 small can tomato purée
1 onion, peeled and chopped	1 can red kidney beans
½ green pepper, seeded and chopped	salt, pepper
	1 can tomatoes

1 Cut sausages into 2 or 3 portions, chop ham and sauté for a few minutes in oil. Remove to a casserole.

2 Add onion and pepper to remaining oil and cook till onion is lightly browned.

3 Put all other ingredients into casserole. Cover and cook in a slow oven (350°F. – Gas Mark 3) about 1½ hours.

4 Add stock if necessary during cooking.

Spanish casserole

you will need for 4 servings:

8 oz. salt pork	1 teaspoon tomato purée (see page 85)
1 tablespoon olive oil	*bouquet garni* (see page 85)
1 large onion, peeled and chopped	1½ pints stock (see page 84) or water (approximately)
1 large carrot, peeled and chopped	2 saveloy sausages
2 cloves garlic, crushed	8 oz. tomatoes
2 red peppers, seeded and sliced thinly	seasoning
1 can red kidney beans	parsley

1 Blanch pork, then simmer for about 30 minutes.

2 Heat oil, add onion, carrot, garlic and peppers and cook for about 5 minutes.

3 Remove to a casserole, add beans, tomato purée, *bouquet garni* and stock which should only just cover.

4 Cover casserole and put into a slow oven (350°F. – Gas Mark 3) for about 30 minutes.

5 Add pork cut into pieces and continue cooking for 1½ hours.

6 Add sausages, blanched and cut into thick slices and tomatoes, peeled and thickly sliced.

7 Continue cooking for 30 minutes.

8 Before serving, correct seasoning and sprinkle with chopped parsley.

Ham, egg and sweet corn casserole

you will need for 4 servings:

1 tablespoon corn oil	2–3 oz. ham, chopped
1 oz. cornflour	3 hard-boiled eggs,
1 chicken stock cube	shelled, and
½ pint milk	quartered
¼ pint water	1 tablespoon
3 oz. grated cheese	breadcrumbs
1 11-oz. can corn	
kernels	

1 Heat corn oil, add cornflour and stock cube and mix well.
2 Add milk and water, stir till boiling and boil for 1 minute.
3 Remove from heat, add cheese (reserving 1 tablespoon) sweet corn and ham.
4 Place eggs in a buttered casserole.
5 Pour sauce mixture on top.
6 Mix remaining cheese and breadcrumbs and sprinkle on top.
7 Bake for 15 minutes in a moderate oven (350°F.– Gas Mark 3), then brown under the grill.

Sauerkraut and pork

you will need for 4 servings:

1–1½ lb. sauerkraut	8 oz. pickled pork,
boiling water	blanched
1 oz. bacon fat	stock (see page 84)
1 onion, peeled and	*bouquet garni*
sliced	(see page 85)
1 carrot, peeled and	salt, freshly ground
sliced	black pepper
1 pig's trotter	3 frankfurters
	parsley

1 Put sauerkraut into boiling water and cook for 10 minutes, then drain well and put into a casserole.
2 Heat bacon fat, add onion and carrot, sauté till brown, then put into casserole.
3 Add pig's trotter and pork and enough stock to moisten well. Add *bouquet garni*, salt and pepper.
4 Cover tightly and cook in a slow oven (350°F.–Gas Mark 3) for about 1¾ hours.
5 About 30 minutes before serving, blanch frankfurters and add to casserole.
To serve: pile sauerkraut on to a serving dish, slice meats and arrange on top. Sprinkle well with parsley. Serve a good brown sauce or gravy separately.

Sweet corn and ham casserole

you will need for 4 servings:

1 oz. butter	2 oz. grated cheese
1 oz. flour	1 can sweet corn
1 chicken stock cube	kernels
½ pint milk	6 oz. cooked ham,
¼ pint water	diced
2 oz. white	little pimento,
breadcrumbs	chopped

1 Heat butter, stir in flour and stock cube and mix well. Cook for 1 minute, then add milk and water. Stir till boiling and boil 1 minute.
2 Remove from heat, add 1 oz. breadcrumbs and 1 oz. cheese, sweet corn, ham and pimento.
3 Correct seasoning and pour into a greased casserole.
4 Sprinkle remaining breadcrumbs and cheese on top and bake for about 20 minutes in a moderate oven (375°F.– Gas Mark 4).
5 Brown under grill before serving.

Company casserole

you will need:

1 small onion	4 slices ham
1 oz. butter	½ can sweet corn
½ packet (3	niblets
tablespoons) dried	1 tablespoon sherry
tomato soup	(optional)

1 Peel and chop onion, fry in melted butter for 5 minutes.
2 Blend in soup and cook for a further 3 minutes.
3 Gradually stir in ½ pint water and bring to boil.
4 Heap a tablespoon of sweet corn on each slice of ham, roll ham up and place in bottom of a greased oven-proof dish.
5 Add sherry, if used, to sauce, pour over ham.
6 Cover and bake in a moderate oven (350°F.–Gas Mark 3), for 30 minutes.
7 Serve with thick slices of French or garlic bread or potato crisps heated through in the oven.

Note: The ham and corn may be cooked in the sauce if an oven is not available. Cover and simmer gently for 20 minutes.

Variation
With celery and cheese sauce – use canned celery hearts in place of sweet corn and a cheese sauce. Pour cheese sauce over the ham, bake in a moderately hot oven for 30 minutes

Murphy's casserole

you will need for 4 servings:

1½ lb. potatoes	1 can condensed
1 lb. leeks	mushroom soup
6 oz. ham or bacon	1 tablespoon chopped
	parsley

1 Peel and cut potatoes into ½-inch thick slices. Cook for 4 minutes in boiling salted water.
2 Prepare and slice leeks and chop ham.
3 Grease a deep casserole and arrange potatoes, leeks and ham in layers, finishing with potato.

4 Pour over soup, cover and cook in a slow oven (325°F. – Gas Mark 2) about 2 hours.
5 Sprinkle with parsley before serving.

Turkey and ham casserole

you will need for 4–6 servings:

1 tablespoon corn oil	6 oz. cooked ham, chopped
1 small onion, chopped	2 medium-sized cooking apples, peeled and sliced
1 small green pepper, chopped	1 packet tomato soup
1–2 sticks of celery, chopped	1 pint water
1 lb. cooked potatoes, sliced	1 oz. breadcrumbs
12 oz. cooked turkey, chopped	butter

1 Heat the corn oil and lightly sauté onion, pepper and celery.
2 Place the potatoes, turkey, ham, vegetables and apples in layers in a deep casserole finishing with potatoes.
3 Make up the tomato soup as directed on the packet using only 1 pint water, and pour over the ingredients in the casserole.
4 Sprinkle with breadcrumbs, dot with butter and bake in a moderately hot oven (375°F. – Gas Mark 4) for 40–45 minutes.

Braised ham

you will need for 4–6 servings:

2–2½ lb. collar or slipper of bacon, soaked overnight in cold water	bouquet garni (see page 85)
½ oz. bacon fat	freshly ground black pepper
1 onion, peeled and chopped finely	about ¾ pint good stock (see page 84) (made with a stock cube if necessary)
1 carrot, peeled and chopped finely	1 teaspoon cornflour
2 oz. mushrooms, chopped	2 tablespoons sherry

1 Drain bacon, scrape it and dry well.
2 Heat fat, put in bacon and sauté for about 10 minutes, turning from time to time. Then remove.
3 Sauté the onion, carrot and mushrooms in remaining fat for about 5 minutes, then remove to a casserole.
4 Put bacon into casserole on top of the vegetables. Add *bouquet garni*, pepper and stock. Cover casserole with paper and then with the lid, so that it is really tightly covered. Cook in a slow oven (350°F. – Gas Mark 3) until the bacon is tender, about 1½–2 hours.
5 When cooked, remove bacon to a serving dish.
6 Strain liquor into a pan and remove excess fat. Mix cornflour smoothly with sherry, add to pan and stir till boiling. Correct seasoning and boil for 1 minute.
To serve: the gravy can be served separately or the required amount of ham can be carved and arranged on a bed of spinach, with some of the gravy poured over.

Ham jambalaya

you will need for 3 servings:

2 tablespoons oil	4 oz. mushrooms, sliced
1 medium-sized onion, peeled and chopped	4 oz. rice
1 medium-sized green pepper, seeded and thinly sliced	8 oz. cooked ham, diced
	½ pint water
	1 teaspoon chilli sauce
1 can condensed tomato soup	seasoning
	chopped parsley

1 Heat oil, add onion and pepper and sauté until onion is transparent.
2 Add tomato soup, mushrooms, rice and ham and trasfer to a casserole.
3 Mix water with chilli sauce and stir into the other ingredients. Season carefully.
4 Cover very tightly and cook in a slow oven (350°F. – Gas Mark 3) about 40–45 minutes or until rice is tender.
5 Add a little extra water if required during the cooking. Sprinkle with parsley and serve.

Ham and tomatoes provençal

you will need for 4 servings:

8 slices bread	1½ oz. butter
olive oil	1 clove garlic, peeled and finely chopped
4 large slices ham	1 dessertspoon finely chopped parsley
4 large tomatoes	
1 teaspoon castor sugar	½ teaspoon salt

1 Cut a circle out of each slice of bread using a biscuit or pastry cutter. Fry until crisp in olive oil. Arrange in a shallow casserole or roasting tin.
2 Cut rounds of ham to cover each piece of bread. Cut tomatoes in half. Place ham and tomatoes, cut side uppermost, on each piece of bread.
3 Sprinkle cut side of tomatoes with sugar.
4 Cream butter with garlic, parsley and salt and spread garlic butter over top of each tomato.
5 Bake in a moderately hot oven (375°F. – Gas Mark 4) for about 15 minutes.

Tomatoes provençal as an accompaniment – Omit bread and ham. Prepare tomatoes as in previous recipe, sprinkling each, when spread with butter, with freshly made breadcrumbs (2 tablespoons required) or packet bread sauce mix. Serve with roast or grilled meat.

Winter casserole

you will need for 4 servings:

1–1½ lb. collar bacon	1 small turnip, peeled and chopped
1 oz. fat	1 parsnip, peeled and cut into thin pieces
1 onion, peeled and chopped	½ oz. flour
2 carrots, peeled and chopped	½ pint water

1 Soak bacon overnight in cold water. *[continued*

2 Remove rind and excess fat and cut into 1-inch cubes.
3 Heat fat, brown bacon cubes and remove from pan.
4 Add all vegetables and sauté for 5 minutes. Put into a casserole and arrange bacon on top.
5 Add flour to remaining fat and cook for a few minutes, add water, stir till boiling.
6 Strain into casserole, cover and cook in a slow oven (350°F.–Gas Mark 3) for 2–2¼ hours.

Somerset pot roast

you will need for 6 servings:

2½–3 lb. middle cut gammon, soaked overnight
2 tablespoons oil
2 medium-sized onions, peeled and sliced
8 oz. carrots, peeled and sliced
1 small parsnip, peeled and chopped
¼ teaspoon powdered mace
freshly ground black pepper
¼ pint water
½ pint cider
8 oz. cooking apples
1 tablespoon honey

1 Trim bacon and remove rind.
2 Heat oil, add vegetables and sauté for 5 minutes, then put all into a casserole.
3 Arrange bacon on vegetables, add mace, pepper, water and cider. Cover tightly and cook for about 1½ hours in a slow oven (350°F.–Gas Mark 3).
4 Peel, core and slice apples and arrange round gammon.
5 Brush over with honey and continue cooking for 30 minutes.

Spiced gammon casserole

you will need for 6 servings:

3–3½ lb. middle gammon
8–9 peppercorns
5–6 cloves
1 tablespoon dark treacle
8 oz. shallots
boiling water

for the sauce:
2 teaspoons cornflour
1 teaspoon dry mustard
1 teaspoon brown sugar
¼ pint stock from gammon and water

1 Soak gammon overnight, then scrape it well and put into a large saucepan with peppercorns and cloves.
2 Trickle treacle over gammon and arrange the shallots around.
3 Add enough boiling water to come a good half way up gammon. Cover tightly and cook in a slow oven (325°F.–Gas Mark 2) about 3½ hours.

To make the sauce
1 Mix cornflour, mustard and sugar together smoothly with a little of the liquid.

2 Put the rest on to heat, add mixed cornflour, stir till boiling and boil for 2 minutes.
3 Correct seasoning and serve in a sauce boat.

Honeyed gammon casserole

you will need for 4 servings:

4 oz. Patna rice
2 oz. honey
3 tablespoons melted butter
1 medium-sized green pepper, seeded and chopped
1 teaspoon Tabasco sauce
1 teaspoon made mustard
1 lb. cold cooked gammon, cut into pieces
8 oz. dried apricots, soaked and chopped

1 Cook rice in boiling salted water for 12 minutes, drain.
2 Add all other ingredients to rice and mix well, then put into a greased casserole.
3 Cover and cook in a slow oven (350°F.–Gas Mark 3) for about 1 hour.

Note: During the cooking, if the mixture looks a little dry, add a small quantity of stock or water.

Casseroled hock

you will need for 4–6 servings:

2½–3 lb. hock of bacon
12 very small onions or white cocktail onions
2–3 sharp dessert apples, peeled and sliced thickly
1 teaspoon dry mustard
1 tablespoon brown sugar
little freshly ground pepper
½ pint cider
4 oz. seedless raisins

1 Put bacon into a deep casserole, add onions and cover with apple slices.
2 Mix mustard, sugar and pepper smoothly with cider, add raisins and pour over contents of casserole.
3 Cover with foil and then with the lid, and cook for 2–2½ hours in a slow oven (350°F.–Gas Mark 3).

Haricot beans with bacon

you will need for 3 servings:

8 oz. haricot beans, soaked overnight
12 oz. streaky bacon
1 oz. bacon fat or dripping
3 medium-sized onions, peeled and sliced
1 tablespoon chopped parsley
pinch mixed herbs

1 Cook beans in boiling salted water for 30 minutes, strain, and keep liquor.
2 Remove rind from bacon and cut it into cubes.
3 Heat fat, and fry onions until lightly browned.
4 Arrange alternate layers of bacon, beans, onions, parsley and herbs in a casserole, finishing with beans.
5 Add liquor in which the beans were cooked so casserole is about ⅔ full.
6 Cover, and cook about 2 hours in a slow oven (325°F. – Gas Mark 2).

Bacon and sausage casserole

you will need for 4 servings:

8 oz. streaky bacon rashers	salt, pepper
12 oz. sausage meat	pinch mixed herbs
1 medium-sized onion, peeled and sliced	1 sprig thyme
1 large cooking apple, peeled, cored and sliced	½ pint stock (see page 84) or water

1 Remove rind from bacon, divide sausage meat into small portions and roll up in bacon.
2 Put half the onion and apple into a casserole, put half the rolls on top, cover with remaining onion and apple and then add the rest of the bacon rolls.
3 Season lightly, add herbs, and pour stock over.
4 Cover, and cook in a slow oven (350°F. – Gas Mark 3) about 1½ hours.
5 Remove lid about 15 minutes before the end of the cooking, if preferred, brown under grill.

Bacon and bean casserole

you will need for 4–6 servings:

1½–2 lb. collar or forehock of bacon	3–4 tomatoes, peeled and sliced
8 oz. butter beans, soaked overnight	1 green pepper, seeded and chopped
1 small onion, peeled and chopped	1 chicken stock cube
2–3 carrots, peeled and chopped	¾ pint boiling water
1 stick celery, chopped	

1 Cut bacon into pieces and put into a casserole with beans and vegetables.
2 Dissolve stock cube in boiling water and pour over contents of casserole.
3 Cover tightly and cook in a slow oven (350°F. – Gas Mark 3) for 2½–3 hours.

Bacon and apple casserole

you will need for 4 servings:

4 fairly thick gammon rashers	1 oz. seedless raisins
2 medium-sized dessert apples	pinch freshly ground pepper
4 tomatoes	¼ pint cider
1 onion, peeled and sliced thinly	

1 Remove skin from gammon and score fat in two or three places. Put into a casserole.
2 Core, but do not peel apples, cut through centres and put into the casserole with whole tomatoes.
3 Add onion, raisins, pepper and cider.
4 Cover and cook in a moderate oven (375°F. – Gas Mark 4) for about 1 hour.

Peperoni casserole

you will need for 3 servings:

2 large green peppers	8 oz. bacon
1 lb. tomatoes	8 oz. cooked rice
salt, pepper, sugar	1 small can tomato purée
1 tablespoon oil	
1 small onion, peeled and finely chopped	

1 Cut peppers in half lengthwise, remove seeds and blanch in boiling water for 5 minutes.
2 Chop tomatoes and put into a pan with 4–5 tablespoons water, salt, pepper and a pinch sugar. Cook till tender, then sieve.
3 Heat oil, sauté onion until transparent, then add bacon, cut into small pieces and cook for a few minutes.
4 Add rice, and 3–4 tablespoons tomato purée.
5 Fill the halves of pepper with rice mixture and arrange in a casserole.
6 Pour remaining tomato purée round the peppers. Cover, and cook in a moderate oven (375°F. – Gas Mark 4) about 35 minutes.

Bacon and potato casserole

you will need for 4 servings:

1 lb. cooked potatoes	3 hard-boiled eggs, sliced
4 oz. rashers streaky bacon	½ oz. breadcrumbs
¼ pint yoghurt or sour milk	¼ oz. butter

1 Slice potatoes and put half of them into a greased casserole.
2 Cover with half the bacon rashers, pour on half the yoghurt and cover with half the eggs.
3 Continue in layers, finishing with potatoes.
4 Sprinkle breadcrumbs over and dot with butter.
5 Put into a slow oven (350°F. – Gas Mark 3) for 30 minutes until top is nicely browned.

Offal Casseroles

Casserole of kidneys

you will need for 4 servings:

1 lb. kidneys	1 dessertspoon flour
2 oz. fat	½ pint stock (see
3 small onions,	page 84) or water
peeled and	1 lb. mashed cooked
chopped finely	potato
4 oz. rashers streaky	little egg or milk
bacon	1 tablespoon chopped
seasoning	parsley

1 Wash and skin kidneys, remove cores. Put into a pan with cold water, bring to the boil, then drain off the water. Repeat this process once.
2 Heat fat, add onions and fry until golden brown.
3 Put onions into a casserole, arrange kidneys on top and cover with bacon.
4 Season and sprinkle with flour.
5 Add stock, cover and cook in a slow oven (350°F. – Gas Mark 3) till tender, about 35 minutes.
6 While kidneys are cooking, line a fireproof serving dish with potato. Brush with egg or milk and brown in the oven.
7 Pour kidneys into prepared dish and serve sprinkled with parsley.

Sauté of kidney

you will need for 4 servings:

2 tablespoons oil	1 oz. almonds,
2 onions, peeled and	shredded
chopped	pinch garlic salt
2 oz. salt pork, cut	pinch mixed spice
into dice	2 teaspoons brown
1 lb. ox kidney	sugar
½ oz. flour	½ pint brown stock
salt, pepper	(see page 84) or
2 oz. mushrooms,	water
sliced	1 tablespoon tomato
2 tomatoes, peeled	purée (see page 85)
and sliced	

1 Heat oil in a large heavy pan, add onion and pork and fry till well browned.
2 Cut up kidney, coat with seasoned flour and put into pan with onion. Stir till well browned.
3 Remove kidney, pork and onion to a casserole.
4 Put mushrooms, tomatoes, almonds, spices and sugar into pan and mix well.
5 Add stock and tomato purée and stir till boiling. Pour over contents of casserole.
6 Cover and cook in a very slow oven (325°F. – Gas Mark 2) for about 2 hours.
7 Before serving, correct seasoning.

Plain boiled rice goes well with this dish.

Kidney and sausage casserole

you will need for 4 servings:

1½ lb. ox kidney	2 carrots, peeled and
8 oz. pork sausages	sliced
1 oz. flour	1 bay leaf
salt, pepper	½ teaspoon crushed
2 oz. fat	sage
1 medium-sized	½ pint stock (see
onion, peeled and	page 84) or water
sliced	

1 Cut kidney into pieces removing cores and fat. Cover with cold salted water and leave for about 15 minutes. Drain and dry.
2 Cut sausages into two or three pieces.
3 Season the flour and coat kidney and sausage well.
4 Heat fat and fry meat till well browned. Remove to a casserole.
5 Add onion and carrots to remaining fat and brown well, then put with kidney.
6 Add bay leaf and sage.
7 Put any remaining flour with sediment left in pan, mix well, then add stock or water and stir till boiling.
8 Pour over ingredients in the casserole. Cover and cook in a slow oven (325°F. – Gas Mark 2) about 2½ hours. Correct seasoning.

Kidney in sherry sauce

you will need for 4 servings:

1 lb. ox kidney	2 teaspoons
1 oz. seasoned flour	concentrated
1 onion	tomato purée
1 oz. butter	salt, pepper
½ pint water	pinch castor sugar
	2 tablespoons dry
	sherry

1 Remove core from kidney, and cut into 1-inch pieces. Toss in seasoned flour.
2 Peel and chop onion. Gently fry kidney and onion in butter for 3 minutes.
3 Stir in remaining flour. Continue cooking for further 3 minutes stirring all the time. Stir in water and tomato purée, bring to boil.
4 Allow to boil for 3 minutes. Add salt and pepper, if necessary, also a pinch of castor sugar.
5 Add sherry. Pour into casserole.
6 Cover and cook at 325°F. – Gas Mark 2 for 1 hour or until kidney is tender. Serve with boiled rice.

Braised liver and onions

you will need for 3 servings:

12 oz. ox or pig's liver	3 onions, peeled and
½ oz. flour	sliced
salt, pepper	1 pint stock (see
2 tablespoons oil	page 84)
¼ teaspoon grated	juice ½ lemon
lemon rind	

1. Wash and dry liver, cut into ½ inch thick slices.
2. Season the flour, coat liver, and fry in hot oil till brown on both sides. Remove to a casserole and sprinkle with lemon rind.
3. Fry onions till brown, then put with liver. Sprinkle with salt and pepper.
4. Add stock, cover and cook in a slow oven (350°F.– Gas Mark 3) about 2 hours.
5. Add lemon juice before serving.

Liver Italienne

you will need for 4 servings:

1 tablespoon oil	1 oz. butter
4 rashers bacon	¾ oz. flour
1 lb. liver	¾ pint stock (see
3–4 onions, peeled	page 84)
and chopped	12 olives
4 oz. mushrooms,	juice ½ lemon
sliced	

1. Heat oil, and fry bacon for about 2 minutes, then remove to a casserole.
2. Slice liver, brown on both sides, then put with the bacon.
3. Add onions and mushrooms to remaining fat. Cook till onions are lightly browned, then put into casserole.
4. Put butter into pan in which other ingredients have been browned, add flour and cook for a few minutes. Remove from heat, add stock.
5. Return to heat and stir till boiling, then pour into casserole.
6. Cover and cook in a very slow oven (325°F.– Gas Mark 2) about 1 hour.
7. Add olives and juice, and cook for 30 minutes extra.

Liver casserole

you will need for 4 servings:

1 lb. calf's liver	2 medium-sized
1 tablespoon flour	carrots
salt, pepper	1 leek
1 oz. dripping	1 stick celery
4 rashers bacon	pinch mixed herbs
1 lb. potatoes	1 beef stock cube
1 apple	¾ pint water
2 medium-sized	
onions	

1. Wash and trim liver and cut into small pieces.
2. Coat with seasoned flour and fry lightly in hot fat.
3. Cut up bacon and fry.
4. Peel and slice potatoes and put into a casserole, reserving enough for the top.
5. Peel and chop apple and vegetables and put half into casserole.
6. Arrange liver and bacon on top and cover with remaining apple and vegetables.
7. Add a little seasoning and pinch of herbs, then cover neatly with potato.
8. Dissolve stock cube in hot water and add to casserole.
9. Cover with greased paper and then with the lid and cook in a slow oven (325°F.– Gas Mark 2) for about 1½–2 hours.

Liver and bacon casserole

you will need for 4–6 servings:

1 lb. sheep's liver	1 pint stock (see
seasoned flour	page 84)
2 lb. potatoes	6 rashers streaky
2 large onions	bacon

1. Wash and dry liver. Cut into ¼ inch thick slices.
2. Toss in seasoned flour.
3. Arrange layers of liver, sliced potato and chopped onion in a casserole, finishing with potato.
4. Pour on enough stock barely to cover ingredients.
5. Cover and cook in a slow oven (350°F.– Gas Mark 3) for about 1 hour.
6. Remove lid and arrange bacon over potatoes. Cook for 10 minutes, uncovered, until bacon is crisp. Serve at once.

Kidney Espagnole

you will need for 4 servings:

1–1½ lb. ox kidney	¼ teaspoon dried basil
1½ oz. flour	1 lb. tomatoes, peeled
salt, pepper	and chopped
2 oz. butter	3 tablespoons
4 oz. mushrooms,	Marsala or sweet
sliced	sherry
1 clove garlic,	stock or water
crushed and	bacon rolls, grilled
chopped	cooked spaghetti

1. Remove core and any fat from kidney and cut in slices. Leave to stand in cold salted water for 20–30 minutes, then drain and dry.
2. Coat kidney with seasoned flour and brown in hot butter. Remove to a casserole.
3. Add mushrooms and garlic to remaining fat and cook for about 5 minutes, then put with kidney. Add basil.
4. Add any remaining flour to pan in which mushrooms were cooked and mix well.
5. Add tomatoes and wine, and a little stock or water as required. Bring to boiling point, stirring.
6. Pour over ingredients in the casserole, cover and cook in a slow oven (325°F.– Gas Mark 2) about 2 hours.
7. Correct seasoning and serve with bacon rolls and spaghetti.

Country style liver

you will need for 3 servings:

8 oz. streaky rashers	1½ oz. flour
bacon	1 beef stock cube
1 lb. ox liver, sliced	¾ pint water
2 oz. butter	seasoning
4 oz. mushrooms,	lemon juice
sliced	
8 oz. onions, peeled	
and sliced	

1. Cut bacon into pieces and fry lightly.

[continued

2 Remove from pan and brown liver slices on both sides in bacon fat. Remove to a casserole.

3 Add 1 oz. butter to pan, sauté mushrooms for a few minutes and put with liver.

4 Fry onions till lightly browned, then put with mushrooms and liver in the casserole.

5 Melt the remaining butter, add flour and crumbled beef stock cube and mix well. Add water, stir till boiling and boil for 1 minute.

6 Add a little seasoning if necessary and pour over liver. Add bacon.

7 Cover and cook in a slow oven (325°F. – Gas Mark 2) until the liver is tender, about 1½ hours.

8 Before serving, add lemon juice to taste.

Liver bonne femme

you will need for 4 servings:

1 oz. bacon fat or butter	12 small white onions
1–1½ lb. liver (cut in one piece)	1 dessertspoon flour
	⅛ pint cider or white wine
4 oz. lean bacon or ham	½ pint stock (see page 84)
2–3 small potatoes, peeled and cubed	salt, pepper
2 mushrooms, quartered	*bouquet garni* (see page 85)

1 Heat fat, add liver and sauté for about 5 minutes. Remove to a casserole.

2 Add bacon, cut into strips, potatoes, mushrooms and onions. Sauté for a few minutes, then put all into casserole with liver.

3 Add flour to remaining fat in pan and mix well. Add cider and stock and stir till boiling, then pour into casserole. Season.

4 Add *bouquet garni*, cover and cook in a slow oven (325°F. – Gas Mark 2) about 1¼ hours.

5 To serve, remove liver and slice thinly. Keep hot.

6 Remove *bouquet garni* from liquor, pour into a pan and bring to boiling point. Correct seasoning, boil for a few minutes, then pour over liver.

Liver and pork casserole

you will need for 4 servings:

12 oz. ox liver	salt, pepper
1 packet veal stuffing	rind and juice ½ lemon
8 oz. fresh streaky pork rashers	½ pint stock (see page 84)
1 onion, peeled and chopped	

1 Slice liver, cover with cold salted water and leave for 5 minutes.

2 Make up stuffing according to package instructions.

3 Remove rind and cut pork into pieces.

4 Grease a casserole and arrange liver, stuffing, pork and onion in layers. Season lightly. Add lemon rind and juice.

5 Add stock, cover and cook in a slow oven (325°F. – Gas Mark 2) for about 2 hours.

Braised liver

you will need for 4 servings:

1 lb. lamb's liver	2 oz. mushrooms, sliced
2 level tablespoons cornflour	1 packet mushroom soup
salt and pepper	1 pint water
2 tablespoons corn oil	2 oz. peas, cooked
2 onions, sliced	

1 Trim the liver and coat with cornflour to which salt and pepper have been added.

2 Heat the corn oil, add the liver and brown well on both sides. Remove to a casserole.

3 Sauté the onions and mushrooms in the remaining corn oil. Place over the liver.

4 Add the contents of the packet of mushroom soup and the water to the pan. Bring to the boil, stirring, and pour over the liver.

5 Bake in a moderately hot oven (375°F. – Gas Mark 4) for about 45 minutes. Fifteen minutes before the end of the cooking time, add the peas.

Stuffed ox liver

you will need for 2–3 servings:

8 oz. ox liver	4–5 rashers streaky bacon
4 tablespoons veal forcemeat (see page 86)	stock (see page 84)

1 Wash liver in warm water.

2 Cut out any tubes and fat and remove skin.

3 Slice thinly and arrange in a casserole.

4 Make veal forcemeat.

5 Remove bacon rinds, chop one rasher finely and mix with forcemeat.

6 Spread this on top of liver and cover with remaining rashers.

7 Moisten with a little stock.

8 Cover and cook in a moderate oven (375°F. – Gas Mark 4) for 1 hour until liver is tender and bacon cooked.

Serve with creamed potatoes and green peas.

Casserole of stuffed liver

you will need:

for the stuffing:	for the casserole:
2 oz. fresh breadcrumbs	7–8 very thin slices of lamb's liver (about 1 lb.)
1 oz. shredded suet	1 oz. dripping
1 level tablespoon chopped parsley	1 oz. plain flour
salt and pepper	1 dessertspoon instant beef stock powder
1 egg	½ pint water

1 Mix together stuffing ingredients, binding mixture with egg and a little water, if necessary, to make a stiff paste.

2 Lay the liver slices on a board and put a little of the stuffing on each.

3 Roll each firmly and secure with a cocktail stick.

4 Melt the dripping in a frying pan, and fry liver until lightly cooked all over. Transfer rolls to an oven-proof dish.
5 Stir the flour into the dripping in the frying pan adding the stock powder and water. Bring to the boil, stirring throughout. Season to taste.
6 Pour the sauce over the liver, cover and cook in the centre of a moderate oven (350°F.—Gas Mark 3) for 1 hour.
7 Remove cocktail sticks and serve.

Braised oxtail

you will need for 4 servings:

2 lb. oxtail	1 tablespoon tomato
1 oz. dripping	purée (see page 85)
8 oz. carrots	*bouquet garni* (see
4 oz. onions	page 85)
3–4 sticks celery	2 pints beef stock
1 bay leaf	(see page 84)
1 oz. flour	seasoning

1 Trim and remove excess fat from oxtail and cut into 2-inch pieces.
2 Heat dripping and brown oxtail pieces. Remove to a casserole.
3 Add carrots, onion and celery to remaining fat and sauté for a few minutes, then put with oxtail. Add bay leaf.
4 Add flour, cook for a few minutes, then add tomato purée and stock. Stir till boiling and pour over contents of casserole.
5 Add *bouquet garni*, cover and cook for about 3 hours in a slow oven (325°F.—Gas Mark 2).
6 When cooked, remove oxtail to a serving dish. Remove bay leaf and *bouquet garni*. Boil sauce until it is reduced to the right consistency.
7 Correct seasoning and pour over oxtail.
Serve with buttered carrots and potatoes.

Oxtail with carrots

you will need for 4 servings:

1 large or 2 small oxtails	1 strip lemon peel
2 oz. dripping	1 bay leaf
2 onions, peeled and sliced	1 sprig parsley } tied in muslin
8 oz. carrots, peeled and chopped	few pepper-corns
1 stick celery, chopped	
1 tomato, peeled and chopped	1 oz. cornflour
	¾ pint stock (see page 84) or water
	seasoning

1 Wash oxtail and chop into serving pieces.
2 Melt dripping, put in oxtail and onion and brown all well. Remove to a casserole.
3 Put carrots, celery, tomato and *bouquet* of herbs with meat.
4 Mix cornflour with fat remaining in pan and cook for a few minutes.
5 Add stock and stir till boiling.
6 Pour over contents of casserole.

7 Cover and cook in a slow oven (325°F.—Gas Mark 2) for 3–3½ hours.
8 Before serving, remove *bouquet* and correct seasoning.

Oxtail au vin

you will need for 4 servings:

1 oxtail	1 oz. flour
1 oz. fat	1 beef stock cube
2 onions, peeled and sliced	¾ pint water
2 carrots, peeled and quartered lengthways	¼ pint red wine
	seasoning
1 small turnip, peeled and chopped	*bouquet garni* (see page 85)

1 Joint the oxtail, then brown in hot fat and put into a casserole.
2 Put all vegetables into remaining fat and sauté for a few minutes, then put with oxtail.
3 Put flour and crumbled beef stock cube into pan, mix well, then add water and stir till boiling.
4 Add wine and pour into casserole.
5 Season lightly and add *bouquet garni*.
6 Cover closely and cook in a slow oven (325°F.—Gas Mark 2) for about 4 hours.

Oxtail ragoût

you will need for 4 servings:

1 oxtail	*bouquet garni* (see page 85)
¼ oz. flour	
salt, pepper	1 lb. carrots
2 oz. fat	¾ pint tomato juice
4 oz. bacon	1 beef stock cube
1 medium-sized onion, peeled and stuck with 4 cloves	¾ pint water
	2 turnips
	2 leeks
	2 sticks celery

1 Joint the oxtail, wash, dry, then coat well with seasoned flour.
2 Heat fat and brown oxtail pieces, put into a casserole.
3 Cut up bacon, fry lightly and put with oxtail.
4 Add onion and *bouquet garni* and half the carrots, peeled and chopped.
5 Put tomato juice into pan in which oxtail was browned, add stock cube and water and stir till boiling, then pour over contents of casserole.
6 Cover and cook in a slow oven (325°F.—Gas Mark 2) for about 3 hours.
7 Peel and quarter remaining carrots and turnips, cut leeks and celery into pieces and put into casserole.
8 Continue cooking for 1 hour. Correct seasoning before serving.

Oxtail with beans

you will need for 4 servings:

2 oz. dried butter beans	½ level teaspoons pepper
1 carrot	1 beef stock cube
1 onion	¾ pint boiling water
1 oxtail, cut in joints	parsley
2 level teaspoons salt	

1 Place beans in a bowl, cover with cold water and leave to soak overnight.
2 Peel and slice carrot and onion.
3 Remove excess fat from meat.
4 Drain beans and place with meat, carrot and onion in casserole. Sprinkle with salt and pepper.
5 Dissolve stock cube in boiling water, pour over casserole.
6 Cover, and cook at 375°F. – Gas Mark 4 for 1 hour. Reduce heat and cook for further 1½ hours at 350°F. – Gas Mark 3.
7 Sprinkle with coarsely chopped parsley and serve.

Savoury sheep's hearts

you will need for 4 servings:

4 sheep's hearts

stuffing:
2 oz. butter
1 small onion, peeled and chopped
1 stick celery, chopped
4 oz. breadcrumbs
1 orange
salt, cayenne pepper
1 egg

2 onions, peeled and cut into 4 or 8 portions
2 carrots, peeled and cut into quarters
1 beef stock cube
1 pint boiling water

1 Prepare hearts carefully, removing all veins and arteries and wash well in cold water.
2 Melt butter, add onion and celery and cook for a few minutes. Add breadcrumbs, grated orange rind and juice, salt and pepper. Bind with beaten egg.
3 Fill hearts with this stuffing and sew up with needle and thread.
4 Put into a casserole with onion and carrot.
5 Dissolve stock cube in boiling water and pour over hearts.
6 Cover closely and cook in a slow oven (350°F. – Gas Mark 3) till tender, about 2 hours.
7 Before serving, remove thread and, if necessary, thicken gravy with a little cornflour.

Braised sheep's tongues

you will need for 4 servings:

6–8 sheep's tongues
3 oz. streaky bacon
2 medium-sized onions, peeled and chopped
1 oz. butter

salt, pepper
stock (see page 84)
1 tablespoon capers
1 tablespoon chopped gherkins

1 Soak tongues in cold salted water for about 3 hours.
2 Drain, put into boiling salted water and simmer for 30 minutes, then drain off water.
3 Chop bacon and fry with onions in butter for 2–3 minutes, then remove to a casserole.
4 Add tongues and seasoning and enough stock just to cover.
5 Cover tightly and cook in a slow oven (350°F. – Gas Mark 3) for 2–2½ hours, until tongues are tender.

6 Remove tongues, cool a little, then skin carefully.
7 Boil remaining stock until it is reduced a little.
8 Return tongues to stock, add capers and gherkins, correct seasoning and cook for 10 minutes.

Sweetbreads suprême

you will need for 4 servings:

1½ lb. calf's sweetbreads
lemon juice
1½ pints white stock (see page 84)
¼ pint milk
1 onion, peeled and sliced
1 carrot, peeled and sliced

1 bay leaf
1 clove
seasoning
2 oz. butter
1 oz. flour
1 egg yolk
1 tablespoon thin cream

1 Wash and soak sweetbreads in cold water for several hours.
2 Cover with clean cold water, add a squeeze of lemon juice and bring to boiling point. Boil for 5 minutes. Drain, put into cold water and remove any fat and skin.
3 Put prepared sweetbreads into a casserole with stock and milk, onion, carrot, bay leaf and clove. Add a little salt and pepper. Cover and cook for about 2½ hours in a slow oven (350°F. – Gas Mark 3).
4 Remove sweetbreads and keep hot.
5 Melt 1 oz. butter, add flour and cook for a few minutes without browning. Remove from heat and gradually add ¾ pint strained liquor from sweetbreads.
6 Return to heat, stir till boiling and boil for 1 minute. Leave to cool a little, then gradually add remaining butter, egg yolk and cream. Add lemon juice and correct seasoning.
7 Put sweetbreads into sauce and reheat without boiling.

Sweetbreads with prunes

you will need for 4 servings:

2 pairs calf's sweetbreads or 1 lb. lamb's sweetbreads
1 oz. butter
12 small button onions
12 prunes (soaked overnight)
½ oz. flour

⅛ pint red wine
¼ pint white stock (see page 84, or use a chicken stock cube)
seasoning
1 bay leaf
mashed potato
parsley

1 Prepare the sweetbreads as described in previous recipe.
2 Heat butter, add sweetbreads and sauté until golden brown. Remove to a casserole.
3 Lightly brown onions in remaining fat, then put into casserole with sweetbreads, add prunes.
4 Put flour into the pan in which onions were browned and cook for a few minutes. Remove from heat, add wine and stock. Return to heat and stir till boiling. Add seasoning as required and pour over contents of casserole.

5 Add bay leaf. Cover tightly and cook in a slow oven (350°F. – Gas Mark 3) about 1 hour.

6 When sweetbreads are cooked, the sauce should have reduced considerably. Slice sweetbreads, and serve on a bed of mashed potato, garnished with prunes and the sauce poured over. Finally sprinkle with parsley.

Casserole of sweetbreads

you will need for 4 servings:

2 pairs calf's sweetbreads	1 carrot, peeled and diced
2 oz. butter	1 small onion, peeled and chopped
½ pint brown stock (see page 84)	¼ pint shelled peas
3–4 tablespoons Madeira or sherry	

1 Soak sweetbreads in cold water for 1 hour.

2 Put into a pan with clean cold water, bring to boiling point and simmer for 10 minutes, then drain and press between plates until cold.

3 Trim sweetbreads, removing all skin, fat and gristle.

4 Heat butter and brown sweetbreads, then remove to a casserole.

5 Add stock, Madeira and vegetables, cover and cook in a slow oven (350°F. – Gas Mark 3) about 45 minutes. Correct seasoning before serving.

Tongue and lentil casserole

you will need for 4 servings:

4 sheep's tongues	8 oz. carrots, peeled and sliced
1 oz. fat	
2 onions, peeled and chopped	pinch mixed herbs
8 oz. lentils, soaked overnight	salt, pepper
	1 small clove garlic

1 Soak sheep's tongues for 3–4 hours, drain, cover with cold water, bring to boiling point and simmer 10–15 minutes. Drain, cover with fresh cold water and simmer for 1 hour. Pour off and retain water.

2 Leave tongues to cool a little, then remove skin very carefully. Slice tongues and put into a casserole.

3 Melt fat, add onions and fry till brown, then put with tongues.

4 Add drained lentils and carrots to remaining fat and cook for a few minutes, then put into casserole with herbs, salt, pepper and crushed garlic.

5 Cover with stock in which tongues were cooked.

6 Put the lid on the casserole and cook in a slow oven (350°F. – Gas Mark 3) for 1½ hours.

Tripe and tomato casserole

you will need for 4 servings:

2 lb. tripe	2 tablespoons oil
1 onion, peeled and chopped finely	4 oz. mushrooms, chopped
1 green pepper, seeded and chopped	1 can tomato purée
	¾ pint milk and water
1–2 sticks celery, chopped	salt, pepper
	2–3 oz. grated Parmesan cheese

1 Wash tripe in several waters, cut into 2-inch strips and simmer in boiling salted water for about 2 hours.

2 Fry onion, pepper and celery in heated oil until onion begins to colour. Add mushrooms, tomato purée and milk and water. Bring to boiling point.

3 Drain tripe, and arrange in a casserole in alternate layers with the sauce, sprinkling each layer with grated cheese and seasoning.

4 Cover and cook in a slow oven (350°F. – Gas Mark 3) about 1 hour.

Tripe in the French style

you will need for 4 servings:

1 oz. bacon fat or dripping	pinch mixed spice salt, pepper
1½ lb. tripe	½ pint stock (see page 84) or water
1 carrot, peeled and sliced	1 bay leaf
1 onion, peeled and sliced	1 sprig parsley
4 oz. thinly sliced streaky bacon	1 clove garlic, peeled

1 Grease a casserole thickly with bacon fat or dripping.

2 Wash and dry tripe and cut into pieces.

3 Put into casserole in layers alternating with vegetables and chopped bacon.

4 Sprinkle each layer with a little spice and seasoning and pour stock over.

5 Put bay leaf, parsley and garlic on top, so they can be easily removed.

6 Cover very tightly and cook in a slow oven (350°F. – Gas Mark 3) for 4–4½ hours.

Tripe jardinière

you will need for 4 servings:

1½ lb. tripe	4 oz. mushrooms, sliced
½ oz. butter	
1 tablespoon oil	¼ pint stock (see page 84) or water
1 medium-sized carrot, peeled and sliced	1 small can tomato purée
1 medium-sized onion, peeled and sliced	salt, pepper
	bouquet garni (see page 85)
1 leek, sliced	1 clove garlic, crushed
2 sticks celery, sliced	

1 Wash tripe thoroughly and cut into strips.

2 Heat butter and oil, add onion, carrot, leek and celery and cook until vegetables begin to soften.

3 Add mushrooms and tripe and continue cooking for 2–3 minutes. Transfer all to a casserole.

4 Mix stock and tomato purée and pour into casserole, barely covering the tripe.

5 Add salt, pepper, bouquet garni and garlic.

6 Cover and cook in a slow oven (350°F. – Gas Mark 3) about 1½ hours.

Casserole of tripe

This dish needs very long slow cooking but requires no attention during the cooking and is a famous old recipe.

you will need for 6 servings:

2 lb. tripe
1 ox foot
1 calf's foot
2 strips pork rind
2 carrots, peeled and chopped
4 medium onions, peeled and chopped

bouquet garni (see page 85)
1 clove garlic
4 cloves
salt
cayenne pepper
1 liqueur glass brandy
dry cider

1 Wash and blanch tripe in boiling water for 30 minutes, drain, and cut into small pieces.
2 Cut off meat from ox and calf's foot.
3 Put pork rind and bones from two feet into a deep casserole with carrots, onions, *bouquet garni* and seasoning.
4 Add tripe and meat, pour over brandy and enough cider to cover contents of casserole.
5 Cover with a double piece of aluminium foil and then put the lid on the casserole. The casserole must be very tightly sealed.
6 Cook in a cool oven (300°F. – Gas Mark 1) for about 7½–8 hours. Remove excess fat before serving.

Chicken Casseroles

Cantonese chicken

you will need for 4-6 servings:

1 2½–3-lb. chicken
2 tablespoons corn oil
8 water chestnuts, sliced
1 8-oz. can bean sprouts
2 oz. mushrooms, sliced
1 small red pepper, seeded and chopped

1 clove garlic, crushed
1 chicken stock cube
1 oz. cornflour
1 pint water
1 tablespoon soy sauce
2 tablespoons red wine

1 Joint and skin chicken. Heat oil and fry joints until lightly brown.
2 Put chicken into a deep casserole and add water chestnuts, bean sprouts, mushrooms, red pepper and garlic.
3 Put crumbled stock cube and cornflour into the pan in which chicken was browned. Cook for a few minutes.
4 Add water and stir till boiling.
5 Add soy sauce and red wine and pour over chicken.
6 Cover and cook in a slow oven (350°F. – Gas Mark 3) for 1½–1¾ hours or until chicken is tender.

Casserole of chicken with yoghurt

you will need for 6 servings:

1 boiling fowl, about 3½-lb.
½ oz. flour
salt, pepper
3 tablespoons oil
2 large onions, peeled and thinly sliced

1 clove garlic, crushed
1 tablespoon paprika
1 small can condensed tomato soup
¼ pint yoghurt

1 Joint chicken, coat with seasoned flour.

2 Heat oil, and fry chicken joints till well browned, then transfer to a casserole.
3 Fry onions and garlic in remaining oil, add paprika, tomato soup and half the can of water. Bring to boiling point, then pour over chicken.
4 Cover closely and cook in a slow oven (350°F. – Gas Mark 3) for 2–2¼ hours.
5 Just before serving, correct seasoning and stir in yoghurt.

Country chicken

you will need for 6 servings:

1 chicken, about 2½–3-lb.
salt, pepper
2 oz. flour
2 oz. butter
1 lb. carrots, peeled and sliced
8 oz. onion, peeled and sliced

1 sprig thyme
1 bay leaf
water
½ pint milk
1–2 tablespoons thin cream
lemon juice

1 Joint and skin chicken and toss in seasoned flour.
2 Heat butter, put in chicken and fry till golden brown. Then transfer to a casserole.
3 Add carrots, onion, thyme and bay leaf, just cover with water and add a little salt and pepper. Cover and cook in a slow oven (350°F. – Gas Mark 3) for about 1¾ hours.
4 Mix remaining flour smoothly with milk, stir into the casserole and continue cooking for 15–20 minutes or until chicken is tender.
5 Just before serving, add cream and a squeeze of lemon juice.

Chicken niçoise

you will need for 6 servings:

1 2½–3-lb. chicken
3–4 rashers streaky
  bacon
½ oz. flour
1 medium-sized onion,
  peeled and chopped
2 oz. mushrooms,
  chopped

1 small green pepper,
  seeded and chopped
1 small can tomato
  purée
½ pint chicken stock
  (see page 85)
4–5 black olives
salt, pepper, garlic salt

1 Joint the chicken.
2 Fry bacon until fat begins to run.
3 Sprinkle chicken joints with flour and brown in bacon fat, then remove chicken and bacon to a casserole.
4 Add onion, mushrooms and green pepper to remaining fat and cook for a few minutes.
5 Add tomato purée, stock and olives, stir till boiling then pour over contents of casserole.
6 Add seasonings, cover and cook in a slow oven (325°F. – Gas Mark 2) for about 1¾ hours.

Chicken cacciatore

you will need for 6 servings:

1 2½–3-lb. chicken
salt, pepper
1 oz. flour
1½ oz. butter
1 large onion, peeled
  and chopped
1 can tomatoes
1 clove garlic,
  crushed and
  chopped

1 chicken stock cube
1 green pepper,
  seeded and
  chopped
½ pint water
⅛ pint dry white wine
1 tablespoon chopped
  parsley

1 Joint and skin chicken.
2 Season flour and coat chicken well.
3 Heat butter, brown chicken joints and put into a casserole.
4 Add onion to remaining fat, brown well, then put with chicken.
5 Add any remaining flour to pan in which chicken and onion were browned and mix well.
6 Add tomatoes, garlic, stock cube, green pepper and water. Stir till boiling. Add wine and pour over ingredients in casserole.
7 Cover and cook in a slow oven (350°F. – Gas Mark 3) for 1 hour or until the chicken is tender.
8 Before serving, check seasoning and sprinkle with parsley.

Chicken en cocotte

you will need for 6 servings:

1 small tender
  chicken
salt, pepper
3 oz. butter
1 onion, peeled and
  chopped
1 carrot, peeled and
  chopped

2–3 tablespoons dry
  white wine
½ pint chicken stock
  (see page 85)
bouquet garni (see
  page 85)
1 strip lemon peel
1 teaspoon cornflour

1 Season chicken with salt and pepper.

2 Heat butter in a thick pan and brown chicken all over. Put into a deep casserole.
3 Sauté onion and carrot in remaining fat until golden, then put with chicken.
4 Add wine, stock, *bouquet garni* and lemon peel. Cover and cook in a slow oven (325°F. – Gas Mark 2) for about 1¼ hours or until the chicken is tender.
5 When cooked, remove chicken to a serving dish.
6 Mix cornflour smoothly with a little water and stir into liquor in casserole. Cook until thickened, correct seasoning and strain over chicken.

Chicken Marengo

you will need for 6 servings:

1 tender chicken
2 tablespoons oil
1 small onion, peeled
  and chopped
2 carrots, peeled and
  chopped
8 oz. tomatoes,
  chopped
2 small cans tomato
  purée

1½ oz. cornflour
2 chicken stock cubes
1¼ pints water
⅛ pint sherry
seasoning
4 oz. mushrooms,
  sliced
1 tablespoon chopped
  parsley

1 Joint and skin chicken and put into a casserole.
2 Heat oil, add onion and cook for a few minutes, then add carrots and tomatoes and cook a further 5 minutes.
3 Add tomato purée and cornflour and mix well.
4 Add stock cubes and water, bring to boiling point, stirring, then boil for 5 minutes.
5 Rub through a sieve, add sherry and correct seasoning.
6 Pour over chicken in casserole, add mushrooms.
7 Cover and cook in a slow oven (350°F. – Gas Mark 3) about 45 minutes–1 hour.
  Sprinkle with parsley before serving.

Chicken and mushroom casserole

you will need for 6 servings:

1 chicken
1½ oz. flour
salt, pepper
3–4 oz. butter
2 small onions,
  peeled and
  chopped

8 oz. mushrooms,
  sliced
8 oz. tomatoes,
  peeled and sliced
1 pint chicken stock
  (see page 85) or
  water
⅛ pint sherry

1 Joint and skin chicken and coat well with seasoned flour.
2 Melt butter and brown chicken joints, then remove to a casserole.
3 Add onion to fat, brown well and put with chicken.
4 Put mushrooms and tomatoes in the pan with remaining fat and sediment and cook for a few minutes.
5 Add stock and stir till boiling, then pour all over chicken in casserole.
6 Cover and cook in a slow oven (350°F. – Gas Mark 3) for about 1 hour.
7 Add sherry and correct seasoning and cook for 15 minutes or until chicken is tender.

Chicken peperoni

you will need for 6 servings:

1 chicken	8 oz. tomatoes,
salt, freshly ground	peeled, seeded and
black pepper	chopped
2 tablespoons oil	1 clove garlic,
1 small onion, peeled	crushed
and chopped finely	2 green peppers,
¼ pint dry white wine	seeded and sliced

1 Joint and skin chicken and season with salt and pepper.
2 Heat oil, and brown chicken on all sides then transfer to a casserole.
3 Put onion and wine into pan and cook until wine is reduced by half.
4 Add tomatoes, garlic and peppers and cook for a few minutes, then add to chicken.
5 Cover and cook in a slow oven (325°F. – Gas Mark 2) for 1–1¼ hours or until the chicken is tender.

Chicken and pineapple casserole

you will need for 6 servings:

1 2½–3lb. chicken	1 chicken stock cube
½ oz. cornflour	1 11-oz. can pineapple
salt, pepper	pieces
2 tablespoons oil	1 teaspoon soy sauce
2 oz. blanched	chopped parsley
almonds	
1 onion, peeled and	
chopped	

1 Joint and skin chicken, and coat with seasoned cornflour.
2 Heat oil and brown chicken on all sides. Transfer to a casserole.
3 Brown almonds and keep on one side.
4 Brown onion and put with chicken.
5 Mix any remaining cornflour with sediment and fat left in pan. Add crumbled stock cube.
6 Make pineapple juice up to ¾ pint with water and stir into cornflour mixture. Bring to boiling point, stirring all the time, then add soy sauce and pour over contents of casserole.
7 Cover and cook in a slow oven (350°F. – Gas Mark 3) for about 1½ hours.
8 Add almonds and pineapple pieces, correct seasoning and cook for 15 minutes.
Sprinkle with parsley before serving.

Chicken Palermo

you will need for 6 servings:

1 tablespoon oil	8 oz. pork sausages,
1 medium-sized	cut into 3 or 4
onion, peeled and	pieces
chopped	1 chicken
1 clove garlic,	1 can tomatoes
crushed	1 tablespoon tomato
2 oz. mushrooms,	purée (see page 85)
sliced	3 tablespoons red
	wine
	salt, pepper

1 Heat oil, fry onion and garlic till lightly browned. Add mushrooms and sausages and cook for a few minutes, then put into a casserole.
2 Joint and skin chicken and brown in remaining oil (a little extra oil may be necessary).
3 Put chicken into casserole, add tomatoes and tomato purée.
4 Cook in a slow oven (350°F. – Gas Mark 3) for about 1½ hours.
5 Just before serving, add wine and correct seasoning.

Honeyed chicken with orange

you will need for 4 servings:

1 roasting chicken	1 tablespoon honey
1½ oz. butter	2 tablespoons wine
1 tablespoon cornflour	vinegar
salt and pepper	1 orange and
¼ pint orange juice	watercress for
¼ pint chicken stock	garnishing, if liked

1 Brown chicken in butter in a flame-proof casserole.
2 Blend the cornflour and seasoning with a little orange juice. Pour, with remaining orange juice, stock, honey and vinegar, into a saucepan. Bring to the boil.
3 Allow to boil for 1 minute, pour over chicken.
4 Cover and bake in a slow oven (350°F.–Gas Mark 3) for 1–1½ hours until chicken is tender.
5 Serve garnished with thin slices of orange and watercress, if liked.

Variations

Honeyed chicken with orange and almonds – prepare chicken as above. Blanch and chop 2 oz. almonds, fry in 1 oz. butter and 2 teaspoons lemon juice. Pour over chicken just before serving.

Chicken Hawaiian – prepare chicken with honey, using pineapple juice in place of orange juice. Serve garnished with pineapple rings and almonds which have been fried in butter.

Chicken paprika (1)

you will need for 6 servings:

1 3-lb. chicken	2 green peppers,
salt, pepper	seeded and sliced
1 oz. butter	4 tomatoes, peeled,
2 medium-sized	seeded and
onions, peeled and	chopped
chopped	water or stock (see
2 small cloves garlic,	page 84)
crushed	½ oz. flour
1 dessertspoon	¼ pint sour cream
paprika	

1 Joint chicken, season with salt and pepper and put into a deep casserole.
2 Heat butter, add onion and garlic and sauté till golden brown. Add paprika and cook for a few minutes, then put into casserole.
3 Add peppers and tomatoes and enough stock or water to barely cover. Season carefully.

4 Cover and cook in a slow oven (350°F. – Gas Mark 3) for 1½ hours.

5 Mix flour smoothly with cream, stir into casserole and cook for a few minutes.

Chicken paprika (2)

you will need for 4 servings:

4 chicken joints	1 tablespoon
salt and pepper	concentrated
2 oz. butter	tomato purée
1 medium onion,	1 8-oz. can tomatoes
peeled and	chicken stock cube
chopped	5 fluid oz. natural
1 tablespoon flour	yoghurt
1 teaspoon paprika	
pepper	

1 Rub chicken joints with salt and pepper. Fry in butter until golden brown. Remove from pan.

2 Fry onion until transparent. Add flour, paprika and tomato purée. Stir until well blended.

3 Strain the tomatoes and make juice up to ½ pint, using a stock cube and hot water. Stir tomatoes and stock into pan containing flour and paprika.

4 Bring to boil and allow to boil for 1 minute.

5 Place chicken joints in a casserole, pour tomato mixture over. Cover and cook in a moderate oven for 45 minutes.

6 Remove from oven, stir in yoghurt and serve.

Variations

Chicken de luxe – omit paprika pepper, use dry sherry instead of stock and soured cream in place of yoghurt.

Chicken de luxe with mushrooms – make as above. Prepare boiled rice to serve with chicken, adding 4 oz. sautéed small, whole mushrooms and 2 tablespoons finely chopped parsley to rice, just before serving.

Chicken with peaches and pilaff

you will need for 6 servings:

1 2½–3-lb. chicken	**for the pilaff:**
2 oz. butter	1 oz. butter
2 large onions,	1 teaspoon finely
peeled and sliced	chopped onion
2–3 peaches, fresh	8 oz. rice
or canned	1 dessertspoon
1 lemon	turmeric
salt, freshly ground	paprika
black pepper,	1½ pints stock (see
pinch nutmeg	page 84) or water
¼ pint stock (see	salt, pepper
page 84) or water	
⅛ pint cream	

1 Joint and skin chicken, brown on all sides in hot butter. Remove to a casserole.

2 Add onions to remaining fat and sauté until beginning to colour. Add peaches (peeled and cut in half if fresh) and continue cooking for a few minutes. Then put onions and peaches with chicken.

3 Add 1–2 strips thinly pared lemon peel, salt, pepper, nutmeg and stock.

4 Cover and cook in a slow oven (350°F. – Gas Mark 3) about 1¼ hours.

To make the pilaff:

1 Heat butter, add onion, rice, turmeric and paprika and cook for a few minutes. Add stock and bring to boiling point.

2 Put into a casserole, add salt and pepper. Cover and cook in oven with the chicken for about 1 hour or until rice is tender and stock absorbed.

3 To serve, put chicken and peaches on to a hot dish, strain liquor into a small pan. Bring to boiling point and reduce a little if necessary. Add lemon juice and cream and correct seasoning, pour over chicken. Serve rice separately.

Chicken and potato casserole

you will need for 4 servings:

1½ lb. potatoes	seasonings
1 lb. leeks	*bouquet garni* (see
1 onion	page 85)
1 oz. pearl barley	1 chicken stock cube
4 oz. streaky bacon	1 pint water
1 small boiling fowl **or**	chopped chives **or**
4 large joints	parsley

1 Peel and slice potatoes thinly and put half into a casserole.

2 Slice leeks, peel and chop onion and put half into casserole.

3 Wash barley and sprinkle on top.

4 Chop bacon and add.

5 Joint and skin chicken and arrange on vegetables. Add seasoning and *bouquet garni*, and cover with remaining vegetables.

6 Arrange remaining potato slices neatly on top.

7 Dissolve chicken stock cube in hot water and pour over contents of casserole.

8 Cover closely and cook in a slow oven (350°F. – Gas Mark 3) 1½–2 hours.

9 Remove *bouquet garni* and sprinkle with chives or parsley before serving.

Chicken sauté estragon

you will need for 6 servings:

1 small tender frying	3 sprigs tarragon
chicken	3 tablespoons cream
salt, pepper	little chopped
1½ oz. butter	tarragon
¼ pint good chicken	
stock (see page 85)	

1 Joint and skin chicken and season with salt and pepper.

2 Heat butter in a sauté pan, add chicken pieces and cook slowly till well browned on all sides. Remove to a casserole.

3 Add stock and tarragon, cover tightly and cook in a

moderate oven (375°F.–Gas Mark 4) for about 40 minutes.

4 Remove chicken to serving dish. Remove tarragon from liquor. Add cream and chopped tarragon and pour over chicken.

Chinese style chicken

you will need for 6 servings:

1 chicken	1 teaspoon sugar
1 oz. cornflour	1 tablespoon soy
2 tablespoons oil	sauce
1 small onion, peeled	1 tablespoon sherry
and sliced	¼ pint water
4 oz. mushrooms,	10 water chestnuts
sliced	2 pieces preserved
1 teaspoon salt	ginger

1 Joint and skin chicken and coat well with cornflour.
2 Heat oil and brown chicken pieces, then remove to a casserole.
3 Sauté onion and mushrooms in remaining oil for a few minutes, then put with chicken.
4 Mix 1 teaspoon cornflour, left from coating the chicken, with salt, sugar, soy sauce and sherry and put into pan with water. Stir till boiling, boil for 1 minute.
5 Add water chestnuts and ginger and pour over chicken.
6 Cover and cook in a moderate oven (375°F.–Gas Mark 4) for about 1 hour.

Curried chicken

you will need for 6 servings:

1 small tender	1 oz. cornflour
chicken	1 chicken stock cube
2 tablespoons oil	⅜ pint water
1 small onion, peeled	1 apple, peeled and
and chopped	chopped
1 clove garlic,	1 dessertspoon
crushed and	redcurrant jelly
chopped finely	juice ½ lemon
2 dessertspoons	1 tablespoon sultanas
curry powder	1 oz. coconut infused
1 teaspoon curry	in 6 tablespoons
paste	boiling water

1 Joint and skin chicken, heat oil and brown chicken lightly on all sides. Remove to a casserole.
2 Add onion and garlic, cook for a few minutes then put with chicken.
3 Add curry powder, curry paste, cornflour and crumbled stock cube to remaining oil, cook all together for 3 minutes.
4 Add water, stir till boiling then pour over contents of casserole.
5 Add apple, jelly, lemon juice, sultanas and water strained from coconut.
6 Cover and cook in a slow oven (325°F.–Gas Mark 2) for about 1 hour.
Correct seasoning before serving, and serve with plainly boiled rice.

Chicken chasseur

you will need for 5–6 servings:

3½–4-lb. chicken	2 cloves garlic
flour	1 teaspoon thyme
4 oz. butter	1 bay leaf
4 oz. bacon	2 fluid oz. brandy
8 oz. mushrooms	½ pint red wine
8 oz. small onions	salt and pepper

1 Cut chicken in pieces and toss in flour. Brown in hot butter in a large flameproof casserole.
2 Cut up bacon, and add to chicken with sliced mushrooms, onions, garlic, thyme and bay leaf.
3 Stir ingredients over a moderate heat until browned. Pour over brandy and ignite. When flame burns out, add wine. Stir well, season with salt and pepper.
4 Cover and cook in a moderate oven (350°F.–Gas Mark 3) for about 1 hour until chicken is tender.

Hacienda chicken

you will need for 6 servings:

1 2½–3-lb chicken	2 oz. mushrooms,
2 tablespoons oil	sliced
1 medium-sized	1 teaspoon paprika
onion, peeled and	1 small can tomatoes
chopped	salt, pepper
6 oz. rice	6–8 olives
1 green pepper,	stock (see page 84)
seeded and sliced	

1 Joint and skin chicken.
2 Heat oil, add chicken and brown on all sides. Remove to a casserole.
3 Add onion, rice, green pepper, mushrooms and paprika and cook for about 5 minutes, then put into casserole.
4 Add tomatoes, salt, pepper and olives and just enough stock to barely cover chicken.
5 Cover tightly and cook in a slow oven (350°F.–Gas Mark 3) for about 1½ hours.

Note: Add extra stock during the cooking if required, but the rice should have absorbed most of the liquid by the time chicken is cooked.

Chicken curaçao

you will need for 4 servings:

4 chicken joints	1 can mandarin
½ oz. cornflour	oranges
salt and pepper	¾ level teaspoon
2 tablespoons corn	tarragon
oil	1 tablespoon curaçao
1 packet savoury	2 oz. peanuts,
white sauce	chopped
½ pint milk	

1 Skin and trim the chicken joints. Coat in the cornflour, to which salt and pepper have been added.
2 Heat the corn oil and lightly brown the chicken joints. Remove to a casserole.
3 Make up the white sauce as directed on the packet, using ½ pint milk.
4 Drain the mandarin oranges and stir the juice of the

oranges, tarragon and curaçao into the sauce. Pour the sauce over the chicken joints.

5 Cover and cook in a moderate oven (350°F. – Gas Mark 3) for 40–45 minutes.
6 Add the mandarin oranges to the casserole and sprinkle the top with peanuts.
7 Return to the oven for a further 10 minutes.

Moroccan chicken

you will need for 6 servings:

1 small chicken	chicken stock (see
salt, freshly ground	page 85)
black pepper	1 sprig coriander or
¼ teaspoon paprika	lemon thyme
2 oz. butter	4 oz. rice
8 oz. Spanish onions,	½ oz. butter
peeled and sliced	lemon juice
¼ teaspoon powdered	2 tablespoons
saffron	chopped parsley

1 Joint and skin chicken, season with salt, black pepper and paprika.
2 Heat butter and fry chicken till lightly browned, then put into a casserole.
3 Fry onions till golden in remaining fat, then put with chicken.
4 Sprinkle with saffron, barely cover with chicken stock and add coriander.
5 Cover and cook in a slow oven (350°F. – Gas Mark 3) about 1¼ hours.
6 While chicken is cooking, cook rice in boiling salted water for 12 minutes. Drain, rinse and keep hot.
7 To serve. Put half the rice into a serving dish, arrange chicken pieces on top. Pour on some of the liquor in which chicken was cooked. Cover with remaining rice, dot with butter, sprinkle with lemon juice and then with parsley.

Hunter's chicken

you will need for 6 servings:

1 small boiling fowl or	2 oz. mushrooms,
4 good-sized joints	peeled and sliced
½ oz. flour	1 can condensed
salt, pepper	tomato soup
2 tablespoons oil	¼ pint cider or dry
2 small onions,	white wine
peeled and sliced	*bouquet garni*
2 small carrots,	(see page 85)
peeled and sliced	1 tablespoon chopped
	parsley

1 Joint and skin chicken, coat with seasoned flour and brown all over in heated oil.
2 Remove chicken and fry vegetables.
3 Put vegetables into a casserole, arrange chicken on top, then add condensed soup and cider or wine. Tuck *bouquet garni* in centre.
4 Cover closely and cook in a slow oven (350°F. – Gas Mark 3) about 1½ hours.
5 Remove *bouquet garni* and correct seasoning. Sprinkle with chopped parsley.

Chinese chicken with cream sauce

you will need for 4 servings:

4 chicken breasts	½ pint water
2 tablespoons corn	2 tablespoons soy
oil	sauce
1 medium onion,	1 tablespoon
finely chopped	cornflour
4 oz. blanched	5 fl. oz. soured cream
almonds	1 9-oz. can bamboo
1 chicken stock cube	shoots

1 Brown chicken joints in oil in a heated flame-proof casserole.
2 Remove from oil, and fry onion for 5 minutes without browning.
3 Return chicken to the casserole, add almonds, stock cube, dissolved in ½ pint boiling water, and soy sauce.
4 Bake in a moderate oven (375°F. – Gas Mark 4) for 1 hour. Remove chicken from casserole and place on hot serving dish and keep warm.
5 Blend cornflour with 2 tablespoons water, stir into casserole. Bring to boil, allow to boil for 1 minute.
6 Remove from heat, stir in soured cream.
7 Meanwhile slice bamboo shoots into half inch strips and cook in boiling water for 5 minutes. Drain and arrange round chicken on serving dish.
8 Pour cream sauce over and serve accompanied by bean shoots, and boiled rice to which raisins or sultanas have been added.

Italian chicken casserole

you will need for 6–8 servings:

8 oz. cooked ham	1 small tender
4 tablespoons fresh	chicken
breadcrumbs	3 oz. butter
1 clove garlic,	¼ pint chicken stock
chopped finely	(see page 85)
2 tablespoons finely	2 tablespoons tomato
chopped parsley	purée (see page 85)
1 egg	6 oz. cooked rice
seasoning	

1 Chop ham and mix with breadcrumbs, garlic and parsley. Bind with beaten egg and season carefully with a little salt and freshly ground black pepper.
2 Stuff chicken with this mixture.
3 Heat butter in a fairly large pan. Put in chicken and brown all over. Remove to a deep casserole.
4 Mix stock and tomato purée and pour over chicken.
5 Cover and cook in a slow oven (325°F. – Gas Mark 2) for 1–1¼ hours or until chicken is tender. Serve with plainly boiled rice.

Mediterranean chicken

you will need for 6 servings:

1 small tender	salt, pepper
chicken	white wine or water
8 oz. green bacon	1 lb. sautéed
3 oz. butter	potatoes
6–8 olives	4 tomatoes
8 oz. small button	
mushrooms	

1 Skin chicken and dice bacon.
2 Heat butter in a fairly deep pan and brown chicken
   and bacon. Remove to a casserole.
3 Add olives, stoned and soaked for 10–15 minutes in
   warm water to remove excess salt.
4 Add mushrooms, salt and pepper and moisten with
   4–5 tablespoons white wine or water.
5 Cover and cook in a slow oven (325°F.–Gas Mark 2)
   for about 1 hour.
6 Add sautéed potatoes and peeled and sliced tomatoes
   and cook for 15 minutes.

Farmhouse casserole

you will need for 4 servings:

1 lb. cooked chicken
4 oz. peas
4 carrots, diced
8 oz. cooked potatoes
1 oz. cornflour
1 15-oz. can chicken soup

salt, pepper
2 oz. Cheddar cheese,
   grated
2 oz. fresh white
   breadcrumbs

1 Slice chicken. Arrange with peas, carrots and sliced
   potatoes in a casserole.
2 Mix cornflour with the chicken soup.
3 Bring to the boil, stirring. Season to taste. Pour into
   casserole.
4 Mix cheese and breadcrumbs, sprinkle over top of
   casserole.
5 Cook in a moderate oven (375°F.–Gas Mark 4) for
   about 35 minutes.

Normandy casserole of chicken

you will need for 6 servings:

1 2½–3-lb. chicken
1 oz. flour
1½ oz. butter
1 medium-sized
   onion, peeled and
   sliced
2 rashers streaky
   bacon

2 apples, peeled,
   cored and quartered
salt, pepper
¼ pint cider
stock (see page 84)
bouquet garni (see
   page 85)

1 Joint and skin chicken and coat well with flour.
2 Heat butter, and fry chicken till brown on all sides.
   Remove to a casserole.
3 Add onion and bacon cut into pieces and cook till
   onion begins to brown. Put into casserole.
4 Add apples, salt, pepper, cider, stock and *bouquet
   garni*. The chicken should be barely covered with
   stock.
5 Cover and cook in a slow oven (350°F.–Gas Mark 3)
   about 1–1½ hours.

Paella

you will need for 6 servings:

1 small tender
   chicken
1 oz. flour
salt, pepper
4 tablespoons oil
8 oz. Italian sausages,
   sliced
8 oz. Patna rice
1 clove garlic,
   crushed
1 bay leaf
pinch saffron

pinch cayenne pepper
1 green pepper,
   seeded and sliced
1 red pepper, seeded
   and sliced
1 chicken stock cube
1 pint water
1 4-oz. can shrimps
1 8-oz. can lobster
1 can peeled
   tomatoes

1 Joint and skin chicken, coat with seasoned flour.
2 Heat oil and fry chicken and sausages till brown.
   Remove to a large casserole.
3 Add rice and garlic to remaining oil and cook till
   lightly brown.
4 Add herbs, peppers, stock cube and water, bring to
   boiling point and pour over ingredients in casserole.
5 Add shrimps, lobster and tomatoes.
6 Cover and cook about 1 hour in a moderate oven
   (375°F.–Gas Mark 4).

Plantation casserole

(Illustrated on the cover)

you will need for 4 servings:

12 oz. cooked
   chicken, thickly
   sliced
4 oz. cooked peas
4 cooked carrots,
   sliced
1 oz. cornflour
1 packet chicken
   vegetable soup

1 11-oz. can cream
   style corn
¾ pint water
1 teaspoon
   Worcestershire
   sauce
salt, pepper
2 oz. cheese, grated
2 oz. fresh white
   breadcrumbs

1 Place chicken, peas and carrots in layers in a casserole.
2 Combine cornflour and chicken vegetable soup, add
   corn, mix well then add water and sauce. Bring to the
   boil, stirring, season to taste.
3 Pour over ingredients in casserole.
4 Mix cheese and breadcrumbs and sprinkle over the
   top.
5 Cook for 25 minutes in a moderately hot oven
   (400°F.–Gas Mark 5).
6 Finally flash under the grill to brown the top.

Stuffed chicken casserole

you will need for 6 servings:

1 2½–3-lb. chicken
8 oz. pork sausage
   meat
salt, pepper
½ oz. flour
1 oz. dripping or
   butter
2 oz. mushrooms,
   sliced

1 small onion, peeled
   and chopped
½ pint cider
12 small button
   mushrooms
12 small button
   onions

1 Stuff neck end of chicken with sausage meat.
2 Season flour and coat chicken well.
3 Heat fat, add mushrooms and onion and cook for a few minutes without browning. Add chicken and brown all over.
4 Remove chicken and vegetables to a casserole, add cider, cover tightly and cook about 1 hour in a moderate oven (375°F. – Gas Mark 4).
5 Add button mushrooms and onions and continue cooking for 30 minutes.

Chicken Catalan

you will need for 4–6 servings:

1 small chicken	salt and pepper
1 oz. seasoned flour	castor sugar
2 oz. butter	8 oz. chipolata
2 tablespoons olive oil	sausages
2 large Spanish onions	4 oz. button mushrooms
¼ pint stock	12 cooked chestnuts
¼ pint dry white wine	or water chestnuts
12 oz. tomatoes	(optional)

1 Cut chicken into 8 joints – removing skin.
2 Dip in seasoned flour. Fry until golden brown in butter heated together with the olive oil. Remove chicken joints and dry well.
3 Slice onions and fry until golden brown. Remove onions and place with chicken in a casserole.
4 Add remaining seasoned flour to the pan, in which chicken was fried. Gradually stir in stock and wine, and bring to the boil.
5 Skin tomatoes and remove pips, chop roughly. Sprinkle with salt, pepper and sugar. Add half the tomatoes to sauce in pan. Season to taste.
6 Pour over chicken, cover and cook at 325°F. – Gas Mark 2 for 1½ hours.
7 Meanwhile, lightly fry sausages, mushrooms and chestnuts, if used. Add to casserole with remainder of the tomatoes 20 minutes before the end of cooking time.
8 Skim off excess fat, adjust seasoning, if necessary, and serve.

Viennese chicken

you will need for 6 servings:

1 chicken	2 oz. dried white
3 oz. butter	breadcrumbs
1 small clove garlic, crushed	1 oz. grated cheese
	1 teaspoon salt
	pinch cayenne pepper

1 Joint and skin chicken.
2 Melt butter, add garlic.
3 Mix breadcrumbs, cheese, salt and pepper.
4 Dip chicken joints into butter, then coat well with breadcrumb mixture.
5 Put into a shallow casserole.
6 Remove garlic and pour butter over chicken.

7 Cover and cook in a moderate oven (375°F. – Gas Mark 4) about 1 hour.
8 Remove lid and continue cooking for 15 minutes or until chicken is brown and tender.

Braised chicken in casserole

you will need for 4–6 servings:

1 3-lb. chicken	4 rashers bacon, diced
1 carrot, peeled and diced	salt, pepper
1 onion, peeled and chopped	2 oz. butter
1–2 sticks celery	½ pint chicken stock (see page 85)

1 Prepare chicken and truss as for roasting.
2 Put vegetables and bacon into a deep casserole and put chicken on top.
3 Season and dot with butter.
4 Cover and cook in a moderate oven (375°F. – Gas Mark 4) about 30 minutes, then reduce the heat to 325°F. – Gas Mark 2 and continue cooking for 45 minutes.
5 When chicken is tender, remove from casserole and untruss. Keep hot.
6 Pour off excess fat from casserole, add stock and bring to boiling point.
7 Correct seasoning and return chicken to casserole. Reheat for a few minutes and serve.

Chicken bonne femme

you will need for 6 servings:

2–3 rashers streaky bacon	6–8 button onions
½ oz. butter	4 oz. mushrooms
1 tender chicken, quartered	4 oz. cooked ham
12 oz. potatoes, peeled and fairly thickly sliced	salt, pepper

1 Dice bacon and fry in butter until fat runs. Remove to a casserole.
2 Brown chicken on all sides and put with bacon.
3 Add potatoes, onions, mushrooms and chopped ham to remaining fat and cook for a few minutes.
4 Turn all into casserole, season, cover tightly and cook in a moderate oven (375°F. – Gas Mark 4) about 1 hour.

Variation

With veal stock – a little veal stock (see page 85) may be added towards the end of the cooking.

Chicken and macaroni

you will need for 2 servings:

3 oz. macaroni	8 oz. cooked chicken, diced
½ small onion, peeled and grated	¼ teaspoon paprika
2–3 cooked carrots, diced	2 eggs
salt, pepper	¼ pint milk
¼ small green pepper, seeded and chopped	

1 Cook macaroni in boiling salted water till tender, then drain well.
2 Add onion, carrot, seasoning, green pepper, chicken and paprika. Mix all well and put into a buttered casserole.
3 Beat eggs, add milk and pour over mixture.
4 Cover and stand casserole in a pan of hot water.
5 Cook for about 1 hour in a slow oven (350°F. – Gas Mark 3).

Chicken with olives

you will need for 6 servings:

1 2½–3-lb. chicken	1 tomato, peeled,
3 tablespoons oil	seeded and
3 oz. butter	chopped
1 onion, peeled and	12 large olives
chopped	3 tablespoons tomato
1 carrot, peeled and	purée (see page 85)
chopped	salt, pepper

1 Cut chicken into small joints.
2 Heat oil and butter, brown chicken on all sides, then transfer to a casserole.
3 Add onion, carrot and tomato to remaining fat and sauté until onion is lightly browned, then put with chicken.
4 Chop half the olives and put into casserole. Add remaining whole olives and just cover with stock.
5 Cover and cook in a slow oven (325°F. – Gas Mark 2) for 1½ hours.
6 Add tomato purée and season carefully.
7 Continue cooking a further 30 minutes.

Variation
With flour – the liquor can be thickened with a little flour before serving.

Chicken with peas and rice

you will need for 6 servings:

1 2½–3-lb. chicken	3 oz. rice
3 tablespoons oil	½ pint chicken stock
2–3 medium-sized	(see page 85)
onions, peeled and	¼ pint white wine
chopped	salt, pepper
8 oz. shelled peas	

1 Divide chicken into small joints and brown in hot oil, then remove to a casserole.
2 Brown onions in remaining oil and put with chicken.
3 Add peas, rice, stock, wine and seasoning.
4 Cover and cook in a slow oven (350°F. – Gas Mark 3) for 1–1¼ hours.
If necessary, add a little extra stock during the cooking.

Chicken Salvatore

you will need for 6 servings:

1 3-lb. chicken	2–3 small carrots,
salt, pepper, garlic	peeled and
salt	chopped
3 tablespoons oil	1–2 sticks celery
1 small onion, peeled	4 tablespoons red
and chopped finely	wine
	¼ pint thin cream

1 Joint chicken and sprinkle with salt, pepper and garlic salt.
2 Heat oil, put in chicken and brown on all sides, then remove to a casserole.
3 Sauté onion, carrot and celery in remaining oil for a few minutes and put with chicken.
4 Add wine and cream.
5 Cover, and cook about 1 hour in a very slow oven (325°F. – Gas Mark 2). Correct seasoning.

Chicken in white wine

you will need for 6 servings:

1 2½–3-lb. chicken	1 teaspoon chopped
½ pint white wine	parsley
2 tablespoons oil	½ oz. flour
salt, pepper	1 tablespoon tomato
¼ teaspoon nutmeg	purée (see page 85)

1 Cut chicken into small joints.
2 Mix wine, oil, seasonings, nutmeg and parsley together. Put in chicken and leave to marinate for about 4 hours.
3 Transfer chicken and marinade to a casserole, cover and cook in a slow oven (350°F. – Gas Mark 3) about 45 minutes.
4 Mix flour smoothly with tomato purée and stir into casserole.
5 Continue cooking for 15 minutes, stirring occasionally. Correct seasoning before serving.

Chestnut chicken

you will need for 4 servings:

2 tablespoons corn	2 tablespoons red
oil	wine
1 chicken, jointed	4 oz. mushrooms,
1 8-oz. can	sliced
chestnuts	8 oz. tomatoes,
½ pint milk	skinned and sliced

1 Heat the corn oil and brown the chicken joints. Remove to a casserole.
2 Drain the chestnuts and rub through a sieve. Stir the milk and wine into the chestnut purée, bring to the boil and pour over the chicken joints.
3 Cover and cook in a moderately hot oven (375°F. – Gas Mark 4) for 1 hour.
4 Add the mushrooms and tomatoes 15 minutes before the end of the cooking time.

Chicken pietro

you will need for 6 servings:

1 tender chicken	6 tablespoons white
½ oz. flour	wine
salt, pepper	½ pint chicken stock
pinch nutmeg	(see page 85)
2 oz. butter	1 tomato
2 tablespoons oil	juice ½ lemon

1 Cut chicken into 6 portions and coat well with flour, seasoned with salt, pepper and nutmeg.
2 Heat butter and oil and sauté chicken until well browned on all sides, then remove to a casserole.
3 Add remaining flour to fat left in pan and mix well, add wine and stock and stir till boiling. Pour over chicken.
4 Cover and cook in a slow oven (350°F. – Gas Mark 3) until the chicken is tender, about 1 hour.
5 10 minutes before serving, add peeled and sliced tomato and lemon juice.

Chicken tarragon

you will need for 6 servings:

1 2½–3-lb. chicken	1 medium-sized
1 tablespoon salt	onion, peeled and
½ teaspoon freshly	chopped
ground pepper	8 oz. mushrooms,
pinch paprika	sliced
3–4 oz. butter	1 tablespoon chopped
	tarragon

1 Cut chicken into small joints and coat with mixed salt, pepper and paprika.
2 Heat butter, fry chicken joints until well browned, then remove to a casserole.
3 Add onion and mushrooms to remaining butter and sauté till onion is transparent. Put with chicken and sprinkle with tarragon.
4 Cover and cook in a slow oven (350°F. – Gas Mark 3) about 45 minutes.

Chicken vilma

you will need for 4 servings:

1 tablespoon corn oil	1 packet tomato soup
1 3-lb. roasting	1 pint water
chicken, cut in	2 tablespoons red
quarters	wine
½ clove of garlic,	4 oz. mushrooms,
finely chopped	peeled and sliced
(optional)	

1 Heat the corn oil and add the chicken and garlic. Brown the chicken quickly on both sides.
2 Remove the chicken. Add the contents of the packet of tomato soup and the water to the pan and bring to the boil, stirring. Stir in the wine and replace the chicken.
3 Cover and cook gently for 30 minutes. Add the mushrooms and continue cooking for a further 15 minutes. Place the chicken on a serving dish and pour the sauce over.

Chicken with mushrooms and spaghetti

you will need for 6 servings:

1 2½–3-lb. chicken	8 oz. tomatoes,
3–4 tablespoons oil	peeled, seeded and
1 onion, peeled and	chopped
chopped	1 teaspoon chilli
1–2 sticks celery,	powder
chopped	salt, pepper
1 small green pepper,	4 oz. spaghetti
seeded and	stock
chopped	2 oz. grated
4 oz. mushrooms	Parmesan cheese

1 Divide chicken into small joints. Brown on all sides in heated oil and remove to a plate.
2 Add onion, celery, green pepper, mushrooms, tomatoes and chilli powder to remaining oil and sauté for 10 minutes. Add seasoning.
3 Break up spaghetti and cook in boiling salted water till just tender.
4 Arrange layers of spaghetti, chicken and sauce in a buttered casserole, adding a little stock if sauce is too thick. Cover and cook in a slow oven (325°F. – Gas Mark 2) about 2 hours.
5 Correct seasoning and sprinkle with cheese before serving.

Chicken with ham and tomatoes

you will need for 5–6 servings:

3½-lb. roasting	½ teaspoon basil
chicken	1 heaped teaspoon
2 oz. butter	sugar
6 oz. ham or cooked	1 5-oz. can concen-
bacon	trated tomato purée
1 medium onion	½ pint chicken stock
2 stalks celery	

1 Cut chicken into serving pieces, and brown in hot butter in a large flameproof casserole.
2 Remove chicken. Add ham, cut into cubes, sliced onion and celery. Add basil and sugar, and simmer for 5 minutes.
3 Replace chicken, add tomato purée and stock.
4 Cover and cook in a moderate oven (375°F. – Gas Mark 4) for about 1 hour until chicken is tender.

Chicken and tomato supper dish

you will need for 4 servings:

2 oz. butter	½ pint white wine
3 tablespoons oil	2 chicken stock cubes
3 small onions,	½ pint water
peeled and sliced	salt, pepper
1 clove garlic,	1 bay leaf
crushed	8 oz. spaghetti
12 oz. cooked	3 oz. Parmesan
chicken, diced	cheese
½ pint tomato purée	
(see page 85)	

1 Heat butter and oil, add onion and garlic and sauté until onion is transparent.
2 Transfer to a casserole and add chicken.
3 Put tomato purée, wine, crumbled stock cubes and

water into pan in which onion was cooked and stir till boiling. Add seasoning and pour over chicken in the casserole. Add bay leaf.

4 Cover and cook about 30 minutes in a moderate oven (375°F. – Gas Mark 4).

5 Meanwhile, cook spaghetti in boiling salted water, then drain.

6 Put spaghetti into a hot clean casserole, pour chicken mixture on top and sprinkle with grated cheese.

Spanish style chicken

you will need for 4 servings:

1 medium-sized onion	1 level dessertspoon concentrated tomato purée
1 green pepper	
4 chicken joints	1 chicken stock cube
2 tablespoons corn oil	½ pint hot water
	8 oz. tomatoes
2–3 puffs lazy garlic	1 level tablespoon cornflour

1 Peel and slice onion. Cut pepper in half, remove pith and seeds and cut into strips.

2 Fry chicken joints in oil for 5 minutes, turning joints to brown on all sides. Add onion and pepper, cook further 5 minutes.

3 Add garlic, tomato purée, chicken stock cube and water.

4 Cover and cook in a moderate oven for 30–40 minutes until chicken is tender.

5 Skin tomatoes and cut into quarters.

6 Place chicken joints on a warm plate, keep warm.

7 Blend cornflour with a little cold water, stir into the liquid in the casserole. Bring to the boil.

8 Add tomatoes and allow to boil for 3 minutes. Add salt and pepper if necessary. Pour over chicken and serve at once.

Game Casseroles

Casserole of hare

you will need for 4 servings:

for the marinade:

½ pint red cooking wine	1 hare
	1 oz. flour
1 slice onion	salt, pepper
2 strips thinly cut orange peel	2 oz. belly of pork
	1 medium-sized onion, peeled and chopped
little freshly ground pepper	
⅛ pint oil	1 carrot, peeled and chopped
	4 oz. mushrooms, sliced
	stock (see page 84) or water

1 *To prepare the marinade:* Put all ingredients except oil into a pan and simmer for 5 minutes. Leave to get cold, then stir in oil.

2 Have hare jointed (the butcher will do this for you). Cover with marinade and leave for several hours or overnight. Then remove joints, dry and coat with seasoned flour.

3 Cut pork into small pieces, fry in a heavy pan until fat has run out and meat is brown.

4 Add joints of hare and brown quickly on all sides, then transfer to a casserole.

5 Brown onion, carrot and mushrooms in remaining fat and put with hare.

6 Strain marinade into pan with any remaining fat and sediment, and bring to boiling point, stirring well. Pour over contents of casserole.

7 Add sufficient stock or water just to cover.

8 Cover tightly and cook in a slow oven (325°F. – Gas Mark 2) for about 3 hours.

9 Correct seasoning before serving.

Jugged hare

you will need for 6 servings:

1 hare	1 large carrot, peeled and sliced
marinade:	1–2 sticks celery, sliced
¼ pint red wine	*bouquet garni* (see page 85)
⅛ pint vinegar	
1 shallot, peeled and sliced	pinch allspice
1 small carrot, peeled and sliced	thinly cut rind 1 orange
1 sprig thyme	1¼ pint stock (see page 84)
1 bay leaf	
few parsley stalks	2 oz. butter
1 oz. bacon fat	2 oz. flour
1 onion, peeled and stuck with 3 cloves	1 glass port wine
	1 dessertspoon redcurrant jelly
	forcemeat balls (see page 86)

1 Prepare hare and cut into small joints.

2 Mix all ingredients for marinade, add pieces of hare and leave for at least 12 hours.

3 Remove joints and dry.

4 Heat bacon fat and brown hare in it, then transfer to a heavy casserole.

5 Add shallot and carrot from marinade, onion stuck with cloves, carrot, celery, *bouquet garni* and orange rind.

6 Cover with stock. Cover casserole with a tightly fitting lid and cook about 3 hours in a slow oven (325°F. – Gas Mark 2).

7 Remove hare to another casserole.

8 Strain liquor into a saucepan. Mix butter and flour together and add gradually to liquor until consistency is creamy.

9 Simmer for 5 minutes, add port wine and redcurrant jelly. Reheat and pour over hare. Garnish with forcemeat balls.

Variation

With blood of hare – if the blood of the hare is available, a little should be added to the sauce.

Braised grouse

you will need for 6 servings:

1 brace grouse	*bouquet garni* (see page 85)
2 carrots, peeled and sliced	¾ pint good stock (see page 84)
2 onions, peeled and sliced	¼ oz. cornflour
1 small turnip, peeled and sliced	1 tablespoon sherry
1–2 sticks celery, chopped	½ teaspoon soy sauce
	1 teaspoon redcurrant jelly
	salt, pepper

1 Prepare grouse as for roasting.

2 Put all vegetables into a casserole with *bouquet garni*. Put grouse on top and barely cover with stock.

3 Cover and cook in a slow oven (350°F. – Gas Mark 3) about 1½ hours.

4 Put grouse and vegetables on to a dish.

5 Mix cornflour smoothly with a little stock from casserole. Add remaining stock and stir till boiling. Boil for 3 minutes, then add soy sauce, sherry and redcurrant jelly.

6 Correct seasoning before serving.

Partridge with cabbage

you will need for 4 servings:

1 medium-sized cabbage	2 partridge
4 oz. streaky bacon (in one piece)	*bouquet garni* (see page 85)
1 oz. bacon fat or butter	salt, pepper
2 medium-sized onions, peeled and thinly sliced	¼–½ pint stock (see page 84)
	4 oz. pork sausages
2 medium-sized carrots, peeled and thinly sliced	flour
	parsley

1 Wash cabbage well, remove outer leaves and cut cabbage in four. Put into boiling water with bacon pieces and boil for 6–7 minutes. Drain well, squeeze as much water from cabbage as possible and cut each quarter into two or three.

2 Put half the cabbage into a casserole. Remove rind from bacon, cut into strips and put with cabbage.

3 Heat bacon fat, add onions and carrots and sauté until beginning to soften, then put into casserole.

4 Split partridge in halves, brown well in remaining fat, then remove to casserole.

5 Add *bouquet garni* and cover with remaining cabbage.

6 Add seasoning and stock.

7 Cover with foil or greaseproof paper and then with casserole lid, so it is tightly covered.

8 Cook in a slow oven (350°F. – Gas Mark 3) about 1½ hours.

9 Add sausages, cut into thick slices and continue cooking for 30 minutes.

10 Thicken gravy with a little flour before serving and sprinkle with parsley.

Casserole of pheasant

you will need for 4 servings:

3 oz. cooked ham	2 rashers streaky bacon
3 tablespoons cooked rice	3 oz. butter
2 tablespoons sherry	2–3 shallots, peeled and chopped
pepper, salt	8 oz. small button mushrooms
pinch marjoram	stock (see page 84)
pinch powdered thyme	lemon juice
egg to bind	
1 young pheasant	

1 Chop ham and mix with rice, sherry, seasonings and herbs. Bind with a little beaten egg and use to stuff pheasant.

2 Wrap bacon rashers over breast of the pheasant.

3 Heat butter and brown pheasant all over. Put into a casserole.

4 Sauté shallots and mushrooms in remaining butter and put into casserole.

5 Moisten with a little stock, cover and cook in a slow oven (325°F. – Gas Mark 2) about 1½ hours.

6 Just before serving, check seasoning and sprinkle with lemon juice.

Braised pigeons

you will need for 6 servings:

4 pigeons	1 teaspoon cornflour
2 small oranges, peeled and halved	¼ pint Marsala or brown sherry
4 rashers streaky bacon	½ pint stock (see page 84)
2 oz. butter	seasoning
4 oz. mushrooms, sliced	*bouquet garni* (see page 85)
1 small onion, peeled and sliced	chopped parsley

1 Prepare pigeons, put ½ orange in each and truss, wrapping a slice of bacon over the breasts.

2 Heat butter and fry pigeons till lightly browned, then transfer to a casserole.

3 Add mushrooms and onion to remaining butter and cook until onion is transparent.

4 Add cornflour and mix well.

5 Add wine and stock, stir till boiling, season, and pour over pigeons.

6 Add *bouquet garni*. Cover and cook about 1½ hours in a slow oven (350°F. – Gas Mark 3).

7 When birds are tender, remove to a serving dish and strain sauce over. Sprinkle with parsley before serving.

Normandy pheasant

you will need for 4 servings:

1 pheasant
3 oz. butter
1½ lb. cooking apples
¼ pint thin cream
salt, pepper

1 Prepare bird as for roasting.
2 Melt butter, put in pheasant and brown it on all sides.
3 Peel, core and slice apples thinly and put half into a deep casserole. Pour over a little butter and then put pheasant on top. Surround with remaining apples.
4 Pour remaining butter and cream on top, season with salt and pepper.
5 Cover tightly and cook in a slow oven (350°F. – Gas Mark 3) for 1–1¼ hours.

Casserole of pigeons

you will need for 4 servings:

2 pigeons
1 oz. flour
salt, pepper
2 oz. butter
1 onion, peeled and chopped
8 oz. carrots, peeled and sliced
½ small turnip, peeled and chopped
1 chicken stock cube
¾ pint water
8 oz. tomatoes, peeled and sliced
1 bay leaf

1 Halve the pigeons, and coat with seasoned flour.
2 Heat butter and brown pigeons on all sides, then remove to a casserole.
3 Put vegetables into pan and sauté for a few minutes in remaining fat, then remove to a casserole.
4 Put any remaining flour and crumbled stock cube into pan. Add water and stir till boiling.
5 Pour over contents of casserole.
6 Add tomatoes and bay leaf.
7 Cover and cook for about 2 hours in a slow oven (325°F. – Gas Mark 2).
8 Remove bay leaf and check seasoning.

Pigeon with cherries

you will need for 4 servings:

2 pigeons
2 oz. bacon fat or butter
2 shallots, peeled and sliced
1 oz. flour
1 chicken stock cube
1½ pints water
bouquet garni (see page 85)
1 tablespoon sour cream
8 oz. red cherries
½ oz. butter

1 Split pigeons in half and brown well in hot bacon fat, then remove to a casserole.
2 Brown shallots and put with pigeons.
3 Add flour and crumbled stock cube to fat in pan. Cook for a minute and then add water. Stir till boiling. Add *bouquet garni*.
4 Cover casserole tightly and cook in a slow oven (350°F. – Gas Mark 3) about 1½ hours.
5 When pigeons are tender, remove to a serving dish and keep hot.
6 Strain sauce into a pan, add cream and boil rapidly to reduce a little. Correct seasoning and pour over pigeons.

7 Sauté stoned cherries for a few minutes in butter, then sprinkle over pigeons.

Pigeon with raisins

you will need for 4 servings:

1 oz. butter
2 pigeons
2 rashers streaky bacon
6 small onions, peeled
½–¾ pint stock (see page 84)
salt, pepper
2 oz. seedless or seeded raisins
1 teaspoon cornflour
2 tablespoons sherry

1 Heat butter, split pigeons in half and brown on all sides in hot butter. Remove to a casserole.
2 Add bacon cut into strips and onions, cut into quarters if not very small, and brown in remaining butter. Add to casserole.
3 Add enough stock to come about ¾ up the birds, add seasoning.
4 Cover and cook in a moderate oven (375°F. – Gas Mark 4) about 1 hour.
5 While pigeons are cooking, soak raisins in a little warm stock and add to casserole 30 minutes before the end of cooking.
6 When ready, remove pigeons to a serving dish. Mix cornflour smoothly with sherry and add to liquid left in casserole. Bring to boiling point and boil for 3 minutes. Correct seasoning.

Pigeon with water chestnuts

you will need for 4 servings:

2 young pigeons
1 oz. flour
1 oz. butter
1 chicken stock cube
¾ pint water
1 teaspoon sugar
salt, pepper
2 dessertspoons soy sauce
1 tablespoon sherry
2 spring onions or 1 shallot, chopped
10 water chestnuts, sliced thinly

1 Cut each pigeon into quarters, coat with flour and brown on all sides in hot butter. Remove to a casserole.
2 Put remaining flour into pan with stock cube and cook for 1 minute. Add water and bring to boiling point, stirring.
3 Add sugar, seasoning, soy sauce, sherry, onions and chestnuts and pour over pigeons.
4 Cover and cook for 45 minutes to 1 hour in a slow oven (350°F. – Gas Mark 3).

Stewed pigeons

you will need for 4 servings:

2 pigeons
2–3 oz. butter
4 oz. bacon rashers
4 tablespoons red wine
4–6 shallots
4 oz. mushrooms
little veal or chicken stock

1 Cut each pigeon in half and brown lightly in butter. Remove to a casserole.

2 Fry bacon lightly, then put with pigeons.

3 Put wine into pan in which pigeons have been browned, let it boil for a minute, then pour over pigeons.

4 Put shallots or very small onions and mushrooms into casserole, moisten with stock.

5 Cover very tightly and cook in a slow oven (325°F. – Gas Mark 2), for about 1–1½ hours.

Note: Young pigeons should require about 1 hour, allow longer for older birds.

Stuffed pigeon casserole

you will need for 4 servings:

2 pigeons	salt, pepper
8 oz. raw chicken	1 tablespoon cream
1 oz. butter	2 oz. butter
1 oz. flour	¼ pint brown stock
⅜ pint chicken stock	(see page 84)
1 egg	

1 Prepare pigeons.

2 Remove skin and any sinew from chicken and mince finely.

3 Make a thick panada with butter, flour and ⅛ pint stock.

4 Add chicken, egg, seasoning and cream and beat all well together.

5 Stuff pigeons with this forcemeat and truss into shape.

6 Heat butter in a casserole, add pigeons and brown carefully.

7 Add sauce and remaining stock and season lightly.

8 Cover tightly and cook in a slow oven (350°F. – Gas Mark 3) about 45 minutes.

Pigeons with beer

you will need for 4 servings:

2 pigeons	1 pint stock (see page 84)
stuffing:	½ pint ale
4 oz. breadcrumbs	1 onion, peeled and chopped
1 tablespoon chopped parsley	1 bay leaf
1 teaspoon mixed herbs	few parsley stalks
salt, pepper, nutmeg	1 oz. flour
grated rind ½ lemon	1 oz. butter
2 oz. suet, shredded	
egg to bind	

1 Prepare pigeons, wash and blanch livers and use for stuffing.

2 Mix all ingredients for stuffing with chopped livers. Bind with egg and stuff birds.

3 Put pigeons in a casserole, add stock, ale, onion, bay leaf and parsley stalks.

4 Cover and cook in a slow oven (350°F. – Gas Mark 3) about 1¾–2 hours.

5 When pigeons are tender, move on to a serving dish.

6 Drain off liquor from casserole and thicken with butter and flour mixed.

7 Correct seasoning and serve sauce separately.

Casserole of rabbit

you will need for 6 servings:

1 rabbit	salt, pepper
4 oz. streaky bacon, diced	1 chicken stock cube
2 oz. butter or bacon fat	1 pint water
	6 peppercorns
12–18 small button onions	2 cloves
	bouquet garni (see page 85)
½ oz. flour	¼ pint red wine

1 Wash, dry and joint rabbit.

2 Fry bacon, butter and onions till lightly browned, then remove to a casserole.

3 Season the flour and coat the rabbit, then fry till the joints are golden brown. Put into casserole with onions.

4 Crumble stock cube and put into pan with any remaining flour. Add water and stir till boiling.

5 Pour over contents of casserole.

6 Add cloves, peppercorns and *bouquet garni.*

7 Cover and cook in a slow oven (350°F. – Gas Mark 3) for 2 hours.

8 Add wine, correct seasoning and continue cooking for 30 minutes.

Rabbit chasseur

you will need for 6 servings:

1 rabbit	1 teaspoon tomato purée (see page 85)
2 tablespoons oil	
½ oz. butter	¼ pint white wine
1 tablespoon finely chopped shallot	½ pint stock (see page 84)
¼ oz. flour	4 oz. mushrooms
	chopped parsley

1 Wash and joint rabbit.

2 Heat oil and butter in a sauté pan. Add shallot and rabbit joints and sauté gently for about 15 minutes. Then remove rabbit to a casserole.

3 Put flour and tomato purée into the sauté pan, cook for a few minutes, then add wine and stock and stir till boiling. Season and pour over rabbit.

4 Cover and cook in a slow oven (350°F. – Gas Mark 3) about 1¼ hours.

5 Add sliced mushrooms and continue cooking for 40–45 minutes.

6 Sprinkle with parsley before serving.

Rabbit and prune casserole

you will need for 6 servings:

1 rabbit	2 oz. butter
¾ pint red wine	1½ oz. flour
2 tablespoons vinegar	seasoning
2 bay leaves	1 tablespoon redcurrant jelly
6 peppercorns	
4 oz. prunes	

1 Joint rabbit, put into a bowl and add wine, vinegar and herbs. Leave overnight.

2 Wash and soak prunes in cold water overnight.

3 Remove rabbit from marinade and dry it.

4 Heat butter, put in rabbit and cook for a few minutes, then remove to a casserole and add well-drained prunes.

5 Add flour to butter in pan, and cook for a few minutes. Remove from heat and gradually add strained wine. Season.

6 Return to heat and stir till boiling. Boil for 3 minutes, then pour over rabbit.

7 Cover and cook in a slow oven (350°F. – Gas Mark 3) for about 2 hours.

8 Just before serving, stir in jelly and correct seasoning.

Jugged rabbit

you will need for 6 servings:

1 rabbit	1 teaspoon lemon
1 oz. flour	juice
salt, pepper	*bouquet garni* (to
2 oz. butter or	include 1 sprig
dripping	thyme, 6
1 onion stuck with	peppercorns, see
2 cloves	page 85)
¼ pint red wine	1 oz. butter
1 pint stock (see	redcurrant jelly
page 84) or water	

1 Wash and dry the rabbit and cut into joints.

2 Coat well with seasoned flour and brown on all sides in hot fat.

3 Remove to a deep casserole.

4 Add onion, wine, stock, lemon juice and *bouquet garni.* Cover tightly and cook in a slow oven (350°F. – Gas Mark 3) about 2½–3 hours.

5 30 minutes before serving, mix remaining flour (about 1 tablespoon) with butter and stir into casserole. Add a little more wine if liked and correct seasoning. Then continue cooking. Serve with redcurrant jelly.

Rabbit and tomato casserole

you will need for 6 servings:

1 rabbit	1 lb. tomatoes, peeled
vinegar	and chopped
½ oz. flour	¼ pint red wine
salt, pepper	pinch rosemary
garlic salt	sprig thyme
2 oz. butter	
1 small onion, peeled	
and chopped	

1 Wash and cut up the rabbit and soak for 2 hours in equal parts vinegar and water. Drain and dry.

2 Coat rabbit pieces with flour seasoned with salt, pepper and garlic salt and brown in heated butter. Remove to a casserole.

3 Add onion and tomatoes and any remaining flour to butter left in pan and cook for a few minutes.

4 Add wine, stir till boiling, then pour over rabbit. Add rosemary and thyme.

5 Cover and cook in a slow oven (325°F. – Gas Mark 2) for 1½ hours.
Correct seasoning before serving.

Rabbit with sour cream

you will need for 6 servings:

1 rabbit	6 tablespoons white
vinegar	wine
½ oz. flour	1 chicken stock cube
salt, pepper	1 tablespoon chopped
½ teaspoon oregano	parsley
2 tablespoons oil	¼ pint sour cream

1 Wash and joint rabbit and leave to soak for 2 hours in equal parts of vinegar and water.

2 Drain and pat dry, then coat with flour seasoned with salt, pepper and oregano.

3 Heat oil and brown rabbit on all sides, then put into a casserole.

4 Put wine and stock into pan in which rabbit was browned and stir till boiling. Pour over rabbit and add parsley.

5 Cover and cook in a slow oven (325°F. – Gas Mark 2) about 1 hour.

6 Add cream, and continue cooking a further 30 minutes. Correct seasoning and consistency before serving.

Rabbit Sicilian

you will need for 6 servings:

1 rabbit	2–3 sticks celery,
1 can tomato purée	chopped
¼ pint wine vinegar	1 oz. sugar
6 olives	salt, pepper
1 tablespoon capers	white stock (see
	page 84)

1 Wash and cut up rabbit and put into a casserole.

2 Mix tomato purée and wine vinegar together and pour over rabbit.

3 Add olives, capers, celery and sugar.

4 Season lightly and add enough stock barely to cover.

5 Cover casserole and cook about 1½ hours in a slow oven (325°F. – Gas Mark 2).
If necessary, thicken with flour before serving.

Salmis of game

you will need for 4 servings:

1 partly roasted	4 tablespoons port
pheasant or other	wine
game bird	mushroom stalks
¾ pint good brown	4 glacé cherries
stock (see page 84)	12 button
1 tablespoon	mushrooms
redcurrant jelly	butter

1 Joint pheasant, remove skin and put into a casserole.

2 Add stock, jelly, wine and mushroom stalks.

3 Cover tightly and cook in a slow oven (350°F. – Gas Mark 3) for 1–1½ hours.

4 Remove pheasant to a serving dish.

5 Remove any excess fat from sauce and strain over pheasant.

6 Garnish with cherries, and mushrooms, sautéed in a little butter.

Fish Casseroles

Casseroled cod cutlets

you will need for 4 servings:

4 cutlets cod
½ oz. flour
salt, pepper
1 oz. butter
2 small onions, peeled and sliced thinly
1 clove garlic, crushed
4 oz. mushrooms, sliced
1 bay leaf
1 sprig thyme
½ pint cider
3 tablespoons cream
paprika

1 Wash and dry cutlets and coat with seasoned flour.
2 Butter a casserole, put in fish and sprinkle with onion. Add garlic, mushrooms, bay leaf and thyme and dot with butter.
3 Add cider, cover and cook about 30 minutes in a moderate oven (375°F. – Gas Mark 4).
4 Put fish on to a serving dish.
5 Remove garlic, bay leaf and thyme and stir cream into sauce. Correct seasoning and pour sauce over fish. Sprinkle with paprika.

Casserole of brill

you will need for 4–6 servings:

2 medium-sized carrots, peeled and sliced
1 small turnip, peeled and sliced
1 medium-sized onion, peeled and sliced
bouquet garni (see page 85)
4–5 tablespoons white stock (see page 84)
salt, freshly ground pepper
1 1½–2 lb. brill
4 tomatoes, peeled and sliced
1 teaspoon chopped parsley
pinch mixed herbs
½ pint cider
1 oz. butter
¾ oz. flour
1 teaspoon lemon juice
¼ pint cream or top of the milk

1 Put vegetables and *bouquet garni* into a buttered casserole. Add stock and seasonings. Cover with buttered paper, then put casserole lid on and cook in a moderate oven (375°F. – Gas Mark 4) till vegetables are tender and stock absorbed.
2 Trim fish and put in casserole on bed of vegetables.
3 Cover with tomatoes, sprinkle with parsley and herbs and pour cider over.
4 Cover and cook in a slow oven (350°F. – Gas Mark 3) for about 30 minutes.
5 When fish is cooked, carefully pour off liquor and put into a small pan.
6 Mix butter and flour and add gradually to liquor, stir till boiling, then add lemon juice and cream. Correct seasoning, thin sauce with a little milk or stock, if too thick. Pour over fish.

Casserole of cod with prawns

you will need for 4–6 servings:

2 tablespoons oil
2 large onions, peeled and sliced
4 tablespoons tomato purée (see page 85)
¼ pint white wine
¼ pint fish stock (see page 67) or water
salt, pepper
2 lb. cod fillet
1 teaspoon chopped parsley
1 packet frozen prawns
1 lemon

1 Heat oil, sauté onion until transparent.
2 Pour off excess oil, add tomato purée, wine and water and just bring to boiling point. Add salt and pepper as required.
3 Skin fish, cut into convenient sized pieces and arrange in a casserole. Pour tomato mixture on top and sprinkle with parsley.
4 Cover and cook in a moderate oven (375°F. – Gas Mark 4) about 20 minutes.
5 Add prawns and continue cooking for another 10 minutes. Serve with wedges of lemon.

Cod with wine sauce

you will need for 4 servings:

1–1½ lb. fillet of cod
salt, pepper, garlic salt
1 tablespoon oil
2 tablespoons finely minced onion
½ oz. flour
½ pint milk
6 tablespoons white wine
1 tablespoon chopped parsley

1 Wash fish, cut into serving pieces and arrange in a casserole. Sprinkle with salt, pepper and garlic salt.
2 Heat oil, add onion and sauté until transparent. Add flour and mix well.
3 Add milk, stir till boiling and boil 3 minutes.
4 Gradually stir in wine and more seasonings and pour over fish.
5 Cover and cook in a slow oven (350°F. – Gas Mark 3) for about 30 minutes.
Sprinkle with parsley before serving.

Cod Bolognese

you will need for 4 servings:

1–1½ lb. fillet cod
2 tablespoons oil
salt, pepper
1 clove garlic, minced
1 tomato, peeled, seeded and chopped
1 oz. butter
juice ¼ lemon
1 tablespoon chopped parsley

1 Wash fish and arrange in one piece in a casserole in which oil has been heated.
2 Sprinkle with salt, pepper and garlic.
3 Add tomatoes and dot with butter.

[*continued*

4 Cover and cook in a slow oven (350°F. – Gas Mark 3) for 30 minutes.

5 Before serving, sprinkle with lemon juice and parsley.

Cod steaks Valencia

you will need for 4 servings:

4 cod steaks	1 oz. butter
2 tablespoons white wine	grated rind ½ orange
3 tablespoons orange juice	salt and pepper

1 Prepare the fish and put it into a fireproof dish.

2 Pour over the wine and orange juice and leave for 10 minutes.

3 Mix the butter with the grated orange rind and put in small pieces over the fish. Season with salt and pepper.

4 Cover the dish tightly with a lid, or cover with aluminium foil and bake in a moderate oven (350°F. – Gas Mark 3) for about 20 minutes.

5 Drain off the liquor from the fish, put into a small pan and reduce a little by boiling and then pour over the fish.

6 Garnish with segments of orange.

Cod Portugaise

you will need for 4 servings:

4 cod steaks	2 tablespoons grated cheese
4 tomatoes, peeled and sliced thickly	2 tablespoons breadcrumbs
1 onion, peeled and sliced very thinly	1 oz. butter
salt, pepper	1 lemon
¼ pint cider	parsley
2 teaspoons chopped parsley	

1 Put cod steaks into a casserole, cover with tomatoes and onions, season with salt and pepper and pour cider on top.

2 Sprinkle with chopped parsley, cover and cook in a slow oven (350°F. – Gas Mark 3) for about 1 hour.

3 Remove lid, sprinkle with cheese and breadcrumbs and dot with butter.

4 Put under the grill for a few minutes to brown. Garnish with wedges of lemon and parsley.

Cod and macaroni casserole

you will need for 4–6 servings:

2 oz. macaroni	3 oz. fresh breadcrumbs
1½–2 lb. cod	¼ pint milk
salt, pepper, lemon juice	1 egg
1 teaspoon finely chopped parsley	butter

1 Break macaroni into 1-inch lengths and cook in boiling salted water for about 10 minutes. Drain.

2 Put fish into a casserole, season with salt, pepper and lemon juice and sprinkle with parsley.

3 Arrange macaroni and some breadcrumbs round fish.

4 Heat milk and pour on to beaten egg, then pour over fish.

5 Sprinkle with remaining breadcrumbs and dot with butter.

6 Cover and cook for about 45–50 minutes in a moderate oven (375°F. – Gas Mark 4).

7 Remove lid for the last 10–15 minutes to brown the top.

Variation

With tomato – if liked, some slices of peeled tomato can be put round the edge while the breadcrumbs are browning.

Casseroled eels

you will need for 4 servings:

2 lb. eels	6 tablespoons red wine
1 tablespoon oil	8 oz. button mushrooms
1 large onion, peeled and chopped finely	1 teaspoon oregano
1 clove garlic, chopped finely	1 bay leaf
2 teaspoons flour	salt, pepper
1 pint fish stock (see page 67) or water	parsley

1 Clean, skin and cut eels into 1-inch pieces and put into a casserole.

2 Heat oil, add onion and garlic and sauté until onion begins to brown.

3 Add flour and mix well.

4 Add stock and wine, stir till boiling and boil for 3 minutes. Add mushrooms, oregano, bay leaf and seasoning and pour over the eels.

5 Cover and cook in a slow oven (350°F. – Gas Mark 3) for about 1¼ hours. Sprinkle with chopped parsley before serving.

Crumble top fish casserole

you will need for 4–6 servings:

1½ lb. cod or haddock fillet	salt, pepper, paprika
2 oz. butter	**for crumble top:**
1 small onion, peeled and sliced	6 oz. flour
2 oz. mushrooms, sliced	pinch salt
2 oz. flour	4 oz. butter
¼ pint milk	¼ teaspoon basil
¼ pint white wine or cider	pinch chopped tarragon

1 Poach fish very lightly and retain liquor. Divide fish into convenient sized pieces.

2 Heat butter and sauté onion and mushrooms.

3 Add flour and mix well.

4 Measure liquor from fish and make up to 1 pint with milk and wine.

5 Add to pan, stir till boiling and boil for 2 minutes.

6 Season carefully, add fish, then pour all into a casserole.

7 Sift flour and salt together, rub in butter, add basil and tarragon.

8 Cover fish with this mixture and cook about 40–45 minutes in a moderately hot oven (400°F. – Gas Mark 5).

Cold terrine of fish

you will need for 6 servings:

1 lb. turbot or halibut	pinch cayenne pepper
6 oz. butter	¼ teaspoon ground
8 oz. white	mace
breadcrumbs	1 egg yolk
1 tablespoon chopped	¼ pint milk
parsley	1 lb. fresh haddock
salt, freshly ground	
black pepper	

1 Bone and skin turbot and chop roughly.

2 Cream 4 oz. butter, add to fish with breadcrumbs, parsley, seasonings and mace.

3 Bind with egg yolk and milk.

4 Skin and bone haddock and cut into thin oblong pieces.

5 Put a layer of turbot mixture into a deep casserole, well greased, and cover with a layer of haddock.

6 Repeat the layers, sprinkle each with a little pepper and mace, until all fish is used up. Dot with remaining butter.

7 Cover with aluminium foil and put on lid.

8 Stand casserole in a baking tin half filled with water and cook in a slow oven (325°F. – Gas Mark 2) about 2½–3 hours.

Keep covered until cold and serve with salad.

Fish custard

you will need for 2 servings:

2 fillets sole	¼ pint milk
1 egg	salt, pepper

1 Skin the fillets and roll up with the skinned side inside. Place in a buttered basin.

2 Beat egg, add milk and seasoning and pour over fish.

3 Cover with buttered paper and stand the basin in a pan of boiling water.

4 Reduce heat at once, cover and simmer gently for about 20–25 minutes.

5 Remove paper and serve immediately.

Fish hot pot

you will need for 4 servings:

1½ lb. white fish	8 oz. tomatoes,
fish stock (see next	peeled and sliced
column) or water	salt, pepper
1 lb. potatoes, peeled	*bouquet garni* (see
and sliced	page 85)
2 small onions,	½ oz. butter
peeled and sliced	

1 Remove skin and bone from fish and cut into pieces.

2 Arrange vegetables and fish in layers in a casserole, sprinkling each with a little salt and pepper. Add *bouquet garni*, half cover with fish stock and finish with a layer of potatoes. Dot with butter.

3 Cover and cook in a fairly slow oven (350°F. – Gas Mark 3) for about 1 hour.

To make fish stock

Take the skin, bones and trimmings and simmer in ¾ pint water, seasoning, 1 sliced shallot and a strip of lemon peel for 20 minutes, then strain.

Fish Portugaise

you will need for 4 servings:

1 lb. fillets white fish	2 tablespoons grated
salt and pepper	cheese
lemon juice	2 tablespoons
1 small onion, sliced	breadcrumbs
very thinly	½ oz. butter
4 tomatoes, peeled	
and sliced	

1 Trim the fish, season with salt and pepper and lemon juice and arrange in a fireproof dish.

2 Add the onion and tomatoes.

3 Mix the cheese and breadcrumbs together and sprinkle on top.

4 Dot with butter and bake about 20 minutes in a moderate oven (375°F. – Gas Mark 4).

Fish Espagnole

you will need for 4–6 servings:

1½–2 lb. white fish	salt, pepper
1½ oz. fat	1 teaspoon finely
1 small carrot, peeled	chopped fennel or
and chopped	parsley
1 small onion, peeled	1 dessertspoon
and chopped	Worcestershire
1 tomato, peeled and	sauce
chopped	gravy browning,
1 oz. flour	optional
1 pint stock (see	
page 84) or water	

1 Prepare fish and put into a casserole.

2 Heat fat, add carrot and onion, cover and cook gently for about 10 minutes.

3 Add tomato and continue cooking, uncovered, for a few minutes.

4 Stir in flour and mix well.

5 Gradually add stock, stir till boiling and boil for 1 minute. Add salt, pepper, parsley, Worcestershire sauce and a few drops of gravy browning.

6 Pour over fish, cover, and cook in a slow oven (325°F. – Gas Mark 2) for 1 hour.

Fish maître d'hôtel

you will need for 4 servings:

1 lb. white fish, cod, hake or haddock
½ oz. butter
salt, pepper
1 shallot, peeled and chopped finely
3 tablespoons white wine
3 tablespoons fish stock (see page 67) or milk
½ pint white sauce (see page 85)
juice ¼ lemon
2 teaspoons chopped parsley
1 lemon

1 Prepare fish, cut into pieces and put in a buttered casserole.
2 Sprinkle with salt, pepper and shallot. Add wine and stock, cover and cook in a very slow oven (325°F. – Gas Mark 2) for 15 minutes.
3 Remove from oven, carefully drain off the liquor. Add it to sauce with lemon juice and parsley. Correct seasoning, pour over fish, cover and continue cooking for 15 minutes.
Serve with wedges of lemon.

Casserole of fish

you will need for 4 servings:

1½ lb. fillets of fresh haddock
1 oz. butter
1 medium-sized onion, thinly sliced
salt and pepper
pinch paprika
pinch nutmeg
2 eggs
1 oz. flour
juice 1 lemon

1 Prepare the fish and cut into pieces and put into a casserole.
2 Melt the butter and cook the onion until soft.
3 Sprinkle the onion on top of the fish and add salt, pepper, paprika and nutmeg.
4 Moisten with a little milk and water. Cover and bake for about 15 minutes in a moderately hot oven (375°F. – Gas Mark 4).
5 Mix the eggs, flour and lemon juice together. Add any liquid from the fish and mix in well.
6 Pour over the fish, return to the oven and cook uncovered for a further 10 minutes.

Quick fish casserole

you will need for 4 servings:

1 oz. fat
1 onion, peeled and chopped
2 sticks celery, chopped
1 small red pepper, seeded and sliced thinly
1–1½ lb. fillets fish (cod, hake, haddock as available)
½ oz. flour
salt, pepper
lemon juice
1 can condensed tomato soup
1 tablespoon chopped parsley

1 Heat fat, add onion, celery and pepper and cook for a few minutes over low heat.
2 Remove vegetables to a casserole and keep any fat left in the pan.
3 Cut fish into 4 pieces, coat with seasoned flour and place in casserole on top of vegetables.

4 Add any fat left from frying vegetables or dot with butter.
5 Sprinkle with lemon juice.
6 Cover and cook for about 10 minutes in a moderate oven (375°F. – Gas Mark 4).
7 Pour tomato soup over, cover and continue cooking for 15–20 minutes.
8 Sprinkle with parsley before serving.

Spiced fish casserole

you will need for 4 servings:

1½ lb. fillet of cod, haddock or other white fish
salt, pepper
lemon juice
1 bay leaf
1 oz. butter
paprika
for the sauce:
1 oz. butter
1 oz. flour
¾ pint water
¼ teaspoon anchovy essence
2–3 cloves
pinch mixed spice
½ teaspoon chilli sauce
8 oz. tomatoes, peeled and chopped
few drops Tabasco
1 teaspoon parsley, finely chopped

1 Cut fish into serving pieces and put into a casserole.
2 Sprinkle with salt, pepper and lemon juice. Add bay leaf and dot with the butter.
3 Cover and put into a slow oven (350°F. – Gas Mark 3) for about 30 minutes. While the fish is cooking, make the sauce.

To make sauce
1 Melt butter, add flour and cook for a few minutes.
2 Remove from heat and add water, return to heat, stir till boiling and boil for 1 minute.
3 Add anchovy essence and all other ingredients except paprika.
4 Simmer for about 20 minutes.
5 Pour sauce over fish and continue cooking for 15 minutes.
6 Just before serving, sprinkle with paprika.

Super fish pie

you will need for 4 servings:

1 lb. cooked white fish, haddock or cod
salt and pepper
2 oz. butter
1 onion, peeled and chopped finely
2 oz. flour
¾ pint milk
2 hard-boiled eggs
4 heaped tablespoons sweet corn
1 2½-oz. packet instant potato
egg for glaze

1 Flake fish roughly, sprinkle lightly with salt and pepper.
2 Melt butter, fry onion, without browning, for 10 minutes. Stir in the flour. Allow to cook for two minutes.
3 Remove from heat, stir in milk. Bring to the boil, stirring throughout.
4 Slice eggs. Add with fish and sweet corn to sauce.

Pour into flameproof casserole (1 pint size).

5 Make up potato, according to instructions on packet. Spread over fish mixture and brush with beaten egg.

6 Bake in a hot oven (400°F. – Gas Mark 5) for 30 minutes.

Variations

Parsley pie – follow previous recipe, omitting onion and sweet corn, and use 1 packet parsley sauce mix made up with ¾ pint milk. Sprinkle mashed potato topping with finely grated cheese. Bake as above.

Mushroom pie – make as for Super fish pie, using one packet mushroom sauce mix made up with ¾ pint milk. Omit sweet corn and add 4 oz. sliced mushrooms or small, whole mushrooms, sautéed in butter.

Spanish fish casserole

you will need for 4 servings:

4 cutlets of hake or cod	8 oz. tomatoes, peeled and chopped
1 small can shrimps	¼ pint dry white wine
2 tablespoons oil	juice 1 lemon
1 clove garlic, chopped finely	salt, pepper
1 small onion, chopped finely	chopped parsley

1 Put fish and drained shrimps into a casserole.

2 Heat oil, fry garlic and onion till golden brown. Add tomatoes and continue cooking for a few minutes.

3 Add wine and lemon juice and stir till boiling. Season carefully and pour over fish.

4 Cover and cook in a moderate oven (375°F. – Gas Mark 4) for about 30 minutes.

5 Sprinkle with parsley before serving.

Haddock casserole No. 1

you will need for 4 servings:

1½ lb. fresh haddock	½ pint milk
1 small onion, peeled and minced	salt, pepper
2 oz. fine oatmeal	1 oz. butter

1 Prepare fish and put into a buttered casserole.

2 Sprinkle with onion, add oatmeal, milk and seasoning.

3 Dot with butter, cover and cook about 30 minutes in a slow oven (325°F. – Gas Mark 2).

Haddock casserole No. 2

you will need for 4–6 servings:

1½ lb. fresh haddock fillet	½ pint milk
1 small onion stuck with 2 cloves	1 tablespoon chopped parsley
1 bay leaf	2 oz. grated cheese
1 strip lemon peel	1 hard-boiled egg
few peppercorns	seasoning
2 oz. butter	3 tomatoes, peeled and sliced
1½ oz. cornflour	

1 Wash fish and put into a pan with onion, bay leaf, lemon peel and peppercorns.

2 Just cover with water, bring slowly to boiling point, then simmer till the fish is cooked (about 7–10 minutes).

3 Strain off liquor and keep for sauce.

4 Remove skin and any bone from fish and cut into pieces.

5 Melt butter, add cornflour and mix well. Add ¼ pint liquor in which fish was cooked to milk. Gradually add to butter and cornflour mixture and stir till boiling.

6 Add parsley, cheese, chopped egg and seasoning.

7 Arrange alternate layers of fish and sauce in a greased casserole. Cover with slices of tomato and bake in a moderately hot oven (400°F. – Gas Mark 5) for about 20 minutes.

Haddock and bacon casserole

you will need for 4 servings:

1½–2 lb. fresh haddock	8 oz. cooked potatoes, sliced
1 oz. flour	1 teaspoon curry powder
salt, pepper	½ pint tomato juice
¼ teaspoon powdered tarragon	2 tablespoons Worcestershire sauce
6 oz. streaky bacon	
8 oz. onions, peeled and sliced	

1 Cut fish into serving pieces and coat with flour seasoned with salt, pepper and tarragon.

2 Remove rind from bacon, cut into pieces and fry till crisp. Remove from pan.

3 Fry onions till lightly browned in bacon fat.

4 Mix bacon, onions and potatoes and put half into a casserole.

5 Arrange fish on top and cover with remaining vegetables and bacon.

6 Mix any remaining flour with curry powder. Add tomato juice and sauce and mix smoothly.

7 Pour over ingredients in casserole. Cover and cook in a slow oven (350°F. – Gas Mark 3) about 45 minutes to 1 hour.

Haddock Crécy

you will need for 4 servings:

2 oz. butter	1 lb. fresh haddock fillet
4 oz. carrots, peeled and chopped	1 bay leaf
1 small turnip, peeled and chopped	seasonings
1 stick celery, chopped	½ oz. cornflour
½ small onion, peeled and chopped	½ pint milk, approx.
2 tomatoes, peeled, seeded and chopped	lemon juice, optional
	3–4 tablespoons cooked green peas

1 Melt 1 oz. butter, add vegetables and sauté for about 5 minutes.

2 Add tomatoes, then put all into a casserole, cover

and cook in a slow oven (350°F. – Gas Mark 3) for about 30 minutes.

3 Cut fish into serving pieces and place on top of vegetables. Add bay leaf.

4 Cover and cook a further 20–25 minutes or until the fish is cooked.

5 Carefully strain off liquor and remove bay leaf.

6 Melt remaining butter, add cornflour and mix.

7 Make up fish liquor to about ½ pint with milk, gradually add to cornflour mixture, stir till boiling and boil for 1 minute. Correct seasoning and add a little lemon juice.

8 Pour over fish and garnish with peas.

Haddock and tomato casserole

you will need for 4 servings:

3 oz. butter	2 lb. fresh haddock
2 medium-sized	fillet
onions, peeled and	salt, pepper
chopped	4 oz. fresh white
2 tablespoons finely	breadcrumbs
chopped parsley	
1 lb. tomatoes, peeled	
and sliced	

1 Spread bottom of a casserole generously with some butter.

2 Cover with half the onion, parsley and tomatoes.

3 Cut fish into pieces and arrange on top. Season.

4 Cover with remaining onion, parsley and tomato.

5 Add breadcrumbs and dot with remaining butter.

6 Cover and cook in a moderate oven (375°F. – Gas Mark 4) for 25–30 minutes.

Stuffed haddock casserole

you will need for 4 servings:

for the stuffing:	salt, pepper
2 oz. butter	1 teaspoon grated
1 small onion, very	lemon rind
finely chopped	
8 tablespoons fresh	1½ lb. fresh haddock
white breadrumbs	milk
4 oz. mushrooms,	3 oz. grated cheese
finely chopped	
2 teaspoons chopped	
parsley	

To make the stuffing:

1 Heat butter and fry onion till tender.

2 Add breadcrumbs and other ingredients and mix well together.

3 Put half the fish into a greased casserole. Press stuffing on top then cover with remaining fish.

4 Add a little milk, cover and cook in a moderate oven (350°F. – Gas Mark 3) for about 30–35 minutes.

5 Before serving, sprinkle with cheese and brown under the grill.

Variation

Stuffed haddock and cheese sauce – substitute cheese sauce for grated cheese.

Fresh haddock with cider

you will need for 4 servings:

1½–2 lb. fresh	½ lemon, cut into
haddock fillet	thick slices
2 oz. butter	salt and pepper
¼ pint cider	little chopped parsley
2–3 tomatoes, peeled	1 small shallot,
and sliced	chopped finely
4–6 mushrooms,	
sliced	

1 Cut the fish into pieces and put into a greased fire-proof dish.

2 Put small pieces of butter on top and then add the cider.

3 Cover with tomatoes, mushrooms and lemon.

4 Season carefully, cover and bake in a moderately hot oven (375°F. – Gas Mark 4) for 20–25 minutes.

5 Before serving, sprinkle with parsley and shallot.

Haddock and onion casserole

you will need for 4 servings:

1½ lb. fillets fresh	pinch paprika
haddock	pinch nutmeg
1 oz. butter	milk and water
1 medium-sized	2 eggs
onion, thinly sliced	1 oz. flour
salt, pepper	juice 1 lemon

1 Prepare fish and cut into pieces, put into a casserole.

2 Melt butter and cook onion until soft.

3 Sprinkle onion on top of fish, add salt, pepper, paprika and nutmeg.

4 Moisten with a little milk and water.

5 Cover and cook about 15 minutes in a moderate oven (375°F. – Gas Mark 4).

6 Mix eggs, flour and lemon juice. Add any liquid from the fish and mix in well.

7 Pour over the fish, return to oven and cook, uncovered, for a further 10 minutes.

Hake and tomato casserole

you will need for 4 servings:

8 oz. onions	3 tablespoons
8 oz. tomatoes	browned crumbs
salt, pepper	1 oz. butter
4 cutlets hake	1 lemon
1 chicken stock cube	parsley
¾ pint boiling water	

1 Peel and slice onions and parboil for 3 minutes, then drain.

2 Put into a casserole with tomatoes, peeled and sliced. Add salt and pepper.

3 Arrange fish on top.

4 Dissolve stock cube in water and pour over fish.

5 Sprinkle with breadcrumbs and dot with butter.

6 Bake in a slow oven (350°F. – Gas Mark 3) about 40–45 minutes.

7 Garnish with lemon and parsley.

Halibut with celery and bacon

you will need for 4 servings:

2 large or 4 small steaks of halibut	milk
salt	1 oz. butter
1 small head celery	½ oz. cornflour
4 oz. streaky bacon	seasoning
1 teaspoon chopped parsley	**for garnish:**
½ teaspoon grated lemon rind	grilled bacon rolls parsley

1 Put halibut into a dish, sprinkle with a little salt and leave to stand about 30 minutes.
2 Wash celery and cook in boiling salted water till tender. Drain, retain stock and chop celery.
3 Dice and fry bacon lightly.
4 Put fish into a greased casserole. Add any liquor from it to celery stock.
5 Mix bacon with celery, add parsley and lemon rind and pile on top of fish.
6 Cover and cook for about 30 minutes in a moderate oven (375°F. – Gas Mark 4).
7 Measure celery stock and make up to ½ pint with milk. Use this to make a sauce with butter and cornflour. Season carefully.
8 When fish is cooked, pour sauce over and garnish with bacon rolls and chopped parsley.

Halibut and bacon casserole

you will need for 4 servings:

2 large or 4 small steaks halibut	½ pint milk
½ oz. flour	2 Spanish onions
salt, pepper	½ oz. butter
1 teaspoon grated lemon rind	4 rashers bacon
	2–3 tomatoes

1 Coat fish with flour, seasoned with salt, pepper and lemon rind.
2 Put into a buttered casserole and cover with milk. Cover and cook in a slow oven (350°F. – Gas Mark 3) for about 10 minutes.
3 Peel onions, slice thickly and fry in butter till lightly browned.
4 After 10 minutes cooking, remove fish from oven. Cover with onion slices and arrange bacon on top.
5 Return to oven and cook for 15–20 minutes.
6 Garnish with tomato slices, heated through in the oven.

Casserole of halibut

you will need for 4 servings:

4 steaks halibut	Juice 2 lemons
4 strips salt pork	2 tablespoons oil
salt, pepper	
2 bay leaves	**to serve:**
few peppercorns	tomato sauce (see
1 teaspoon allspice	page 85)
2 cloves	

1 Arrange fish in a shallow casserole, put a strip of salt pork on each and sprinkle with salt and pepper.

2 Add all other ingredients and leave to marinate for 2 hours.
3 Cover and cook in a moderate oven (375°F. – Gas Mark 4) about 25 minutes.
Serve with tomato sauce.

Halibut with mushrooms

you will need for 4 servings:

1 small onion	1 tablespoon lemon juice
4 oz. mushrooms	
2 level tablespoons finely chopped parsley	4 tablespoons single cream
4 halibut steaks	3 tablespoons breadcrumbs
salt and pepper	2 oz. butter

1 Finely chop onion and mushrooms. Mix with parsley.
2 Arrange halibut steaks in a greased shallow ovenproof dish. Sprinkle steaks with salt, pepper and lemon juice.
3 Divide mushroom mixture in four and heap onto each halibut steak. Pour a spoonful of cream over each and sprinkle liberally with breadcrumbs.
4 Dot with butter and bake in the centre of a moderately hot oven (375°F. – Gas Mark 4) for 35 minutes.
5 Serve fish with liquid from the dish as a sauce.

Variation

Halibut au gratin – prepare as above omitting cream and butter. Make ½ pint cheese sauce, pour over fish. Sprinkle with breadcrumbs and grated cheese.

Casseroled herrings

you will need for 4 servings:

4 herrings	1 bay leaf
freshly ground black pepper, salt	1 can tomatoes
1 onion, peeled and sliced	chopped parsley

1 Bone and fillet herrings, sprinkle with pepper and salt and roll up.
2 Put into a casserole with onion, bay leaf and tomatoes.
3 Cover and cook in a moderate oven (375°F. – Gas Mark 4) about 30–40 minutes.
4 Sprinkle with chopped parsley before serving.

Herrings almondine

you will need for 4 servings:

4 fresh herrings	1 tablespoon melted butter
3 tablespoons white breadcrumbs	**for the sauce:**
1 dessertspoon finely chopped onion	1 oz. butter
	1 oz. flour
1 dessertspoon chopped capers	½ pint milk
1 teaspoon grated lemon rind	1 teaspoon made mustard
salt, pepper	salt, pepper
	2 oz. chopped blanched almonds

1 Prepare herrings, remove tails, split and remove backbones. *[continued*

2 Mix all ingredients for stuffing, spread a quarter on each herring and roll up. Put into a shallow greased casserole, cover and put into a moderate oven (375°F. – Gas Mark 4) for 30 minutes.
3 *To make the sauce.* Melt butter, add flour and cook for 1 minute. Add milk, stir till boiling and boil for 3 minutes.
4 Add mustard, seasoning and 1 oz. almonds.
5 Pour sauce over fish, sprinkle with remaining almonds.
6 Return to oven, and cook for 10 minutes, uncovered.

Herrings and tomato casserole

you will need for 4 servings:

4 fresh herrings	1 bay leaf
salt, pepper	1 4-oz. can tomatoes
1 small onion, peeled and chopped	1 small can or 1 small packet frozen peas

1 Prepare herrings, split and remove backbones and remove tails. Sprinkle with salt and pepper, roll up and put into a casserole.
2 Add onion and bay leaf, tomatoes and drained peas.
3 Cover and cook in a moderate oven (375°F. – Gas Mark 4) about 30 minutes.

Herring hot pot

you will need for 4 servings:

4 fresh herrings	2 bay leaves
1 onion, peeled and grated or minced	4 tablespoons vinegar
2 tablespoons capers	1 lb. potatoes, peeled and sliced
salt, pepper	

1 Prepare fish, remove heads and tails, split and remove roes if any. Flatten fish and remove backbones.
2 Cut each herring into four and put into a casserole with onion, capers, salt, pepper and bay leaves.
3 Add vinegar and enough water just to cover.
4 Cover with potato.
5 Put lid on casserole and cook in a slow oven (350°F. – Gas Mark 3) about 1½ hours.

Stuffed herring casserole

you will need for 6 servings:

6 herrings with soft roes	**stuffing:**
1 tablespoon dry mustard	1 small onion, peeled and finely chopped
½ oz. brown sugar	1 oz. butter
little vinegar	6 oz. white breadcrumbs
about ¼ pint dry white wine	2 tablespoons finely chopped parsley
	1 large egg
	salt, pepper

1 Prepare fish, remove roes, heads and tails and take out backbones.
2 *For stuffing:* cook onion in butter for a few minutes without browning. Add roes and continue cooking

for about 10 minutes. Add all other ingredients and mix well together.
3 Lay herrings flat, skin side downwards. Mix mustard and sugar to a paste with a little vinegar and spread over herrings.
4 Put a spoonful of stuffing on each fish and roll up.
5 Put into a greased casserole, cover with wine and sprinkle with salt and pepper.
6 Cover closely and cook in a slow oven (325°F. – Gas Mark 2) for about 2½ hours.

Note: This dish requires long slow cooking and if preferred the herrings may be served cold.

Normandy herrings

you will need for 4 servings:

4 herrings	1 teaspoon chopped chives
1 medium-sized onion, peeled and chopped very finely	½ teaspoon chopped thyme
1 large apple, peeled and finely chopped	salt, pepper
1 teaspoon chopped parsley	1 oz. butter
	2 tablespoons vinegar

1 Clean and split herrings and remove backbones. Put on a board, skin side downwards.
2 Mix onion, apple and herbs.
3 Sprinkle fish with salt and pepper, put a spoonful of onion mixture on each and roll up, head to tail.
4 Put into a buttered casserole, dot with butter and add vinegar.
5 Cover and cook in slow oven (350°F. – Gas Mark 3) about 45–50 minutes.

Soused herrings

you will need for 4 servings:

4 fresh herrings	⅛ pint tarragon vinegar
salt, freshly ground black pepper	¼ pint water
1 bay leaf	1 shallot, peeled and chopped finely
⅛ pint malt vinegar	

1 Clean and scale fish, split and remove backbones.
2 Sprinkle with salt and pepper and roll up.
3 Arrange in a casserole and add bay leaf.
4 Cover with vinegar and water and sprinkle shallot on top.
5 Cover and cook in a slow oven (350°F. – Gas Mark 3) about 45 minutes–1 hour.
Leave to cool in the liquor.

Yorkshire herring casserole

you will need for 4 servings:

4 fresh herrings	1 small onion or shallot, peeled and chopped
4 potatoes	salt, pepper
2 cooking apples, peeled and chopped	¼ pint water

1 Clean and split herrings, remove backbones and cut

into fillets. Cover with cold salted water and leave for 10–15 minutes.

2 Peel potatoes, put into cold salted water, bring to boiling point, boil for 5 minutes, then drain and slice.

3 Butter a casserole, put in a layer of potatoes, cover with some of the drained herring fillets and sprinkle with apple and onion. Add salt and pepper. Repeat till ingredients are used up, finishing with potato.

4 Add water, then cover and cook in a moderate oven (375°F. – Gas Mark 4) for about 1 hour.

Mackerel with basil

you will need for 4 servings:

4 mackerel	6 tablespoons red
salt, pepper	wine
3–4 tomatoes, peeled	½ teaspoon oregano
and sliced	2 teaspoons chopped
1 oz. butter	basil
1 oz. flour	2 tablespoons finely
½ pint chicken stock	chopped chives
(see page 85)	

1 Prepare mackerel and put into a buttered casserole. Sprinkle with salt and pepper and arrange tomato slices on top.

2 Melt butter, add flour and mix well. Add stock and red wine, stir till boiling and boil for 3 minutes. Add oregano and basil and pour over fish. Sprinkle with chives.

3 Cover and cook in a moderate oven (375°F. – Gas Mark 4) about 40 minutes.

Soused mackerel

you will need for 4 servings:

4 mackerel	1 onion, peeled and
4 cloves	sliced thinly
few chillis	salt
12 peppercorns	vinegar
1 bay leaf	
1 blade of mace	**for garnish:**
few parsley stalks	1 lemon
	2 gherkins

1 Clean and wash mackerel and remove heads and fins.

2 Put into a casserole with herbs and flavourings and sprinkle with a little salt.

3 Cover with equal parts of vinegar and water.

4 Cover and cook in a slow oven (350°F. – Gas Mark 3) for 1–1½ hours.

5 Move fish carefully into a serving dish and strain liquor over. Leave to get cold. Garnish with slices of lemon and gherkin.

Plaice and mushroom casserole

you will need for 4 servings:

1 large or 2 medium-	salt, pepper
sized plaice	8 oz. mushrooms,
1 oz. butter	sliced
1 oz. flour	1 lb. parboiled
milk	potatoes

1 Fillet the fish.

2 Put bones and skin into a pan. Cover with water, bring to boiling point and boil for 15 minutes, then strain.

3 Melt butter, add flour and cook for a few minutes without browning.

4 Make fish stock up to ¾ pint with milk. Add gradually to butter and flour mixture. Stir till boiling and boil for 3 minutes. Season carefully.

5 Put half the fish into a casserole, cover with mushrooms and add remaining fish. Pour sauce on top.

6 Slice potatoes and arrange neatly on top.

7 Cover and cook in a moderate oven (375°F. – Gas Mark 4) for about 1 hour.

8 When half cooked, remove casserole lid so potatoes will brown.

Fillets of sole in cider

you will need for 4 servings:

4 good-sized fillets of	⅛ pint fish stock (see
sole	page 67) or water
1 shallot, peeled and	¾ oz. butter
finely chopped	¾ oz. flour
1 bay leaf	1 teaspoon chopped
salt, pepper	parsley
⅛ pint cider	

1 Skin fillets and put into a shallow casserole with shallot and bay leaf.

2 Add salt and pepper, cider and water.

3 Cover and cook in a moderate oven (375°F. – Gas Mark 4) about 25 minutes.

4 Drain off liquid, make up to ½ pint with fish stock.

5 Melt butter, add flour and cook for a few minutes. Remove from the heat.

6 Add liquid and mix well. Return to heat, stir till boiling and boil for 3 minutes.

7 Add parsley, correct the seasoning and pour over fish.

Plaice and onion casserole

you will need for 4 servings:

1 oz. butter	⅛ pint cider or white
8 oz. onions, peeled	wine
and sliced thinly	⅛ pint water
1 teaspoon salt	lemon juice
1 teaspoon sugar	½ oz. butter
freshly ground pepper	1 teaspoon flour
1½ lb. plaice, filleted	chopped parsley

1 Heat butter, add onions, salt, sugar and pepper, cover and cook till onions are soft, but not brown. Transfer to a casserole.

2 Arrange fish on bed of onions, add wine, water and a good squeeze of lemon juice.

3 Cover and cook about 25 minutes in a slow oven (350°F. – Gas Mark 3).

4 Carefully drain off liquor and put in a small pan. Mix butter and flour and add gradually to fish liquor, stir till boiling.

5 Correct seasoning and pour over fish. Sprinkle with parsley.

Casserole of plaice

you will need for 2 servings:

1 large plaice
2 oz. butter
2 onions, peeled and sliced
1 tablespoon chopped parsley

salt, pepper
3 tomatoes, peeled and quartered
1 tablespoon vinegar
¼ pint fish stock (see page 67) or water

1 Fillet plaice and cut each fillet in half.
2 Heat butter, fry onions till lightly browned.
3 Put half onions into a casserole, arrange fish on top, and sprinkle with parsley, salt and pepper. Cover with remaining onions.
4 Add the tomatoes, vinegar and fish stock.
5 Cover and cook in a moderate oven (375°F. – Gas Mark 4) about 30–35 minutes.

Shrimps and rice casserole

you will need for 2 servings:

1 oz. butter
4 oz. mushrooms
3 oz. rice
2 5-oz. cans shrimps or 8 oz. frozen shrimps
6 oz. grated cheese
1 6-oz. can cream

1 tablespoon tomato ketchup
½ teaspoon Worcestershire sauce
salt, pepper
potato crisps

1 Heat butter, add sliced mushrooms and sauté till tender.
2 Cook rice in boiling salted water till just tender, then drain.
3 Mix rice, shrimps, cheese and mushrooms.
4 Add cream, ketchup, sauce and seasoning and mix.
5 Turn into a casserole and cook for 40 minutes in a slow oven (350°F. – Gas Mark 3).
6 Remove the lid for the last 5 minutes and sprinkle over crushed potato crisps.

Trout with tarragon

you will need for 4 servings:

4 trout
salt and pepper
2 oz. unsalted butter

2 tablespoons chopped tarragon
2 tablespoons water
1 lemon

1 Clean trout and season with salt and pepper.
2 Cream butter, adding chopped tarragon. Divide butter into four portions and place one inside each fish.
3 Place the fish in an ovenproof dish. Add water.
4 Cover dish tightly. Cook at 350°F. – Gas Mark 3 for about 40 minutes until fish is tender.
5 Squeeze lemon juice over and serve.

Variation

Trout with parsley butter – butter flavoured with lemon juice with chopped parsley added, may be used instead of the tarragon flavoured butter in this recipe. Omit lemon juice before serving.

Egg and shrimp savoury

you will need for 4 servings:

4 eggs, boiled for 6 minutes
1 oz. butter
1 tablespoon chopped parsley
1 teaspoon chopped chervil, if available

½ teaspoon French mustard
1 4-oz. can shrimps
1 small can evaporated milk
seasoning
1 tablespoon grated cheese

1 Peel and slice eggs.
2 Mix all ingredients together, except cheese, and season carefully.
3 Put into a greased casserole, sprinkle with cheese and cook in a moderately hot oven (375°F. – Gas Mark 4) for 20 minutes.

Turbot provençale

you will need for 4 servings:

1 lb. turbot
salt, pepper
1 shallot, peeled and chopped finely
4 tablespoons white wine
1 oz. butter

½ pint white sauce (see page 85)
1 egg yolk
1 teaspoon anchovy essence
Juice ¼ lemon

1 Wash fish and put into a shallow buttered casserole.
2 Sprinkle with pepper, salt, and shallot and add wine and a few pats butter. Cover and cook about 30 minutes in a slow oven (325°F. – Gas Mark 2).
3 Remove from oven and carefully pour off liquor from fish.
4 Add liquor to white sauce, add egg yolk, anchovy essence, lemon juice and remaining butter.
5 Correct seasoning, pour over fish and continue the cooking for 10 minutes.

Turbot Auvin

you will need for 4 servings:

4 oz. butter
2 onions, finely sliced
4 turbot steaks
salt and pepper
lemon juice

8 oz. button mushrooms
2 firm tomatoes
pinch castor sugar
¾ pint red wine

1 Melt butter and fry onions gently for 5 minutes, turning once in fat.
2 Place turbot steaks on onions, sprinkle with salt, pepper and lemon juice.
3 Fry steaks for 5 minutes, turn over and continue frying over low heat. Add mushrooms, spoon butter over.
4 Cut tomatoes in half, and place cut side up in casserole. Sprinkle cut surface with castor sugar.
5 Pour in wine. Cover and cook in a moderate oven (350°F. – Gas Mark 3) for 20 minutes.

Tuna casserole

you will need for 4 servings:

3 oz. macaroni
2 tablespoons oil
1 small onion, peeled and chopped
1 small green pepper, seeded and chopped
½ oz. flour
½ pint milk
1 can cream of chicken soup
1 can tuna
1 tablespoon pimento, chopped
salt, pepper
1 oz. almonds

1 Cook macaroni in boiling salted water till tender, then drain and chop.
2 Heat oil, add onion and green pepper and sauté until the onion is transparent.
3 Add flour and mix well, add milk and stir till boiling.
4 Add chicken soup, tuna and seasoning.
5 Put macaroni into a casserole, cover with fish mixture and sprinkle with almonds.
6 Cover and cook in a slow oven (350°F. – Gas Mark 3) for 20 minutes.
7 Remove lid and cook for 10 minutes.

Vegetable, Egg and Cheese Casseroles

Aubergines à la Provence

you will need for 4 servings:

2 aubergines
salt
8 oz. tomatoes, peeled and sliced
1 oz. butter
¼ small onion, finely chopped
2 tablespoons breadcrumbs
seasoning

1 Wipe the aubergines. Cut in half lengthways and remove the pulp (do not peel).
2 Sprinkle a little salt into the aubergine cases. Turn upside down and leave for 30 minutes. This is to remove excess water.
3 Fry the tomatoes in the butter with the onion and pulp from the aubergines.
4 Add the breadcrumbs and season with salt and pepper.
5 Drain and wipe the aubergine shells and pile in the filling.
6 Sprinkle a few more breadcrumbs over the filling and bake in a moderate oven (375°F. – Gas Mark 4), for about 20–30 minutes.

Aubergines with meat filling

you will need for 4 servings:

2 aubergines
2 tablespoons chopped cooked meat
1 tablespoon finely chopped onion
1 teaspoon chopped parsley
1 oz. mushrooms, chopped
salt, pepper
1 egg
breadcrumbs
½ oz. butter

1 Wipe aubergines. Cut in half lengthways and remove the pulp.
2 Sprinkle a little salt into aubergine cases. Turn upside down and leave for 30 minutes. This is to remove excess water.
3 Mix pulp with meat, onion, parsley and mushrooms and season well. Bind with beaten egg.
4 Drain and wipe aubergine cases and pile in filling. Arrange in a casserole.
5 Sprinkle with breadcrumbs, dot with butter and cook in a moderate oven (375°F. – Gas Mark 4) for 25–30 minutes.

Aubergines with rice and cheese

you will need for 4 servings:

2 aubergines
1 shallot, finely chopped
¼ small clove garlic
2 oz. grated cheese
2 oz. cooked rice
salt and pepper

1 Prepare the aubergines as described in the recipe for Aubergines à la Provence.
2 Put the pulp into a basin with the shallot, garlic, most of the cheese, rice, salt and pepper. Mix all well together.
3 Pile into the aubergine shells, sprinkle with the remaining cheese and bake in a moderate oven (375°F. – Gas Mark 4) for about 25 minutes.

Boston bean casserole

you will need for 4–6 servings:

4 oz. haricot beans
1½ lb. spare rib of pork
1 oz. cornflour
salt and pepper
2–3 tablespoons corn oil
2 sticks celery, diced
2 carrots, sliced
1 level tablespoon sugar
1 tablespoon golden syrup
¾ pint stock

1 Soak the beans overnight. Cut the pork into cubes and coat with the cornflour, seasoned with salt and pepper.
2 Heat the corn oil and sauté the meat. Add the celery and carrots and sauté a further minute.
3 Remove to a casserole and place the beans on top.
4 Add any remaining cornflour, the sugar, syrup and

stock to the pan. Bring to the boil stirring and pour over the ingredients in the casserole. Season to taste.

5 Cover and cook in a slow oven (325°F. – Gas Mark 2) for 1½–2 hours.

Bean and sausage crumble

you will need for 4 servings:

1 10½-oz. can cream of tomato soup	**for crumble topping:**
1 16-oz. can baked beans with sausages	3 oz. flour
	salt, pepper
	2 oz. margarine or butter
	2 oz. grated cheese

1 Mix soup with beans and sausages and put into a casserole.
2 Sieve flour and seasoning.
3 Rub in fat, add cheese and mix well.
4 Sprinkle mixture over beans and sausages.
5 Cook in a moderately hot oven (400°F. – Gas Mark 5) for 30 minutes.

Savoury bean casserole

you will need for 4 servings:

1 large onion	water
4 oz. fresh white breadcrumbs	salt, pepper
2 teaspoons sage	1 16-oz. can baked beans with pork

1 Peel and roughly chop onion.
2 Put in a pan with cold water to cover. Bring to the boil and simmer until tender. Drain.
3 Mix onion with breadcrumbs, sage and bind with a little water. Season lightly.
4 Place half the beans in a greased casserole.
5 Cover with half the stuffing. Add remaining beans and top with remaining stuffing.
6 Cover and cook in a moderate oven (375°F. – Gas Mark 4) for 15 minutes. Remove lid and finish cooking.

Hungarian hot pot

you will need for 4 servings:

1 lb. cooked potatoes	3 hard-boiled eggs, sliced
4 oz. rashers streaky bacon	1 tablespoon breadcrumbs
¼ pint yoghurt or sour milk	½ oz. butter

1 Slice the potatoes and put half of them into a greased fireproof dish.
2 Cover with half the bacon rashers and then pour on half the yoghurt and cover with half the eggs.
3 Continue in layers finishing with potatoes.
4 Sprinkle the top with breadcrumbs and dot with butter.
5 Put into a moderate oven (350°F. – Gas Mark 3) for about 25–30 minutes to brown.

Baked bean hot pot

you will need for 4 servings:

1½ lb. neck of lamb	1½ pints water
2 large onions	3 tomatoes
1½ lb. potatoes	1 16-oz. can baked beans
salt, pepper	

1 Wipe meat and place in a large casserole.
2 Slice onions and add to casserole.
3 Peel and slice potatoes, add to casserole.
4 Season with salt and pepper and add water.
5 Cover and cook in a slow oven (350°F. – Gas Mark 3) for 1 hour 30 minutes.
6 Skin tomatoes and cut into quarters. Add to hot pot with baked beans and cook for a further 10 minutes. Serve.

Stuffed cabbage (Dutch style)

you will need for 4 servings:

1 medium-sized cabbage	2 oz. rice
1 tablespoon corn oil	1 chicken stock cube
1 small onion, chopped	¾ pint boiling water
4 oz. mushrooms, chopped	4 tomatoes
2 oz. minced veal or pork	4 cooked rashers streaky bacon

1 Remove the leaves of the cabbage and cut away any tough stalk. Blanch the leaves in boiling water for 3–4 minutes.
2 Heat the corn oil and sauté the onion with the mushrooms and meat. Add the rice, stir very thoroughly.
3 Dissolve the chicken stock cube in the water and add ½ pint to the rice mixture. Cover and cook until the rice is tender and the stock absorbed.
4 Divide this mixture among eight blanched cabbage leaves and roll up.
5 Chop the remaining cabbage, place in a dish and arrange the stuffed leaves and the halved tomatoes on top.
6 Pour over the remaining stock and cover.
7 Cook in a moderately hot oven (375°F. – Gas Mark 4) for about 1 hour.
8 Cut up the bacon and sprinkle over the cabbage before serving.

Casserole of cabbage and potato

you will need for 4 servings:

1 lb. cooked cold potatoes	1 lb. cooked well-drained cabbage
4–6 oz. rashers streaky bacon	little milk
	1 oz. butter

1 Slice potatoes and put a layer into the bottom of a well greased fireproof dish.
2 Add some of the rashers, cut into pieces.
3 Cover with a layer of chopped cabbage.

4 Repeat layers until all ingredients are used up, finishing with potato.

5 Pour over enough milk to moisten.

6 Dot with butter and bake about 30 minutes in a moderate oven (375°F. – Gas Mark 4).

Potato casserole

you will need for 4–6 servings:

1½ lb. potatoes	1 egg
2 oz. butter	1 pint milk
salt and pepper	6 oz. grated cheese
nutmeg	

1 Scrub potatoes and peel if necessary. Cut into thin slices. Place in layers in well buttered casserole.

2 Sprinkle each layer with salt, pepper and nutmeg.

3 Beat the egg into the milk, adding 4 oz. cheese. Pour over the potatoes.

4 Sprinkle with remaining cheese and dot with remaining butter.

5 Cover and cook in a moderately hot oven (375°F. – Gas Mark 4) for 40 minutes.

Variations

With onion – proceed as above, using 1 lb. potatoes, 8 oz. Spanish onions.

Potato casserole with chives – proceed as above, omitting nutmeg. Sprinkle each layer of potato with finely chopped chives.

Swiss savoury potatoes

you will need for 4–6 servings:

2 lb. potatoes	1 pint chicken stock
2 onions	4 oz. Gruyère cheese
4 oz. unsalted butter	pepper

1 Scrub and peel potatoes if necessary. Cut into thin slices. Peel onions and slice thinly.

2 Fry onions in melted butter until lightly browned. Arrange layers of potatoes and onions with butter, in a casserole.

3 Pour stock over the vegetables, to three-quarter way up sides of dish. Top with Gruyère cheese, cut into slices.

4 Sprinkle with freshly ground pepper.

5 Bake in a moderately hot oven (375°F. – Gas Mark 4) for 45 minutes–1 hour until potatoes are tender.

Cheese casserole

you will need for 4 servings:

6–8 slices bread and butter	2 teaspoons Worcestershire sauce
2 eggs	4 oz. grated cheese
salt, pepper	1 pint milk
¼ teaspoon made mustard	1 tablespoon breadcrumbs
1 small onion, finely chopped	

1 Put bread and butter into a greased fireproof dish.

2 Beat eggs with seasonings, add onion, sauce and most of the cheese.

3 Stir in milk, then pour into a casserole and allow to stand for about 10 minutes.

4 Mix remaining cheese and breadcrumbs, sprinkle over top and cook in a slow oven (350°F. – Gas Mark 3) for 25–30 minutes until set.

Cheese and onion pudding

you will need for 4 servings:

8 oz. onions	4 oz. grated cheese
1 pint milk	salt, pepper
6 oz. fresh breadcrumbs	cayenne pepper
3 eggs	chopped parsley

1 Peel and slice onions thinly and cook slowly in milk until just tender.

2 Remove from heat, add breadcrumbs and beaten eggs and most of the cheese.

3 Season very carefully with salt, pepper and a little cayenne pepper.

4 Turn into a greased fireproof dish, sprinkle with the remaining cheese and bake about 20 minutes in a moderate oven (375°F. – Gas Mark 4). Serve sprinkled with parsley.

Cheese and tomato savoury

you will need for 4 servings:

1 oz. butter	½ teaspoon chopped fresh basil or 1 teaspoon chopped parsley
¾ oz. flour	
¼ pint canned tomato juice	
salt, cayenne pepper	2 eggs
½ teaspoon sugar	2 oz. grated cheese

1 Melt butter, add flour and mix well. Add tomato juice, stir till boiling, then boil for 3 minutes, stirring all the time.

2 Remove from heat, add seasoning, sugar and herb.

3 Separate eggs, beat yolks and add to sauce. Add cheese.

4 Beat egg whites stiffly and fold into mixture.

5 Pour into a buttered fireproof dish and bake in a moderate oven (350°F. – Gas Mark 3) for 25–30 minutes.

Cheese and vegetable casserole

you will need for 4 servings:

1 lb. parboiled potatoes	salt, pepper
2 medium-sized onions	4 tablespoons thick cream or milk
8 oz. Cheddar cheese	butter

1 Slice potatoes and put a layer into a well greased casserole.
2 Cover with half the onion, finely chopped, then add a layer of very thinly sliced cheese.
3 Repeat the layers, seasoning each.
4 Moisten with cream or milk and top with final layer of potatoes.
5 Dot with butter, cover and cook for about 20 minutes in a slow oven (350°F. – Gas Mark 3).
6 Remove lid and continue cooking until potatoes are brown.

Cheese macaroni and cauliflower

you will need for 4 servings:

8 oz. cauliflower, cooked	2½ oz. grated cheese
salt, pepper	1½ oz. butter
4 oz. macaroni, cooked	1½ oz. flour
	¾ pint milk
	1 egg, beaten

1 Break cauliflower into sprigs and put a layer in the bottom of a greased casserole.
2 Season lightly, then cover with a layer of macaroni and cheese.
3 Repeat these layers, finishing with cheese.
4 Melt butter, add flour and a little seasoning.
5 Gradually add milk and stir until boiling. Cool slightly and add egg.
6 Pour this over the vegetables and cook in a slow oven (350°F. – Gas Mark 3) for 30 minutes.

Variation

Cheese macaroni and tomato casserole – substitute tomatoes for cauliflower and add pinch lemon balm, chopped, if available.

Egg and celery casserole

you will need for 4 servings:

1½ oz. butter	4 oz. grated cheese
1 medium-sized onion, peeled and chopped	3–4 tablespoons cooked peas
1 can condensed celery soup	4 hard-boiled eggs
3 tablespoons milk	1 tablespoon breadcrumbs

1 Melt ¾ oz. butter, add onion and cook till soft but not coloured.
2 Add soup, milk and most of the cheese.
3 Stir over low heat for 3–4 minutes.
4 Add peas, chopped eggs; put in buttered fireproof dish.
5 Mix remaining cheese with breadcrumbs and sprinkle on top.
6 Dot with butter and put into a moderate oven (375°F. – Gas Mark 4) for 15–20 minutes.

Savoury egg casserole

you will need for 6 servings:

6 hard-boiled eggs	salt, pepper
4 oz. cooked ham	1 tablespoon breadcrumbs
2 oz. cooked tongue	½ oz. butter
¼ pint white sauce (see page 85)	triangles of toast for garnish
3 oz. grated cheese	

1 Slice eggs thickly and place in a casserole.
2 Chop ham and tongue and mix with white sauce.
3 Add 1½ oz. cheese, correct seasoning, then pour mixture over eggs.
4 Mix remaining cheese with breadcrumbs and sprinkle on top.
5 Dot with butter and brown in a hot oven (400°F. – Gas Mark 5) for about 20 minutes.
6 When cooked, arrange toast round the edge of the dish and serve with salad.

Egg and cheese casserole

you will need for 4 servings:

4 tomatoes	3 oz. grated Parmesan cheese
salt, pepper	1½ lb. creamed potatoes
sugar	
4 eggs	4 rashers streaky bacon
¾ pint thick white sauce (see page 85)	

1 Cut tomatoes into thick slices and sprinkle with salt, pepper and a little sugar.
2 Hard-boil eggs and slice them.
3 Make sauce. Stir in cheese and season to taste.
4 Pipe or spread potato round inside edge of a greased casserole.
5 Arrange eggs in the bottom of the dish.
6 Place tomatoes around the edge next to potato and pour in cheese sauce.
7 Arrange bacon rashers on top.
8 Cook, uncovered, in a moderate oven (375°F. – Gas Mark 4) for 30 minutes.

Egg and cheese supper savoury

you will need for 4 servings:

4 oz. macaroni	6 oz. grated cheese
2 oz. butter	1 small packet frozen peas (cooked) or
2 oz. flour	4 oz. cooked peas
1 pint milk	4–6 rashers lean bacon
salt, pepper	
4 hard-boiled eggs	

1 Break macaroni and cook in boiling salted water for 10–12 minutes. Drain well.
2 Make a white sauce with butter, flour and milk, boil for 3 minutes and season carefully.
3 Add chopped eggs, most of the cheese and the peas.
4 Pour into a buttered fireproof dish with the macaroni and cover with remaining cheese.
5 Roll bacon rashers and arrange on top.
6 Cook in a moderate oven (375°F. – Gas Mark 4) for about 30–35 minutes.

Casserole of red cabbage

you will need for 4–6 servings:

2 lb. red cabbage	4 oz. butter
salt and pepper	8 oz. eating apples
ground cinnamon	1 tablespoon castor
1 tablespoon vinegar	sugar

1 Remove damaged leaves. Cut cabbage in quarters, removing stalk and thick ribs. Wash well and chop coarsely.
2 Place cabbage in casserole, season with salt, pepper and a good pinch of cinnamon. Sprinkle with vinegar.
3 Cut the butter into small pieces, and mix through cabbage. Cover with greased paper or foil and lid.
4 Cook in a moderate oven (375°F. – Gas Mark 4) for 1 hour.
5 Peel apples, remove core and pips. Sprinkle with sugar.
6 Arrange pieces of apples, evenly through cabbage. Cook for a further 30 minutes.

Egg and ham charlotte

you will need for 4 servings:

3 oz. breadcrumbs	seasoning
8 oz. ham, chopped finely	4 hard-boiled eggs, sliced
½ pint cheese sauce (see page 85)	1 oz. butter

1 Grease a pie dish and sprinkle thickly with breadcrumbs.
2 Mix ham with sauce and correct seasoning.
3 Put half the mixture into pie dish and add 2 of the sliced hard-boiled eggs. Cover with remaining meat mixture and put remaining egg slices on top.
4 Cover with the rest of the breadcrumbs, dot with butter and cook about 20 minutes in a moderate oven (375°F. – Gas Mark 4).

Italian casserole

you will need for 4 servings:

2 oz. macaroni	1 pint boiling water
4 eggs	3 oz. grated cheese
1 oz. butter	4 oz. cooked ham or
1 oz. flour	bacon
1 chicken stock cube	buttered breadcrumbs

1 Cook macaroni until tender. Boil eggs for 10 minutes.
2 Melt butter, blend in flour and cook over a gentle heat for 3 minutes.
3 Dissolve stock cube in boiling water, gradually stir into flour and bring to the boil.
4 Reduce the heat and stir in the cheese.
5 Pour a little sauce into the bottom of a greased casserole, add half the macaroni, shelled eggs and roughly chopped ham. Cover with sauce, then with remaining macaroni.

6 Top with sauce and sprinkle with breadcrumbs.
7 Put into a slow oven (350°F. – Gas Mark 3) for 30 minutes until crumbs are well browned.

Savoury bake

you will need for 4 servings:

4 oz. fresh breadcrumbs	6 oz. grated cheese
½ pint milk	6 oz. bacon, chopped
3 eggs, separated	1 small onion, peeled
salt, pepper	and chopped finely
½ teaspoon dry mustard	8 oz. cooked vegetables (carrots, peas, beans, etc.)

1 Put breadcrumbs into a large basin, add milk and leave to stand about 15 minutes.
2 Stir in egg yolks and all the other ingredients, seasoning carefully.
3 Whip egg whites stiffly and fold into mixture.
4 Turn into a buttered fireproof dish and bake in a moderate oven (375°F. – Gas Mark 4) till well risen and golden brown, about 45–50 minutes.

Scalloped mushrooms

you will need for 4 servings:

1 oz. butter	8 oz. mushrooms
1 oz. cornflour	4 hard-boiled eggs
¾ pint milk	2 tomatoes
salt, pepper	breadcrumbs
nutmeg	chopped parsley

1 Make a sauce with butter, cornflour and milk and season with salt and pepper and pinch nutmeg.
2 Add thinly sliced mushrooms and simmer for about 10 minutes.
3 Put sliced eggs and peeled and sliced tomatoes into a fireproof dish.
4 Pour mushrooms and sauce over.
5 Sprinkle with breadcrumbs and put into a moderately hot oven (400°F. – Gas Mark 5) until brown and crisp, about 20 minutes.
6 Sprinkle with parsley before serving.

Marrow savoury

you will need for 4 servings:

cooked marrow ⎫ about	4 oz. grated cheese
cooked rice and ⎬ 8 oz.	salt, pepper
cooked potato ⎭ each	2 oz. butter

1 Mix diced marrow, rice and diced potato with about 1 oz. cheese. Season carefully.
2 Put layer into a greased fireproof dish, sprinkle with some of the remaining cheese and a few flakes of butter.
3 Add another layer of vegetables, sprinkle with cheese and continue until the ingredients are used up, finishing with cheese and flakes of butter.
4 Bake for about 20 minutes in a moderate oven (375°F. – Gas Mark 4).

Baked onion

you will need for 2 servings:

1 large Spanish onion	salt and pepper
olive oil	dry white wine

1 Peel onion, cut in half. Place cut side uppermost in a baking dish.
2 Sprinkle the surface of each with olive oil, salt and freshly ground black pepper.
3 Bake at 375°F. – Gas Mark 4 for 30 minutes.
4 Spoon dry white wine over the top of each onion and cook for a further 30 minutes.

Variation

Baked onion with cloves – cook as Baked onions, sticking 1 or 2 cloves in each onion half. Sprinkle castor sugar on surface of onion with oil, salt and pepper. Omit wine, but add 2–3 tablespoons water to baking dish.

Stuffed onion casserole

you will need for 4 servings:

4 medium-sized onions	salt, pepper
2 tablespoons breadcrumbs	¼ pint white sauce (see page 85)
3 oz. grated cheese	butter

1 Peel onions and parboil in boiling salted water.
2 Drain and cool a little, then remove some of the centres with a small teaspoon.
3 Chop centres and mix with breadcrumbs and 1½ oz. cheese. Season carefully.
4 Add a little of the white sauce to moisten if necessary.
5 Fill onions with this mixture, sprinkle with remaining cheese and dot with butter.
6 Put into a casserole dish and pour sauce around.
7 Cook in a moderate oven (375°F. – Gas Mark 4) for 30 minutes.

Variation

Potato and onion casserole – prepare as above until Step 5. When onions are stuffed, cover bottom of casserole with mashed potato, arrange onions on top, but do not add sauce. Serve this separately.

Celery au gratin

you will need for 4 servings:

2 heads celery	4 oz. grated cheese
¾ pint white sauce (see page 85)	4 oz. breadcrumbs
1 egg	salt, pepper, cayenne pepper

1 Prepare celery, remove the coarse outer sticks, wash thoroughly.
2 Put into boiling, salted water and cook gently for 8–10 minutes.
3 Drain well and cut into pieces.
4 While celery is cooking, make sauce, cool a little and add beaten egg.

5 Mix cheese and breadcrumbs and add seasoning.
6 Put a layer of celery into a buttered fireproof dish. Cover with sauce and sprinkle with cheese and breadcrumbs.
7 Continue in layers till ingredients are used up, finishing with cheese and breadcrumbs.
8 Dot with butter and brown under the grill.

Leeks au gratin

you will need for 4 servings:

7–8 leeks	½ teaspoon made mustard
2 oz. butter	lemon juice
2 oz. cornflour	2 tablespoons breadcrumbs
½ pint milk	little butter
4 oz. grated cheese, Gruyère or Cheddar	
salt, black pepper	

1 Prepare and wash leeks thoroughly, then cook in boiling salted water until just tender. Drain and put into a greased fireproof dish.
2 Melt butter, add cornflour and mix well. Cook for a few minutes, then remove from heat.
3 Add milk gradually, return to heat, stir until boiling and boil for 1 minute.
4 Add cheese and continue cooking until it has melted, then season carefully with salt, pepper, mustard and a squeeze of lemon juice.
5 Pour sauce over leeks, sprinkle with breadcrumbs and dot with butter.
6 Bake in a moderate oven (375°F. – Gas Mark 4) for 20–25 minutes until the top is brown.

Creamed beetroots

1 Wash small beetroots and place in a casserole with just sufficient water to cover.
2 Cook in a moderate oven (375°F. – Gas Mark 4) until beetroot begins to peel.
3 Rub off skins when beetroot is cooked.
4 Allow to become cold.
5 Serve with a sauce made by adding chopped chives and salt and pepper to single cream.

Alternative

Serve with a **mustard sauce:** stir 1 tablespoon French mustard into 5 fluid oz. sour cream. Pour over beetroot. Serve very cold.

Stuffed marrow No. 1

you will need for 4 servings:

1 medium-sized marrow	½ oz. flour
1 oz. butter	½ pint stock (see page 84) or water
1 medium-sized onion, peeled and chopped finely	1 small can sweet corn
1 lb. stewing beef, minced	3 tomatoes, peeled, chopped and seeded
	seasoning

1 Cut marrow in half lengthways and remove seeds.
2 Heat butter and fry onion till lightly browned.
3 Add beef and cook for 3–4 minutes.
4 Stir in flour.
5 Add stock, stir till boiling and simmer for 5 minutes.
6 Add drained corn and tomatoes, salt and pepper.
7 Divide this mixture between two halves of marrow and press well into cavities.
8 Put marrow together and secure with string.
9 Put into a greased casserole, cover tightly and cook for about 1 hour in a moderate oven (375°F.–Gas Mark 4).

Stuffed marrow No. 2

you will need for 4 servings:

1 medium-sized marrow	1 teaspoon chopped parsley
3 tablespoons chopped cooked meat	little grated lemon rind
3 tablespoons breadcrumbs	1 egg
	salt, pepper

1 Wash and peel marrow, cut lengthways and remove seeds.
2 Mix meat, breadcrumbs, parsley and lemon rind.
3 Bind with egg and season carefully.
4 Put filling on half the marrow and cover with other half.
5 Put into a greased casserole dish, cover and cook in a moderate oven (375°F.–Gas Mark 4) for 25–30 minutes.

Mushroom rice casserole

you will need for 4 servings:

4 oz. mushrooms, washed and chopped	½ pint beef stock (see page 84)
6 oz. rice, cooked	1 dessertspoon parsley, chopped
1 can condensed mushroom soup	seasoning
	grated cheese

1 Mix mushrooms and rice into soup, diluted stock.
2 Add parsley and seasoning.
3 Pour into a greased casserole and sprinkle generously with cheese.
4 Cook in a moderate oven (375°F.–Gas Mark 4) for 30 minutes.

Scalloped onions

you will need for 4 servings:

1¼ lb. onions	cayenne pepper
1 oz. butter	4 oz. cooked ham
1 oz. flour	2 oz. grated Parmesan or Gruyère cheese
½ pint milk	
salt, pepper	

1 Peel onions, slice thickly and cook in boiling salted water until tender.
2 Drain and put half into a greased fireproof dish.

3 Make a sauce with butter, flour and milk. Season well.
4 Pour some sauce over onions.
5 Cover with chopped ham and remaining onions and sauce.
6 Sprinkle with cheese and bake in a hot oven (425°F.– Gas Mark 7) for 20 minutes.

Savoy potatoes

you will need for 4 servings:

1½ lb. potatoes	1 small clove garlic
4 oz. Gruyère cheese	1 chicken stock cube
salt, pepper	¾ pint boiling water

1 Peel potatoes and cut into ¼-inch thick slices.
2 Slice cheese very thinly.
3 Arrange potatoes and cheese in layers in a buttered fireproof dish, sprinkling each layer with seasoning and a little crushed garlic. Finish with a potato layer.
4 Dissolve stock cube in boiling water and pour into the dish. It should not quite cover the top layer of potato.
5 Cook in a moderately hot oven (375°F.–Gas Mark 4) for about 45 minutes when the potatoes should be tender and nearly all the stock absorbed.
6 If liked, garnish with chopped parsley.

Potato and leek scallop

you will need for 4 servings:

1½ lb. potatoes	1 oz. butter
3–4 leeks	¾ pint well flavoured cheese sauce (see page 85)
4 rashers bacon	
salt, pepper	

1 Peel potatoes and slice fairly thickly. Put into boiling salted water and cook gently for 5 minutes, then drain.
2 Prepare leeks carefully, then slice.
3 Chop bacon and fry until crisp.
4 Arrange potatoes and leeks in alternate layers in a well buttered casserole. Sprinkle each layer with a little seasoning and crumbled bacon. Dot potato layers with butter.
5 Pour cheese sauce over.
6 Cover and cook about 1½ hours in a slow oven (325°F.–Gas Mark 2).

Variation

With cheese and breadcrumbs–if you prefer the dish browned, when cooked, sprinkle with a mixture of breadcrumbs and grated cheese and brown under the grill, or raise the casserole to the top of the oven and increase the heat.

Casseroled potatoes

Peel 2 lb. potatoes, cut into equal sized pieces. Place in an ovenproof dish. Pour over ¾ pint chicken or beef stock made using a stock cube. Bake at 375°F.– Gas Mark 4 for 1 hour until the potatoes are cooked. Sprinkle with freshly chopped parsley and serve.

Potatoes au gratin

you will need for 4 servings:

2 lb. potatoes	salt, pepper
2 oz. butter	1 egg, separated
1 oz. flour	4 oz. grated cheese
½ pint milk	pinch nutmeg

1 Parboil potatoes, drain and slice fairly thickly. Put into a buttered fireproof dish.
2 Make a sauce with 1 oz. butter, flour and milk.
3 Add seasoning, egg yolk, most of the cheese and nutmeg.
4 Beat egg whites stiffly and fold into sauce. Pour over potatoes.
5 Sprinkle remaining cheese on top, dot with remaining butter and bake in a moderately hot oven (400°F.– Gas Mark 5) for 40 minutes. Serve with salad.

Potato and egg supper savoury

you will need for 4 servings:

2 lb. potatoes	salt, pepper
4 oz. cream cheese	3–4 tablespoons milk
1 tablespoon finely chopped chives	½ oz. butter parsley sprigs
4 hard-boiled eggs, sliced	

1 Parboil potatoes, drain and slice.
2 Put a layer of potato into a buttered fireproof dish.
3 Mix cream cheese and chives and spread a thin layer over the potatoes. Cover with egg slices.
4 Continue in layers, season lightly and finish with a layer of potatoes.
5 Add milk, dot with butter and cook in a moderately hot oven (400°F.– Gas Mark 5) for about 20 minutes.
6 Serve hot, garnished with parsley sprigs.

Green pepper ragoût

you will need for 4 servings:

12 oz. sliced potatoes	3 tablespoons red wine
12 oz. chuck steak	salt, pepper
12 oz. onions	3 large sliced tomatoes
1 green pepper	breadcrumbs
2 oz. butter	
1 dessertspoon flour	
1 beef stock cube dissolved in ¼ pint water	

1 Butter a large casserole and line with potatoes.
2 Lay steak over this.
3 Slice onions and green pepper and brown in butter.
4 Stir in flour and add stock, wine and seasoning.
5 Pour over meat and cover with tomato. Sprinkle with breadcrumbs and dot with butter.
6 Cook in a cool oven (325°F.– Gas Mark 2) for 1 hour 40 minutes.
7 Raise heat to 350°F.– Gas Mark 3 for the last 20 minutes.

Braised celery

you will need for 4 servings:

2 firm heads celery	salt and pepper
2 onions	½ pint stock
1 carrot	gravy or sauce

1 Wash celery, removing green leaves. Cut each head in 2 or 4, depending on size. Blanch for 15 minutes in boiling water. Drain well.
2 Peel and slice onions and carrot, place in casserole. Sprinkle lightly with salt and pepper.
3 Arrange celery on top of other vegetables.
4 Pour in stock. Cover and cook in a moderate oven (375°F.– Gas Mark 4) for 1½ hours until celery is tender.
5 Drain well, place on serving dish and serve masked with a good gravy, tomato or white sauce.

Stuffed peppers

you will need for 4 servings:

4 good-sized peppers, red or green	1 4-oz. can shrimps
1 small onion	salt, pepper
1 oz. butter	lemon juice
4 oz. cooked rice	½ pint stock (see page 84)

1 Wash peppers, cut off tops and remove seeds and pith.
2 Peel and chop onion finely.
3 Fry in butter until soft.
4 Add rice and shrimps and season carefully, adding lemon juice to taste.
5 Pile into peppers and put into a greased casserole.
6 Pour stock over and cook for about 20 minutes in a slow oven (350°F.– Gas Mark 3).

Variations

Beef stuffed peppers–substitute 4 oz. minced beef for shrimps, omit lemon juice and add pinch cayenne pepper.

Veal and ham stuffed peppers–substitute 4 oz. mixed minced veal and ham for shrimps.

Lamb stuffed peppers – substitute 4 oz. lean minced lamb for shrimps, omit lemon.

Casserole of tomato and spaghetti

you will need for 4 servings:

8 oz. tomatoes, peeled and sliced	4 oz. cooked spaghetti
salt, pepper	3 oz. grated cheese
pinch of sugar	½ pint white sauce (see page 85)
pinch tarragon	1 egg

1 Put half the tomatoes into a greased fireproof dish. Add salt and pepper, a pinch of sugar and a pinch of chopped tarragon.
2 Cover with half the spaghetti and half the cheese.
3 Repeat layers finishing with cheese, reserving a little to sprinkle over the dish before baking.

4 Make white sauce, allow to cool a little, then add beaten egg.
5 Pour sauce over and sprinkle with remaining cheese.
6 Cook for about 25 minutes in a slow oven (325°F.– Gas Mark 2).

Casserole of vegetables

you will need:

1 medium aubergine	2 cloves garlic,
salt and pepper	crushed
1 medium onion	8 oz. tomatoes
olive or corn oil	8 oz. courgettes
	4 oz. mushrooms

1 Slice aubergine, sprinkle with salt and leave to 'sweat'.
2 Slice onion and fry gently in oil for 5 minutes in a flameproof dish.
3 Drain the aubergine, add to the onion and cook for a further 5 minutes.
4 Add the garlic, sliced tomatoes and courgettes, and cook for a further 5 minutes. Add the mushrooms, cover and cook in a moderate oven (375°F.– Gas Mark 4) for 30 minutes.
5 Season with salt and freshly ground black pepper.
6 Serve hot or cold.

Tomato and cheese casserole

you will need for 4 servings:

1 oz. butter	cayenne pepper
¾ oz. flour	½ teaspoon sugar
¼ pint canned tomato	2 eggs
juice	2 tablespoons grated
salt, pepper	cheese

1 Melt butter, add flour and mix. Add tomato juice, stir until boiling and cook for 3 minutes, stirring all the time.
2 Add seasonings and sugar.
3 Add egg yolks and cheese.
4 Beat egg whites until stiff and fold into the mixture.
5 Pour into a greased casserole and cook in a slow oven (350°F.– Gas Mark 3) for about 30 minutes.

Quick casserole

you will need for 4 servings:

2 oz. butter	grated nutmeg
6 small whole onions,	8 oz. spaghetti
parboiled	1 12-oz. can pork
4 sticks celery	luncheon meat
4 oz. mushrooms	2 large tomatoes,
2 teaspoons cornflour	sliced
salt, pepper	2 oz. grated cheese
1 pint milk	

1 Melt butter in a casserole.
2 Add onions, celery, cut in pieces and mushrooms.

Cover and simmer gently on top of the cooker for 20 minutes.
3 Sprinkle cornflour into casserole, add salt and pepper. Cook for 3 minutes, uncovered, over gentle heat.
4 Gradually stir in milk. Cook uncovered until thick and creamy, stirring throughout. Add nutmeg.
5 Cook spaghetti in boiling salted water until tender. Drain.
6 Cube and add luncheon meat and spaghetti to casserole, arrange tomatoes over the top, sprinkle with cheese and cook in a slow oven (350°F.– Gas Mark 3) for 10 minutes.

Variations

Gammon casserole – substitute 8 oz. cooked gammon, cubed, for luncheon meat and omit salt.
Beef casserole – substitute 8 oz. – 12 oz. corned beef for luncheon meat at step 6.

Tomato and mushroom casserole

you will need for 4 servings:

4 large firm tomatoes	1 dessertspoon
2 large mushrooms	breadcrumbs
1 oz. butter	salt, pepper
	4 eggs

1 Cut a slice from the stalk end of each tomato and carefully scoop out the pulp. Remove seeds and chop pulp.
2 Chop mushrooms and fry in butter.
3 Add tomato pulp, breadcrumbs, salt and pepper and mix well.
4 Put a little of this mixture into each tomato case.
5 Break eggs carefully and drop one into each tomato case.
6 Add a little salt and pepper and arrange stuffed cases in a casserole.
7 Cook in a slow oven (350°F.– Gas Mark 3) until eggs are lightly set, about 10–15 minutes.

Summer vegetable casserole

you will need for 4 servings:

1 lb. mixed cooked	3 tomatoes
vegetables (carrots,	1½ oz. flour
peas, beans,	½ pint milk
potatoes, etc., as	2 eggs
available)	salt, pepper
12 chives	pinch nutmeg
3½ oz. butter	4 oz. grated cheese

1 Dice carrots and potatoes, chop chives and sauté all the vegetables in 2 oz. butter.
2 Put into a buttered casserole and cover with slices of peeled tomatoes.
3 Heat remaining butter in a pan, add flour and mix well. Add milk and stir till boiling.
4 Separate eggs, stir yolks into sauce and add seasoning, nutmeg and cheese
5 Beat whites stiffly and fold into sauce.
6 Pour over vegetables; bake in a moderately hot oven (400°F.– Gas Mark 5) for 25 minutes.

Vegetable casserole

(Illustrated on the cover)

you will need for 3 servings:

1 lb. mixed vegetables	1 oz. butter
¼ pint chicken stock	chopped parsley
(see page 85)	

1 Prepare the vegetables, according to type, cutting root vegetables evenly.
2 Melt the butter in the casserole.
3 Add the vegetables, then toss them lightly so they are well coated with butter.
4 Add the stock and cover the casserole closely.
5 Cook in a cool oven (325°F.–Gas Mark 2) for 45 minutes–1 hour, until the vegetables are tender.
6 Remove casserole from oven, take lid off and sprinkle with parsley. Serve very hot.

Ratatouille

you will need for 6 servings:

2 onions	2 tablespoons olive oil
1 lb. courgettes	
1½ lb. tomatoes	2 cloves garlic
1¾ lb. aubergines	salt and pepper
2 peppers	

1 Peel and slice onions. Wash courgettes and cut into dice.
2 Skin tomatoes, remove seeds and chop roughly. Wash and slice aubergines.
3 Remove pith and seeds from peppers, cut into strips.
4 Fry the onions lightly in oil for 5 minutes.
5 Add remaining vegetables, whole cloves of garlic, a good pinch of salt and freshly ground pepper.
6 Cover and cook in a slow oven (325°F.–Gas Mark 3) for 30–40 minutes, until vegetables are tender and all liquid is absorbed.

Recipes for Reference

Stock

This is an important item in meat cookery. All cooks used to make their own and the stock pot was an essential part of the kitchen. Today it is being replaced by ready-prepared stocks made from cubes, by bone stocks made quickly in a pressure cooker and by vegetable stocks, or by mixing two of these (for example, vegetable stock and beef or chicken stock made from a cube).

Bone or white stock

Use any kind of bones, chopped and covered with cold water. For each pint of water, add 1 onion, 1 carrot and a *bouquet garni*. Boil for 2–3 hours, or pressure cook for 45 minutes. Strain and use or, when cold, store in a refrigerator.

Vegetable stock

Use any shredded vegetables or trimmings, add boiling water to come three-quarters of the way up the vegetables, and a few bacon rinds, *bouquet garni*, a few peppercorns and 1–2 cloves. Cover and boil for 20–30 minutes. Strain and use. The liquid from boiled vegetables should be saved for stock and also that from canned vegetables.

Brown stock No. 1

you will need:

1 lb. lean beef (shin or stewing beef)	1 carrot
1 knuckle of veal and veal bones (cut in pieces)	1 onion
	bouquet garni (see page 85)
2 oz. bacon rinds, blanched	1 clove garlic
1 dessertspoon meat dripping	salt
	2½ pints water

1 Put beef, cut in pieces, bones and bacon rinds in hot fat with sliced vegetables, *bouquet garni* and garlic and brown.
2 Add seasoning and 1 pint water and boil down to a jelly.
3 Add ½ pint water and boil down again.
4 Add remaining water and simmer for 1 hour.
5 Skim off fat and strain off liquid.

Note: If not using immediately, allow to cool and store in a refrigerator. The meat can be used in a hash or stew.

Brown stock No. 2

you will need:

1 or 2 beef stock cubes	1 pint boiling water

Dissolve cubes in water, stir thoroughly and use.

Chicken stock

you will need:

bones and carcass of
  1 chicken
1 onion, sliced

bouquet garni (see
  this page)
salt, pepper
water

1 Put bones and carcass, onion, *bouquet garni* and seasoning into a strong pan.
2 Add water to cover.
3 Simmer steadily, with the pan half covered, for 1 hour 30 minutes.* Strain and allow to cool.

*If using a pressure-cooker cook for 45 minutes at 15 lb pressure.

Veal stock

Substitute veal bones, with about ½ lb. veal if available, for children.

Bouquet garni

This is a bunch of fresh herbs used for flavouring and usually consists of 1 bay leaf, 1 sprig thyme and 1 sprig parsley, tied together with thread; sometimes a small piece of celery is included. If the piece of thread is long enough to hang over the edge of the pan, the *bouquet* is more easily removed before the food is served.

Mint jelly (for storing)

you will need:

3 lb. sugar
¼ pint pure lemon
  juice (bottled or
  fresh)

½ pint vinegar
2 oz. mint leaves,
  finely chopped

1 Dissolve sugar in the liquid, bring to boiling point and boil steadily until liquid begins to jell (about 30 minutes).
2 Stir in mint. Pour into warm bottles and seal.

Mint jelly (for immediate use)

you will need:

½ pint lemon or lime
  jelly

½–1 tablespoon mint,
  chopped

1 Make jelly with ⅓ less water than given in packet instructions.
2 Stir in mint. Allow to set. Use immediately.

Tomato purée

you will need:

2 lb. tomatoes,
  chopped
1 large or 2 small
  onions, chopped
1 tablespoon vinegar
1 oz. sugar

bouquet garni
  (see this page)
seasoning
water

1 Put all ingredients into a pan, bring to the boil and simmer gently for 20 minutes.
2 Rub through a fine sieve.
3 Pour into warmed bottles and seal.

Note: If you have an electric blender, use it at Step 2 instead of the sieve.

Tomato sauce

you will need:

2 onions
2 tablespoons oil
1 small can tomato
  paste

pinch thyme
1 pint water
salt, pepper

1 Peel and chop onions.
2 Heat oil and fry onions for about 5 minutes.
3 Add tomato paste and cook a few minutes longer, stirring all the time.
4 Add thyme and water, simmer gently for about 25 minutes. Season to taste.

White sauce

you will need:

1 oz. butter
1 oz. flour

½ pint milk
seasoning

1 Melt butter, stir in flour, using a wooden spoon.
2 Cook over a gentle heat for 3 minutes without browning, stirring all the time.
3 Remove from heat and gradually stir in half the milk, then stir hard until well blended.
4 Return to heat, cook slowly until sauce thickens, stirring all the time. Season.

Variations: Maître d'hôtel sauce–to ½ pint basic white sauce add 1 tablespoon finely chopped parsley and mix well. Add 2 teaspoons lemon juice and 2 tablespoons thin cream or evaporated milk. **Onion sauce**–to ½ pint white sauce (made from ½ milk and ½ liquid in which onions were cooked) add 2 chopped boiled onions and a few drops lemon juice. **Cheese sauce**–to ½ pint basic white sauce add 2–3 oz. grated cheese. **Egg sauce**–to ½ pint basic white sauce add 1 chopped hard-boiled egg. **Mustard sauce**–to ½ pint basic white sauce add 2 level teaspoons dry mustard mixed with 2 teaspoons vinegar. **Fennel sauce**–to ½ pint basic white sauce add 2 tablespoons chopped fennel. **Anchovy sauce**–to ½ pint basic white sauce add 2–3 teaspoons anchovy essence. **Parsley sauce**– to ½ pint basic white sauce add 1–2 tablespoons finely chopped parsley.

Pancakes

you will need for 4 servings:

4 oz. flour
pinch salt

1 egg
½ pint milk

1 Sift flour and salt.
2 Make a well in the centre, add egg and a little of the

milk, beat, then add extra milk to make a smooth thick batter.

3 Beat for 2–3 minutes. Cover and leave to stand for at least 30 minutes, longer if possible.
4 When required for use, stir in remaining milk.

To cook pancakes

1 Melt a little unsalted butter in a small frying pan. There should be only enough fat to give a thin film over the bottom of the pan.
2 Pour in enough batter to make a thick layer, tilting pan so the bottom is evenly covered.
3 Raise heat and move pan around while pancake is cooking and loosen it from the sides.
4 When set and lightly browned on the underside, turn with a palette knife or fish slice and brown the other side. Cooking time about 4–5 minutes.

Note: Pancakes will keep hot in the oven or over a pan of hot water, if stacked with greaseproof paper between each one.

Baked croûtons

Cut bread into small dice. Place on a baking tray at the bottom of the oven. Cook until lightly browned. It is sensible to cook croûtons while oven is on to cook a casserole. When golden and crisp, allow to become cold. Store in an airtight tin. Sprinkle into soup just before serving.

Forcemeat balls

you will need:

4 oz. breadcrumbs	grated lemon rind,
2 oz. suet, finely	lemon juice
chopped	1 teaspoon thyme
2 teaspoons chopped	salt, pepper
parsley	egg or milk to bind

1 Mix all ingredients and bind with egg or milk.
2 Shape into small balls, roll in flour and fry till brown.

Savoury dumplings

you will need:

4 oz. flour (with plain	good pinch salt
flour use ¾ teaspoon	and pepper
baking powder)	water to mix
2 oz. shredded suet	

1 Mix all ingredients, adding enough water to make a firm dough.
2 Lightly flour the hands and roll the dough into 8–12 small balls.
3 Add dumplings to casserole, stew or soup, when it is at simmering point – about 15–20 minutes before the end of the cooking time. Make sure the stew does not go off the boil while the dumplings are cooking.

Bacon dumplings – make as for savoury dumplings, adding 2 rashers of lightly fried bacon, cut into small pieces, 2 tablespoons chopped parsley and 1 tablespoon tomato ketchup. Serve with rabbit or bacon casseroles.

Cornish dumplings – make as for savoury dumplings, but cook in boiling salted water. Drain well and serve with boiled meat.

Mixed herb dumplings – make as for savoury dumplings, adding 1 teaspoon dried mixed herbs or 2 teaspoons freshly chopped mixed herbs.

Parsley dumplings – make as for savoury dumplings, adding 1 tablespoon finely chopped parsley. Make the dough into smaller balls and cook for 10 minutes only. Serve with chicken, rabbit or ham casseroles.

Sausage meat dumplings – make as for savoury dumplings, adding 4 oz. pork sausage meat and ½ teaspoon dried sage.

Kidney dumplings – skin and core 2 sheep's kidneys, cutting each into 4. Divide savoury dumpling dough into 8 balls and tuck 1 piece of kidney into each.

Veal forcemeat or stuffing

you will need:

1–2 oz. suet*	1 teaspoon dried
1 tablespoon chopped	thyme or savory
parsley	pinch mace
½ teaspoon grated	½ teaspoon salt
lemon rind	¼ teaspoon pepper
2 oz. fresh	1 beaten egg and
breadcrumbs	milk to mix

*Use only 1 oz. suet if stuffing fatty meat.

1 Grate the suet.
2 Wash, dry and chop parsley.
3 Finely grate lemon rind.
4 Mix ingredients, binding with beaten egg and some milk if necessary.

Sage and onion stuffing

you will need:

4 large onions	4 oz. fresh
10 fresh sage leaves	breadcrumbs
or 1 teaspoon dried	1 teaspoon salt
sage	¼ teaspoon pepper
1 oz. butter or	
margarine	

1 Peel onions and boil for 5 minutes.
2 If fresh sage leaves are used, dip in boiling water for a minute.
3 Chop or mince onion and sage leaves.
4 Melt fat and thoroughly mix all ingredients.

Suet pastry

you will need:

8 oz. flour (with plain flour use 1 teaspoon baking powder)

pinch salt
4 oz. shredded suet
water to mix

1 Sieve flour and salt (and baking powder, if used).
2 Add suet and mix in, using a long-bladed knife.
3 Stir in enough water to make a firm dough.
4 Knead lightly, roll out as required.

Buttered noodles

you will need for 4 servings:

8 oz. noodles
water

salt
2 oz. butter

1 Put noodles into boiling salted water and boil steadily until noodles are tender, about 20 minutes.
2 Drain and toss in melted butter. Serve.

Desserts

With a savoury casserole as your main dish, it is simple and economical to follow with a dessert which can be cooked in the oven at the same time.

Egg custard

you will need:

1 pint milk
3 eggs
2 tablespoons sugar

¼ teaspoon vanilla essence
nutmeg

1 Heat the milk until it is just coming to the boil. Meanwhile lightly whisk the eggs and sugar together.
2 Pour the milk on to the eggs, stirring. Add vanilla essence.
3 Strain into a 1½ pint buttered ovenproof dish. Sprinkle surface with grated nutmeg.
4 Place dish in a roasting tin containing cold water, to come 1 inch up side of dish.
5 Bake in the centre of a moderate oven (375°F.–Gas Mark 4) for 40–45 minutes.

Variations

Using 2 eggs–this custard will set, if made with 2 eggs. However, it is firmer made with 3 eggs.
Individual or cup custards–make as before, pouring mixture into four individual dishes which have been rubbed inside with buttered paper. Bake for about 25 minutes in a slow oven (325°F.–Gas Mark 2).
Coconut custard pudding–make as Egg custard, omitting nutmeg. When custard is set, spread lightly with warmed jam. Sprinkle with desiccated coconut and serve.
Cup custard de luxe–prepare individual baked custards as described previously. Just before serving, have grill very hot. Top each custard with sour cream, sprinkle thickly with brown sugar and flash under the hot grill. The custard may be hot or cold. It is important that the dishes are flameproof.

Apple custard

you will need for 4 servings:

2 small sponge cakes
1 large apple baked and sieved or 1 small can apple purée

1 egg
1 tablespoon sugar
¼ pint milk

1 Crumble the sponge cakes into a small pie dish.
2 Cover with sieved apple pulp.
3 Beat egg with sugar.
4 Warm the milk and pour over the egg mixture.
5 Strain over apple and leave to stand about 10 minutes.
6 Bake in a slow oven (350°F.–Gas Mark 3) until set and lightly browned, about 40 minutes.
7 Serve either hot or cold, with extra cooked apple, if liked.

Caramel custard

you will need for 4 servings:

4½ oz. sugar
¼ pint water
¼ pint milk

¼ pint thin cream
4 eggs
vanilla essence

1 Put 4 oz. sugar into a small strong saucepan with water. Heat till sugar has dissolved, then boil until it caramelizes.
2 Pour caramel into a 5-inch cake tin or charlotte mould and turn it round until the bottom and sides of the tin are evenly coated.
3 Heat milk, cream and remaining sugar and pour over beaten eggs.
4 Add a few drops of vanilla essence and strain into the prepared tin. Cover with greaseproof paper or aluminium foil.
5 Stand tin in a container with cold water coming about ¼ of the way up the tin and cook for about 45 minutes in a fairly slow oven (350°F.–Gas Mark 3). Then

reduce the heat to 290°F.–Gas Mark 1 for a further 40–45 minutes.

To steam–caramel custard may be steamed. Allow water to simmer only and it will take about 1 hour to cook. If the custard is to be served cold, leave in the tin until cold before turning out.

Sultana rice pudding

you will need:

1½ oz. short grain rice	1 pint milk
2 oz. sugar	nut of butter
2 oz. cleaned sultanas	grated nutmeg

1 Put rice, sugar and sultanas into a buttered 1½ pint pie dish. Add the milk and butter. Sprinkle grated nutmeg over the surface.
2 Bake in a slow oven (325°F.–Gas Mark 2) for 2½–3 hours until set.
3 Stir the rice every ½ hour for the first 2 hours to prevent a skin forming.
4 Serve hot or cold.

Variations

Chocolate rice pudding–omit sultanas and nutmeg. Heat the milk, adding 3 oz. plain chocolate. Pour the chocolate flavoured milk over the rice and sugar and cook as above.

St. Clements rice pudding–omit nutmeg and sultanas. Add thinly pared rind of ½ a lemon, plus 1 oz. mixed, chopped peel, to rice. Proceed as above.

With currants–2 oz. currants may be used instead of sultanas.

Baked trifle

you will need:

1 Swiss roll, jam filled	2 eggs
1 can peach slices	5–6 tablespoons
2 level tablespoons	sugar
custard powder	1 pint milk

1 Slice the Swiss roll and arrange it on the bottom and around the sides of a 1½ pint buttered ovenproof dish.
2 Moisten slices with a little of the peach juice (or sherry if preferred).
3 Drain the peaches and place on the slices of Swiss roll in the bottom of the dish.
4 Blend the custard powder with the yolks of the two eggs, 2 tablespoons of the sugar and a little of the milk. Bring the rest of the milk to the boil.
5 Remove from the heat and pour onto the custard mixture, stirring all the time. Pour the custard into the lined dish.
6 Top with meringue made with the two egg whites and remaining sugar. Bake for 30 minutes in the middle of a moderate oven (375°F.–Gas Mark 4). Serve hot.

Variation

Hot chocolate trifle–make as above using canned pears, and add 2 oz. plain chocolate to the milk. Allow the chocolate to dissolve in the milk before making the custard.

Bread and butter pudding

you will need:

4 thin slices buttered bread	2 eggs
1½ oz. dried fruit	1 pint milk
1½ oz. sugar	grated nutmeg, optional

1 Cut slices of bread into quarters or small squares. Arrange buttered side up in a buttered 2 pint oven-proof dish.
2 Sprinkle the dried fruit and sugar between the layers of bread.
3 Beat the eggs lightly, meanwhile heat the milk until almost boiling. Pour the milk on to the eggs, stirring well.
4 Pour over bread and allow to stand for 10 minutes. Sprinkle with nutmeg.
5 Bake in the middle of a moderate oven (375°F.–Gas Mark 4) for 45 minutes, until set and lightly browned.

Cheese bread and butter pudding

you will need for 4 servings:

4 slices buttered bread	1 egg
3 oz. grated cheese	salt, pepper
½ pint milk	

1 Butter a fireproof dish and arrange alternate layers of bread and cheese, finish with bread.
2 Heat milk, pour over beaten egg and add seasoning.
3 Strain into dish.
4 Bake in a fairly slow oven (350°F.–Gas Mark 3) until firm and lightly browned, about 45 minutes.

Ginger Betty

you will need:

2 lb. cooking apples	2 tablespoons water
juice of 1 lemon	8 oz. ginger biscuits
3 oz. brown sugar	2 oz. butter

1 Peel, core and thinly slice apples.
2 Place in a shallow ovenproof dish, sprinkle with lemon juice, brown sugar and water.
3 Cover and bake at 375°F.–Gas Mark 4 till apples are tender, about 30 minutes.
4 Meanwhile crush biscuits and stir in melted butter. Cover apples with this mixture and bake for a further 15 minutes.
5 Serve hot with custard or cream.

Apricot almond crumble

you will need:

1 large can apricots	2 oz. brown sugar
4 oz. flour	2 oz. butter
1 oz. cornflour	¼ teaspoon almond essence
2 oz. ground almonds	

1 Drain apricots and place them in an ovenproof dish, with 6 tablespoons of the juice.
2 Mix dry ingredients together. Rub in butter, adding

almond essence until mixture resembles fine bread-crumbs.
3 Sprinkle crumble mixture over fruit.
4 Bake at 350°F. – Gas Mark 3 for 40 minutes.
5 Serve hot with cream.

Variations

Pear crumble – follow the Apricot recipe using canned or fresh pears, adding a pinch of ginger instead of almond essence, if liked.
Apple crumble – apples may also be used, flavour with cinnamon instead of almond essence.

Peaches – Spanish style

you will need:

1 1-lb. 4 oz. can peach halves	2 tablespoons blanched, chopped almonds
3 tablespoons sweet sherry	cream or ice cream

1 Drain off half the juice from the peaches.
2 Place peaches, remaining juice and sherry in an oven-proof dish.
3 Cover and cook at 350°F. – Gas Mark 3 for 30 minutes.
4 Serve hot with cream or ice cream sprinkled with almonds.

Variation

With apricots – canned apricots may be used instead of peaches; cook for 20 minutes.

Peaches – Escoffier

you will need:

1 1-lb. 13 oz. can peach halves	2 tablespoons dry sherry
4 tablespoons raspberry jam	flaked toasted almonds

1 Drain juice from peaches, place in an ovenproof dish.
2 Warm raspberry jam with sherry over a gentle heat. Pour over peaches.
3 Cover and bake at 325°F. – Gas Mark 2 for 30 minutes.
4 Sprinkle with almonds and serve.

Variations

Pears Abrocotine – make as before using canned pears and apricot jam.
With apricots – apricots, canned, may be used instead of peaches. Use sweet sherry.

Apple conde

you will need for 4 servings:

4 oz. rice	sugar
1½ pints milk	1 oz. butter
1 lb. apples	2 eggs, separated

1 Wash rice and cook slowly in milk.
2 Peel and core apples and cook with a little water and sugar to taste.
3 Put stewed apple into a buttered fireproof dish.

4 When rice is tender, remove from heat and add butter and egg yolks.
5 Spread rice over apples.
6 Beat egg whites stiffly, beat in 2 tablespoons sugar and pile on top of the rice.
7 Bake in a slow oven (350°F. – Gas Mark 3) for about 25–30 minutes, till crisp and golden brown.

Apple meringue

you will need for 4 servings:

1 lb. cooking apples	1 strip lemon peel
¼ pint water	2 oz. semolina
4 oz. sugar	2 eggs, separated

1 Peel apples, put into pan with water, 2 oz. sugar and lemon peel, cook till tender.
2 Remove peel and beat well or, preferably, rub through a sieve.
3 Measure quantity of purée and make up to 1¼ pints with water or fruit juice.
4 Return to pan, add semolina and cook gently until semolina is soft and transparent.
5 Remove from heat, add beaten egg yolks, a little extra sugar if required and pour into a fireproof dish.
6 Beat egg whites stiffly, fold in remaining sugar and pile on top of pudding.
7 Put into a very moderate oven (350°F. – Gas Mark 3) for about 20 minutes or until meringue is set and lightly browned.

Chocolate custard

you will need for 4 servings:

1 tablespoon grated chocolate	¼ oz. sugar
¼ pint milk	1 egg
	vanilla essence

1 Heat chocolate with milk and sugar until chocolate has melted and milk is just below boiling point.
2 Beat egg and add chocolate milk slowly, stirring all the time.
3 Add a few drops of vanilla essence and strain into a small buttered fireproof dish.
4 Stand in a dish of cold water and cook for about 40 minutes in a slow oven (325°F. – Gas Mark 2) until the custard has set.

Coffee pudding

you will need for 4 servings:

1 pint milk	¼ pint strong coffee
4 eggs	pinch salt
3 oz. sugar	extra sugar

1 Scald milk, then leave to cool a little.
2 Beat eggs and sugar together, add milk, coffee and salt.
3 Strain into a fireproof dish. Stand dish in a baking tin and half fill the tin with warm water.
4 Bake in a slow oven for about 40 minutes (325°F. – Gas Mark 2) until the pudding is firm.
5 Leave to cool and sprinkle with sugar before serving.

Lemon pudding

you will need for 4 servings:

2 eggs, separated
6 oz. sugar
1 lemon
1 oz. cornflour
pinch salt
½ pint milk

1 Beat yolks with sugar and grated lemon rind.
2 Mix cornflour and salt smoothly with lemon juice and add to eggs and sugar.
3 Heat milk almost to boiling point, pour on to egg mixture and stir well.
4 Beat egg whites stiffly and fold into mixture.
5 Pour into buttered custard cups or individual fire-proof dishes. Stand in a baking tin of warm water and bake in a moderate oven (375°F. – Gas Mark 4) for 40–45 minutes. Serve cold.

Queen of puddings

you will need for 4 servings:

½ pint milk
2 oz. cake crumbs or
   breadcrumbs
½ oz. butter
1½ oz. castor sugar
2 eggs
1 tablespoon jam or
   jelly

1 Heat milk and pour over the crumbs.
2 Add butter and ½ oz. sugar and leave for about ½ hour.
3 Beat 1 whole egg and 1 egg yolk and stir into milk and breadcrumbs, then pour into a buttered pie dish.
4 Bake for 30 minutes in a moderate oven (375°F. – Gas Mark 4).
5 When set, spread carefully with jam or jelly.
6 Beat remaining egg white till frothy. Add remaining sugar and beat till stiff.
7 Pile on top of the pudding and return to a slow oven (325°F. – Gas Mark 2) for about 30 minutes or until the meringue is lightly coloured.

Rice meringue

you will need for 4 servings:

1½ oz. rice
1 pint milk
1 lemon
2 eggs, separated
3 tablespoons sugar
jam

1 Wash rice and put into a double pan with milk and thinly pared lemon peel. Cook very gently until rice is soft and creamy (about 1½ hours).
2 Remove from heat, discard lemon peel and allow rice to cool a little.
3 Add lemon juice, egg yolks and 1 tablespoon sugar.
4 Put a layer of jam in the bottom of a fireproof dish and cover with rice mixture.
5 Whisk egg whites with a pinch of salt until frothy. Add remaining sugar and beat until very stiff.
6 Pile meringue on top of pudding, sprinkle with sugar and put into a very moderate oven for about 30 minutes (350°F. – Gas Mark 3) until the meringue is crisp and lightly browned.

Vanilla cream pudding

you will need for 4 servings:

1¼ oz. cornflour
1 oz. sugar
1 pint milk
1 teaspoon vanilla
   essence
3 eggs
2 tablespoons cream
2 tablespoons
   apricot jam

1 Mix cornflour and sugar smoothly with a little cold milk. Put the rest on to heat.
2 Add mixed cornflour, stir till boiling and boil for 3 minutes. Remove from heat and add vanilla essence.
3 Separate eggs, beat yolks with cream and stir into pudding.
4 Fold in stiffly beaten egg whites.
5 Spread jam over the bottom of a fireproof dish and pour in the pudding.
6 Bake for about 20 minutes in a moderate oven (375°F. – Gas Mark 4).

Index

Accompaniments to casseroles 3
American casserole 26
Anchovy sauce 85
Angelino's beef casserole 6
Apple:
  Apple conde 89
  Apple crumble 89
  Apple custard 87
  Apple meringue 89
  Bacon and apple casserole 43
Apricot:
  Apricot almond crumble 88
  Apricots Spanish style 89
Aubergine:
  Aubergines with meat filling 75
  Aubergines à la Provence 75
  Aubergines with rice and cheese 75
Auto-timer cookers, making best use
  of 4

Bacon casseroles:
  Bacon and apple casserole 43
  Bacon dumplings 86
  Bacon and bean casserole 43
  Bacon and potato casserole 43
  Bacon and sausage casserole 43
  Casserole of beef, bacon and
    mushrooms 18
  Casseroled hock 42
  Haddock and bacon casserole 69
  Halibut and bacon casserole 71
  Haricot beans with bacon 42
  Liver and bacon casserole 45
  Murphy's casserole 40
  Peperoni casserole 43
  Steak and bacon casserole 18
  Veal and bacon casserole 23
  Winter casserole 41
Baked bean hot pot 76
Barley lamb casserole 26
Bean and sausage crumble 76
Beef casseroles:
  Angelino's beef casserole 6
  Beef bourgeoise 17
  Beef bourguignon 9
  Beef casserole 83
  Beef cobbler 7
  Beef au gratin 7
  Beef à la grecque 6
  Beef and mushroom casserole 7
  Beef Neapolitan 8
  Beef and onion casserole 6
  Beef olives 8
  Beef and orange casserole 6, 7
  Beef paprika 17
  Beef and potato hot pot 8

Beef provençale 8, 21
Beef in red wine 17
Beef and sausage casserole 6
Beef and spaghetti casserole 18
Beef stew 18
Beef stuffed peppers 82
Beef suprême 9
Beef and tomato casserole 7
Braised beef bourguignon 9
Braised beef casserole 9
Braised silverside of beef 9
Brown stew 18
Burgundian meat balls 10
Californian beef casserole 10
Canadian steak 10
Cantonese beef with ginger rice 10
Carbonade of beef 19
Casserole of beef, bacon and
  mushrooms 18
Casserole Napoli 20
Casseroled beef Palermo 11
Casseroled beef with peppers 11
Casseroled roast beef 19
Chilli con carne 12
Chuck wagon casserole 19
Crusty beef stew 11
Daube of beef 19
Dolmas 12
Exeter stew 12
Farmhouse pot roast 12
Flemish hot pot 13
Goulash 13
Haricot beef 13
Hungarian beef 14
Hungarian herb stew 14
Huntsman's steak 13
Italian beef stew 13
Jugged beef 14
Meat balls with noodles 14
Mexican minced beef 14
Minced beef Marguerite 15
Mock duck 15
Moussaka 15
Old English beef hot pot 16
Priest's goulash 20
Provençal stew 15
Prune hot pot 15
Ragoût of beef 16
Russian beef casserole 16
Simple stroganoff 20
Spiced beef casserole 17
Steak and bacon casserole 18
Steak and kidney casserole 16
Stewed steak and onions 20
Stuffed steak 11
Swedish casserole 10

Sweet-sour meat balls 20
Tyrolean beef casserole 21
Beetroot:
  Creamed beetroots 80
Belly of pork casserole 38
Bitter sweet lamb casserole 27
Bone or white stock 84
Boston bean casserole 75
Bouquet garni 85
Braised beef bourguignon 9
Braised beef casserole 9
Braised celery 82
Braised chicken in casserole 57
Braised grouse 61
Braised ham 41
Braised lamb and green peas 27
Braised lamb with vegetables 35
Braised liver 46
Braised liver and onions 44
Braised mutton ménagère 27
Braised oxtail 47
Braised pigeons 61
Braised sheeps' tongues 48
Braised silverside of beef 9
Braised veal 21
Bread and butter pudding 88

Brill:
  Casserole of brill 65
Brown stew 18
Brown stock 84
Burgundian meat balls 10
Buttered noodles 87

Cabbage:
  Casserole of cabbage and potato
    76
  Casserole of red cabbage 79
  Stuffed cabbage (Dutch style) 76
Californian beef casserole 10
Canadian steak 10
Canterbury casserole 28
Cantonese beef with ginger rice 10
Cantonese chicken 50
Caramel custard 87
Carbonade of beef 19
Casseroles, basic method of
  making 2-4
Casseroles, mock 3
Cauliflower:
  Cheese, macaroni and cauliflower
    78
Celery:
  Braised celery 82

Celery au gratin 80
Egg and celery casserole 78
Cheese:
  Cheese bread and butter
    pudding 88
  Cheese casserole 77
  Cheese, macaroni and cauliflower
    78
  Cheese, macaroni and tomato
    casserole 78
  Cheese and onion pudding 77
  Cheese sauce 85
  Cheese and tomato savoury 77
  Cheese and vegetable casserole 77
  Egg and cheese casserole 78
  Egg and cheese supper savoury
    78
  Tomato and cheese casserole 83
Chestnut chicken 58
Chicken:
  To make chicken stock 85
  Braised chicken in casserole 57
  Cantonese chicken 50
  Casserole of chicken with yoghurt
    50
  Chestnut chicken 58
  Chicken bonne femme 57
  Chicken cacciatore 51
  Chicken Catalan 57
  Chicken chasseur 54
  Chicken en cocotte 51
  Chicken Curaçao 54
  Chicken with ham and tomatoes 59
  Chicken Hawaiian 52
  Chicken de luxe 53
  Chicken de luxe with
    mushrooms 53
  Chicken and macaroni 57
  Chicken Marengo 51
  Chicken and mushroom casserole
    51
  Chicken with mushrooms and
    spaghetti 59
  Chicken niçoise 51
  Chicken with olives 58
  Chicken Palermo 52
  Chicken paprika 52, 53
  Chicken with peaches and pilaff 53
  Chicken with peas and rice 58
  Chicken peperoni 52
  Chicken pietro 59
  Chicken and pineapple casserole
    52
  Chicken and potato casserole 53
  Chicken Salvatore 58
  Chicken sauté Estragon 53
  Chicken tarragon 59
  Chicken and tomato supper dish 59
  Chicken vilma 59
  Chicken in white wine 58

Chinese chicken with cream
  sauce 55
Chinese style chicken 54
Country chicken 50
Curried chicken 54
Farmhouse casserole 56
Hacienda chicken 54
Honeyed chicken with orange 52
Honeyed chicken with orange and
  almonds 52
Hunter's chicken 55
Italian chicken casserole 55
Mediterranean chicken 55
Moroccan chicken 55
Normandy casserole of chicken 56
Paella 56
Plantation casserole 56
Spanish style chicken 60
Stuffed chicken casserole 56
Viennese chicken 57
Chilli con carne 12
Chinese chicken with cream sauce
  55
Chinese style chicken 54
Chocolate custard 89
Chocolate rice pudding 88
Chocolate trifle, hot 88
Chuck wagon casserole 19
Coconut custard pudding 87
Cod:
  Casserole of cod with prawns 65
  Casseroled cod cutlets 65
  Cod Bolognese 65
  Cod and macaroni casserole 66
  Cod Portugaise 66
  Cod steaks Valencia 66
  Cod with wine sauce 65
Coffee pudding 89
Company casserole 40
Cornish dumplings 86
Country casserole 28
Country chicken 50
Country style liver 45
Creamed beetroots 80
Creamy lamb casserole 28
Croûtons 86
Crumble top fish casserole 66
Crusty beef stew 11
Cup custards 87
Curried dishes:
  Curried chicken 54
  Curried mutton 28
  Lamb curry 31
  Lamb curry with yoghurt 31
  Daube of beef 19
Desserts:
  Apple conde 89
  Apple crumble 89
  Apple custard 87
  Apple meringue 89

Apricot almond crumble 88
Apricots Spanish style 89
Baked trifle 88
Bread and butter pudding 88
Caramel custard 87
Cheese bread and butter
  pudding 88
Chocolate custard 89
Chocolate rice pudding 88
Coconut custard pudding 87
Coffee pudding 89
Cup custards 87
Egg custard 87
Ginger Betty 88
Hot chocolate trifle 88
Lemon pudding 90
Peaches Escoffier 89
Peaches Spanish style 89
Pear crumble 89
Pears Abrocotine 89
Queen of puddings 90
Rice meringue 90
St Clement's rice pudding 88
Sultana rice pudding 88
Vanilla cream pudding 90
Devonshire casserole 29
Devonshire pork chops 36
Dolmas 12
Dumplings:
  Bacon dumplings 86
  Cornish dumplings 86
  Kidney dumplings 86
  Mixed herb dumplings 86
  Parsley dumplings 86
  Sausage meat dumplings 86
  Savoury dumplings 86

Eel:
  Casseroled eels 66
Egg dishes:
  Egg and celery casserole 78
  Egg and cheese casserole 78
  Egg and cheese supper savoury 78
  Egg custards 87
  Egg and ham charlotte 79
  Egg sauce 85
  Egg and shrimp savoury 74
  Ham, egg and sweet corn
    casserole 40
  Potato and egg supper savoury 82
  Savoury egg casserole 78
Exeter stew 12

Farmhouse casserole 56
Farmhouse pot roast 12
Fennel sauce 85
Fish casseroles:
  To make fish stock 67
  Casserole of brill 65
  Casserole of cod with prawns 65

Casserole of fish   68
Casserole of halibut   71
Casserole of plaice   74
Casseroled cod cutlets   65
Casseroled eels   66
Casseroled herrings   71
Cod Bolognese   65
Cod and macaroni casserole   66
Cod Portugaise   66
Cod steaks Valencia   66
Cod with wine sauce   65
Cold terrine of fish   67
Crumble top fish casserole   66
Egg and shrimp savoury   74
Fillets of sole in cider   73
Fish custard   67
Fish Espagnole   67
Fish hot pot   67
Fish maître d'hôtel   68
Fish Portugaise   67
Fresh haddock with cider   70
Haddock and bacon casserole   69
Haddock casserole   69
Haddock Crécy   69
Haddock and onion casserole   70
Haddock and tomato casserole   70
Hake and tomato casserole   70
Halibut and bacon casserole   71
Halibut with celery and bacon   71
Halibut au gratin   71
Halibut with mushrooms   71
Herring hot pot   72
Herrings almondine   71
Herrings and tomato casserole   72
Mackerel with basil   73
Mushroom pie   69
Normandy herrings   72
Parsley pie   69
Plaice and mushroom casserole   73
Plaice and onion casserole   73
Quick fish casserole   68
Shrimps and rice casserole   74
Soused herrings   72
Soused mackerel   73
Spanish fish casserole   69
Spiced fish casserole   68
Stuffed haddock casserole   70
Stuffed haddock casserole and
  cheese sauce   70
Stuffed herring casserole   72
Super fish pie   68
Trout with parsley butter   74
Trout with tarragon   74
Tuna casserole   75
Turbot Auvin   74
Turbot provençale   74
Yorkshire herring casserole   72
Flemish hot pot   13
Forcemeat balls   86
Fricassée of veal   22

Fried rice   3

Game casseroles:
  Braised grouse   61
  Braised pigeons   61
  Casserole of hare   60
  Casserole of pheasant   61
  Casserole of pigeons   62
  Casserole of rabbit   63
  Jugged hare   60
  Jugged rabbit   64
  Normandy pheasant   62
  Partridge with cabbage   61
  Pigeon with cherries   62
  Pigeon with raisins   62
  Pigeon with water chestnuts   62
  Pigeons with beer   63
  Rabbit chasseur   63
  Rabbit and prune casserole   63
  Rabbit Sicilian   14
  Rabbit with sour cream   64
  Rabbit and tomato casserole   64
  Salmis of game   64
  Stewed pigeons   62
  Stuffed pigeon casserole   63
Gammon see Ham
Ginger Betty   88
Ginger rice   11
Goulash   13
Grouse:
  Braised grouse   61

Hacienda chicken   54
Haddock:
  Fresh haddock with cider   70
  Haddock and bacon casserole   69
  Haddock casserole   69
  Haddock Crécy   69
  Haddock and onion casserole   70
  Haddock and tomato casserole   70
  Stuffed haddock casserole   70
  Stuffed haddock and cheese sauce
    70
Hake and tomato casserole   70
Halibut:
  Casserole of halibut   71
  Halibut and bacon casserole   71
  Halibut with celery and bacon   71
  Halibut au gratin   71
  Halibut with mushrooms   71
Ham casseroles:
  Braised ham   41
  Company casserole   40
  Egg and ham charlotte   79
  Gammon casserole   83
  Ham, egg and sweet corn casserole
    40
  Ham jambalaya   41
  Ham and tomatoes provençal   41
  Honeyed gammon casserole   42

Murphy's casserole   40
Somerset pot roast   42
Spiced gammon casserole   42
Sweet corn and ham casserole   40
Turkey and ham casserole   41
Hare:
  Casserole of hare   60
  Jugged hare   60
Haricot beans with bacon   42
Haricot beef   13
Haricot cutlets, quick   32
Haricot veal   21
Herring:
  Casseroled herrings   71
  Herring hot pot   72
  Herrings almondine   71
  Herrings and tomato casserole   72
  Normandy herrings   72
  Soused herrings   72
  Stuffed herring casserole   72
  Yorkshire herring casserole   72
Holiday stew   29
Honeyed chicken with orange   52
Honeyed chicken with orange and
  almonds   52
Honeyed gammon casserole   42
Hungarian beef   14
Hungarian herb stew   14
Hungarian hot pot   76
Hungarian mutton   28
Hunter's chicken   55
Huntsman's steak   13

Imperial lamb cutlets   29
Irish stew   29
Italian beef stew   13
Italian casserole   79
Italian chicken casserole   55
Italian veal casserole   24

Jugged beef   14
Jugged hare   60
Jugged lamb cutlets   29
Jugged rabbit   64

Kidney:
  Casserole of kidneys   44
  Kidney dumplings   86
  Kidney Espagnole   45
  Kidney and sausage casserole   44
  Kidney in sherry sauce   44
  Lamb and kidney casserole   31
  Sauté of kidney   44
  Steak and kidney casserole   16

Lamb and mutton casseroles:
  American casserole   26
  Barley lamb casserole   26
  Bitter sweet lamb casserole   27
  Braised lamb and green peas   27

93

Braised lamb with vegetables 35
Braised mutton ménagère 27
Canterbury casserole 28
Casserole of lamb with rice 27
Casserole of shoulder of mutton 28
Casseroled breast of lamb 27
Country casserole 28
Creamy lamb casserole 28
Curried mutton 28
Devonshire casserole 29
Holiday stew 29
Hungarian mutton 28
Imperial lamb cutlets 29
Irish stew 29
Jugged lamb cutlets 29
Lamb casserole with peas 30
Lamb chop casserole 30
Lamb chops créole 30
Lamb curry 31
Lamb curry with yoghurt 31
Lamb cutlets soubise 30
Lamb hot pot 30
Lamb and kidney casserole 31
Lamb and macaroni casserole 31
Lamb with noodles 33
Lamb and potato casserole 31
Lamb stew 32
Lamb stuffed peppers 82
Lamb with sweet red pepper 33
Lamb and tomato casserole 34
Lancashire hot pot 33
Lazy lamb 36
Lazy lamb with garlic 36
Lazy lamb with tomatoes 36
Marinated lamb casserole 32
Navarin of lamb 32
Paprika lamb 32
Quick haricot cutlets 32
Raisin-stuffed shoulder of lamb 34
Scotch hot pot 34
Shank of mutton casserole 33
Spanish lamb casserole 34
Spicy lamb hot pot 35
Spicy lamb noisettes 32
Spring casserole 34
Stuffed breast of lamb en
  casserole 35
Summer casserole 35
Thursday lamb 34
Welsh cowl 36
Lancashire hot pot 33
Lazy lamb 36
Leek:
  Leeks au gratin 80
  Potato and leek scallop 81
Lemon pudding 90
Lemon rice 3
Liver:
  Braised liver 46
  Braised liver and onions 44

Casserole of stuffed liver 46
Country style liver 45
Liver and bacon casserole 45
Liver bonne femme 46
Liver casserole 45
Liver Italienne 45
Liver and pork casserole 46
Stuffed ox liver 46

Mackerel:
  Mackerel with basil 73
  Soused mackerel 73
Maître d'hôtel sauce 85
Marinated lamb casserole 32
Marrow:
  Marrow savoury 79
  Stuffed marrow 80, 81
Meat balls with noodles 14
Mediterranean chicken 55
Mexican minced beef 14
Minced beef Marguerite 15
Mint jelly 85
Mock duck 15
Moroccan chicken 55
Moussaka 15
Murphy's casserole 40
Mushroom:
  Beef and mushroom casserole 7
  Casserole of beef bacon and
    mushrooms 18
  Chicken de luxe with mushrooms
    53
  Chicken and mushroom casserole
    51
  Chicken with mushrooms and
    spaghetti 59
  Halibut with mushrooms 71
  Mushroom pie 69
  Mushroom rice casserole 81
  Plaice and mushroom casserole 73
  Scalloped mushrooms 79
  Tomato and mushroom casserole
    83
  Veal chops with mushrooms 24
Mustard sauce 85

Navarin of lamb 32
Normandy casserole of chicken 56
Normandy herrings 72
Normandy pheasant 62

Offal casseroles:
  Braised liver 46
  Braised liver and onions 44
  Braised oxtail 47
  Braised sheeps' tongues 48
  Casserole of kidneys 44
  Casserole of stuffed liver 46
  Casserole of sweetbreads 49

Casserole of tripe 50
Country style liver 45
Kidney Espagnole 45
Kidney and sausage casserole 44
Kidney in sherry sauce 44
Liver and bacon casserole 45
Liver bonne femme 46
Liver casserole 45
Liver Italienne 45
Liver and pork casserole 46
Oxtail with beans 47
Oxtail with carrots 47
Oxtail ragoût 47
Oxtail au vin 47
Sauté of kidneys 44
Savoury sheeps' hearts 48
Stuffed ox liver 46
Sweetbreads with prunes 48
Sweetbreads suprême 48
Tongue and lentil casserole 49
Tripe in the French style 49
Tripe jardinière 49
Tripe and tomato casserole 49
Old English beef hot pot 16
Onion:
  Baked onion 80
  Baked onion with cloves 80
  Beef and onion casserole 6
  Cheese and onion pudding 77
  Onion sauce 85
  Potato and onion casserole 80
  Scalloped onions 81
  Stewed steak and onion 20
  Stuffed onion casserole 80
Orange:
  Beef and orange casserole 6, 7
  Veal and orange casserole 24
Oriental pork chops 38
Ossobuco 22
Oxtail:
  Braised oxtail 47
  Oxtail with beans 47
  Oxtail with carrots 47
  Oxtail ragoût 47
  Oxtail au vin 47

Paella 56
Pancakes 85-6
Paprika lamb 32
Parsley dumplings 86
Parsley pie 69
Parsley sauce 85
Partridge with cabbage 61
Peach:
  Peaches Escoffier 89
  Peaches Spanish style 89
Pear:
  Pear crumble 89
  Pears Abrocotine 89
Peperoni casserole 43

Peppers:
Green pepper ragoût 82
Peperoni casserole 43
Stuffed peppers 82
Pheasant:
Casserole of pheasant 61
Normandy pheasant 62
Pigeon:
Braised pigeons 61
Casserole of pigeons 62
Pigeon with cherries 62
Pigeon with raisins 62
Pigeon with water chestnuts 62
Pigeons with beer 63
Stewed pigeons 62
Stuffed pigeon casserole 63
Pilaff 53
Pineapple:
Chicken and pineapple casserole 52
Pineapple rice 4
Piquant pork chops 38
Plaice:
Casserole of plaice 74
Plaice and mushroom casserole 73
Plaice and onion casserole 73
Plantation casserole 56
Pork casseroles:
Belly of pork casserole 38
Casserole of pork 37
Casseroled pork chops 37
Devonshire pork chops 36
Liver and pork casserole 46
Oriental pork chops 38
Piquant pork chops 38
Pork and beans 36
Pork chops Italienne 38
Pork chops Milanaise 38
Pork goulash, quick 39
Pork hot pot 38
Pork and macaroni casserole 37
Pork with peppers 37
Pork and prune casserole 37
Pork and quince casserole 39
Ragoût of pork 39
Sauerkraut and pork 40
Sausage and bean casserole 39
Savoury pork chops 37
Spanish casserole 39
Potato:
Bacon and potato casserole 43
Beef and potato hot pot 8
Casserole of cabbage and potato 76
Casseroled potatoes 81
Chicken and potato casserole 53
Hungarian hot pot 76
Lamb and potato casserole 31
Murphy's casserole 40
Potato casserole 77
Potato casserole with chives 77

Potato casserole with onion 77
Potato and egg supper savoury 82
Potato and leek scallop 81
Potato and onion casserole 80
Potatoes au gratin 82
Savoy potatoes 81
Swiss savoury potatoes 77
Priest's goulash 20
Provençal stew 15
Prune:
Pork and prune casserole 37
Prune hot pot 15
Rabbit and prune casserole 63
Sweetbreads with prunes 48
Puddings *see* Desserts

Queen of puddings 90

Rabbit:
Casserole of rabbit 63
Jugged rabbit 64
Rabbit chasseur 63
Rabbit and prune casserole 63
Rabbit Sicilian 64
Rabbit with sour cream 64
Rabbit and tomato casserole 64
Ragoût of beef 16
Ragoût of pork 39
Raisin-stuffed shoulder of lamb 34
Ratatouille 84
Rice:
To cook rice 3
Fried rice 3
Ginger rice 11
Lemon rice 3
Pilaff 53
Pineapple rice 4
Rice meringue 90
Rice puddings 88
Risotto 4
Russian beef casserole 16

Sage and onion stuffing 86
St Clement's rice pudding 88
Salmis of game 64
Sauces:
Anchovy sauce 85
Cheese sauce 85
Egg sauce 85
Fennel sauce 85
Maître d'hôtel sauce 85
Mustard sauce 85
Onion sauce 85
Parsley sauce 85
Tomato sauce 85
White sauce 85
Sauerkraut and pork 40
Sausage:
Bacon and sausage casserole 43
Beef and sausage casserole 6

Kidney and sausage casserole 44
Sausage and bean casserole 39
Sausage meat dumplings 86
Sauté of kidney 44
Savoury bake 79
Savoury bean casserole 76
Savoury dumplings 86
Savoury egg casserole 78
Savoury pork chops 37
Savoury sheeps' hearts 48
Savoy potatoes 81
Scalloped mushrooms 79
Scalloped onions 81
Scotch hot pot 34
Shank of mutton casserole 33
Sherry veal with cream 26
Shrimp:
Egg and shrimp savoury 74
Shrimps and rice casserole 74
Sole:
Fillets of sole in cider 73
Somerset pot roast 42
Soused herrings 72
Soused mackerel 73
Spanish casserole 39
Spanish fish casserole 69
Spanish lamb casserole 34
Spanish style chicken 60
Spanish veal casserole 23
Spiced beef casserole 17
Spiced fish casserole 68
Spiced gammon casserole 42
Spicy lamb hot pot 35
Spicy lamb noisettes 32
Spring casserole 34
Steak and bacon casserole 18
Steak and kidney casserole 16
Stewed pigeons 62
Stewed steak and onions 20
Stock:
Bone or white stock 84
Brown stock 84
Chicken stock 85
Fish stock 67
Veal stock 85
Vegetable stock 84
Stroganoff 20
Stuffed breast of lamb en casserole 35
Stuffed cabbage (Dutch style) 76
Stuffed chicken casserole 56
Stuffed haddock casserole 70
Stuffed haddock casserole and cheese sauce 70
Stuffed herring casserole 72
Stuffed marrow 80, 81
Stuffed onion casserole 80
Stuffed ox liver 46
Stuffed peppers 82
Stuffed pigeon casserole 63

Stuffed steak   11
Stuffing:
  Sage and onion stuffing   86
  Veal forcemeat or stuffing   86
Suet pastry   87
Sultana rice pudding   88
Summer casserole   35
Super fish pie   68
Swedish casserole   10
Sweetbreads:
  Casserole of sweetbreads   49
  Sweetbreads with prunes   48
  Sweetbreads suprême   48
Sweet corn and ham casserole   40
Sweet-sour meat balls   20
Swiss savoury potatoes   77
Terrine of fish   67
Thursday lamb   34
Tomato:
  Beef and tomato casserole   7
  Casserole of tomato and spaghetti
    82
  Cheese and tomato savoury   77
  Chicken and tomato supper dish   59
  Haddock and tomato casserole   70
  Hake and tomato casserole   70
  Ham and tomatoes provençal   41
  Herrings and tomato casserole   72
  Lamb and tomato casserole   34
  Rabbit and tomato casserole   64
  Tomato and cheese casserole   83
  Tomato and mushroom casserole
    83
  Tomato purée   85
  Tomato sauce   85
  Tripe and tomato casserole   49
  Veal and tomato casserole   25
Tongue and lentil casserole   49
Trifle, baked   88
Tripe:
  Casserole of tripe   50
  Tripe in the French style   49
  Tripe jardinière   49
  Tripe and tomato casserole   49
Trout with parsley or tarragon
    butter   74
Tuna casserole   75
Turbot Auvin   74
Turbot provençale   74
Turkey and ham casserole   41
Tyrolean beef casserole   21

Vanilla cream pudding   90
Veal casseroles:
  To make veal stock   85
  Braised veal   21
  Casserole of veal   22
  Casseroled breast of veal   22
  Casseroled knuckle of veal   25
  Fricassée of veal   22
  Haricot veal   21
  Italian veal casserole   24
  Neck of veal with forcemeat
    balls   22
  Ossobuco   22
  Sherry veal with cream   26
  Spanish veal casserole   23
  Veal and bacon casserole   23
  Veal chops Lyonnaise   23
  Veal chops with mushrooms   24
  Veal chops with wine   24
  Veal forcemeat or stuffing   86
  Veal goulash   24
  Veal Marengo   23
  Veal Mozzarella   26
  Veal and orange casserole   24
  Veal paprika   24
  Veal paprika with lemon   26
  Veal Portugaise   25
  Veal rolls   23
  Veal Romano   25
  Veal sauté   25
  Veal and tomato casserole   25
Vegetable, egg and cheese casseroles:
  To make vegetable stock   84
  Aubergines with meat filling   75
  Aubergines à la Provence   75
  Aubergines with rice and cheese   75
  Baked bean hot pot   76
  Baked onion   80
  Baked onion with cloves   80
  Bean and sausage crumble   76
  Boston bean casserole   75
  Braised celery   82
  Casserole of cabbage and potato
    76
  Casserole of red cabbage   79
  Casserole of tomato and spaghetti
    82
  Casserole of vegetables   83
  Casseroled potatoes   81
  Celery au gratin   80
  Cheese casserole   77

Cheese, macaroni and cauliflower
    78
Cheese, macaroni and tomato
    casserole   78
Cheese and onion pudding   77
Cheese and tomato savoury   77
Cheese and vegetable casserole   77
Creamed beetroots   80
Egg and celery casserole   78
Egg and cheese casserole   78
Egg and cheese supper savoury   78
Egg and ham charlotte   79
Green pepper ragoût   82
Hungarian hot pot   76
Italian casserole   79
Leeks au gratin   80
Marrow savoury   79
Mushroom rice casserole   81
Potato casserole   77
Potato casserole with chives   77
Potato casserole with onion   77
Potato and egg supper savoury   82
Potato and leek scallop   81
Potato and onion casserole   80
Potatoes au gratin   82
Quick casserole   83
Ratatouille   84
Savoury bake   79
Savoury bean casserole   76
Savoury egg casserole   78
Savoy potatoes   81
Scalloped mushrooms   79
Scalloped onions   81
Stuffed cabbage (Dutch style)   76
Stuffed marrow   80, 81
Stuffed onion casserole   80
Stuffed peppers   82
Summer vegetable casserole   83
Swiss savoury potatoes   77
Tomato and cheese casserole   83
Tomato and mushroom casserole
    83
Vegetable casserole   84
Viennese chicken   57

Welsh cowl   36
White sauce   85
Winter casserole   41

Yorkshire herring casserole   72